DATE			
NOV 3 1981			
JUL 2 7 1982			
MAR 1 1983			
MAY 1 5 1984			
OCT 2 3 1984			
NOV 1 3 84			
DEC 4 1984			
FEB 2 8 '89			
MAY 1 4 1991			
MAY 2 8 1991			

The Sweetheart of the Silent Majority

CAROL FELSENTHAL

The Sweetheart of the Silent Majority

The Biography of Phyllis Schlafly

DOUBLEDAY & COMPANY, INC.
GARDEN CITY, NEW YORK   1981

ISBN: 0-385-14912-3
Library of Congress Catalog Card Number: 79–6090
Copyright © 1981 by Carol Felsenthal

For my husband, Steve, once again, an inspiration.

Contents

Introduction

In June 1977, the book editor of the Chicago *Tribune* asked me if I considered myself capable of writing an objective review of Phyllis Schlafly's ninth book, *The Power of the Positive Woman.* By then, of course, Schlafly had an entrenched national reputation as the woman who, against all odds, had stalled, and perhaps stopped, the Equal Rights Amendment (ERA)—on its way to easy ratification in 1972 when Schlafly declared all-out war. Among my fellow writers, Phyllis Schlafly was about as popular as Anita Bryant.

"Of course," I replied. I had no ax to grind. I support ERA, but I had never worked actively for it. I considered myself a feminist, but, at times, I had found leaders of the pro-ERA side as ridiculous as leaders of the anti-ERA side. Besides, I liked to think I could, under all circumstances, judge a book by what's between its covers, not by my opinion of its author's politics.

The Power of the Positive Woman, a mix of Schlafly's advice on "How to Be a Happy Housewife" and her seemingly endless parade of arguments against the ERA, was a challenge, to say the least. Parts were well-reasoned and convincing, but it was sprinkled with statements that I considered downright silly. For example: "The small number of women in Congress proves only that most women do not want to do all the things that must be done to win elections. . . ." Or, "The overriding psychological need of a woman to love something alive" is the reason women dominate such low-paying, low-prestige fields as teaching and nursing. "The schoolchild or the patient of any age provides an outlet for a woman to express her natural maternal need."

In my review, published on July 31, 1977, I blasted the book as "irrational, contradictory and simpleminded." Two days later, the letters of protest started coming, and they kept coming—from people who were enraged that I had insulted "Our Savior," as one letter writer called Schlafly, or "Our Wonder Woman," as another called her. One Schlafly fan even took the trouble to rewrite the review. She knew her tribute would never be published, as did the rest of my newfound correspondents, because the *Tribune* book editor does not run a regular "letters" column. These people were writing for one reason only—to convert me, to make me see the light.

By then, I had written hundreds of reviews, including a weekly book column that goes nationwide to seven hundred newspapers, mostly in small and conservative cities and towns. I could count on one hand the number of letters they provoked, and all those letters, except one, were complaints from authors of the criticized books (the sole exception was from an author's mother). Yet here was a stack of letters from relatively disinterested people, aflame with righteousness and indignation. At that point, I stopped being horrified by Phyllis Schlafly and started being fascinated. Anyone who could spark such controversy and passion, such fervor and fury; anyone who seemed to be such a mass of contradictions demanded a closer look. And so I headed for the library to look up articles on her—which left me more confused than ever.

On the one hand, Schlafly seemed the epitome of the liberated woman. On the other, she insisted, at every opportunity, that she could think of not a single good word to say about the women's liberation movement. She preached that "God intended the husband to be the head of the family"; that women are more emotional and mystical and men more analytical and logical, yet she and her husband appeared to have a perfect intellectual partnership. She is a mother of six who claimed mothering was her "No. 1 career," yet, since her oldest was eighteen months, she maintained a hectic pace of travel, writing, speaking, testifying, organizing, lobbying, campaigning. She was constantly vilifying the "eastern establishment," yet she was educated at Harvard and usually included her Phi Beta Kappa key in her self-descriptions. Her background was blue-blooded, yet many of her supporters were blue-collar. As a young woman in St. Louis she made her debut into society, yet she worked nights, forty-eight hours a week, in an ammunition plant, test-firing machine guns, to put herself through college. She was a devout Catholic, yet she looked to the Bible as an irrefutable moral code and believed in the "Holy Scriptures" with the conviction and zeal of a Southern Baptist preacher. She complained incessantly that reporters—especially women reporters whom she labeled "libbers"—distorted her positions. Yet it was these same reporters who transformed her into a household word— a woman who won "most-admired" polls with the regularity of a First Lady.

Then I began reading Schlafly's earlier books, starting with her first and most famous, *A Choice Not an Echo,* which she wrote and self-published during Barry Goldwater's run for the Republican presidential nomination in 1964. The book sold three million copies, was credited with giving Goldwater the nomination, and made Schlafly the most well-known and controversial woman in the Republican Party. By summer's end, I had read them all, except *Kissinger on the Couch*, an eight-hundred-page criticism of the former Secretary of State's pro-détente policies.

At that point, I decided I wanted to be the first to write an in-depth, *objective* article on Phyllis Schlafly—the first because almost everything on her in the major magazines was relentlessly critical, often vicious. (Reporters who normally believe in objectivity as they believe in the First Amendment apparently made an exception for Phyllis Schlafly.)

I found the perfect angle in October 1977 when a Chicago gossip columnist reported that Schlafly was considering challenging Charles Percy, Illinois' liberal incumbent senator, in the Republican primary. I immediately called an editor at *Chicago* magazine to pitch a profile of the potential Senator Schlafly. I got the assignment. In early November, I followed Schlafly to Houston, the site of her "pro-family alternative" to the International Women's Year Conference (IWY), which she denounced as "a federally funded festival for foolish, frustrated feminists." (Its delegates were mostly pro-ERA.)

I planned to stick by Schlafly's side for the duration. The rub was that, to do so, I obviously needed her approval. I had some difficulty mustering the nerve to call her because I was afraid she would recognize me as the "libber" who lambasted the most personal of her books and berate me or, worse yet, hang up on me. As it turned out, she never heard of me. I stuck so close to her that she began calling me "Shadow."

Very late the second night, a CBS newsman corraled her as we were leaving her hotel room for dinner at the lobby coffee shop. Within moments, the television lights were glaring and the interview was conducted right in the corridor, Schlafly positioned just inches from the elevator, facing the door, her red STOP ERA button beaming. She was outlining ERA's legislative history when the elevator door opened. The women inside, mostly IWY delegates, several sporting "ERA NOW!" buttons, in unison, raised their third fingers, just inches from Phyllis' face. One woman spat and, incredibly, missed. Schlafly didn't pause. She didn't even blink. "Good for her," I thought, surprising myself, but beginning to understand why her supporters tout her as the best thing since Joan of Arc.

Having spent three days at her side, I too came away impressed by her articulateness, her energy, her cool, her confidence, her sense of humor, and her lack of vanity. (She wore the same two dresses through a seemingly endless stream of television interviews and televised press conferences.) My experience with Phyllis Schlafly was turning out to be drastically at odds with almost everything I had read and heard. Who was Phyllis Schlafly anyway and why were people saying such terrible things about her? I still wasn't sure about the first part of that question. I decided I needed another interview.

I arranged to meet Schlafly on Pearl Harbor Day (the next December 7) when she was coming to Chicago to lead a rally against the Panama Canal treaties, and to announce that she would not challenge Senator Percy in the primary. Walking to lunch, we were deep in discussion of the treaties when, suddenly, she stopped, looked me in the eye, and said, "By the way, the other day a clip of that ghastly *Tribune* review came across my desk. When I saw that you wrote it, I was just furious. To think of all the time I spent with you!"

The day was frigid, but I could feel my face hot, blushing. To my profound relief, Schlafly was smiling. I steered the conversation back to the Canal and that was the last she ever mentioned the "ghastly review." She had claimed that she never holds grudges against political opponents or reporters. In the case of reporters, at least, that was, apparently, true.

By the time I sat down to write the *Chicago* article—after a couple of months of research and interviewing—I had reached the pivotal conclusion that Phyllis Schlafly's opposition to ERA was sincere, a conclusion that separated me from just about every other journalist I knew. (Conventional wisdom had it that Schlafly was treacherously ambitious. More than one journalist implied that she was fighting ERA not because she really believed there was anything wrong with the Amendment, but because she is a shameless media hound who recognized ERA as a hot, attention-grabbing issue.) Once I concluded that Schlafly was not an unadulterated villain, she became much more complex and interesting. The first draft of my *Chicago* article ran over a hundred pages. Upon presenting the opus to my editor I said, "I could write a book about Phyllis Schlafly." I could, and I decided that I would.

As soon as the article appeared, as a cover story in June 1978, I sent a copy to Susan Schwartz, an editor at Doubleday. A book contract followed quickly. My next task was to convince Schlafly to cooperate with me. I was hopeful because, while she didn't like the article, she considered it at least somewhat objective (which apparently it was, as it generated equal numbers of outraged letters from fans and foes).

I had no desire to write an authorized biography (which invariably gives the subject, who usually commissions the biography in the first place, editorial control over the manuscript). But I did need Schlafly to cooperate (that is, to agree to spend more time with me, to give me names of friends and relatives who knew her before she became a public figure). I saw no alternative to going to the source and forming my own opinions. I could not depend on the public record because, even prior to 1972 and ERA, Schlafly elicited such extreme responses. People have always either idolized or despised her. Strident censure or breathless exaltation are fine if you're out to create a fairy-tale character. I wanted to present a flesh-and-blood person. I needed to talk to Phyllis' children, her relatives, her neighbors, her high-school classmates, her elementary-school teachers, her friends, her enemies.

When I wrote to Schlafly to arrange what I hoped would be the first in a series of interviews, she responded, to my dismay, that, at age fifty-five, she had decided it was much too early in her career for a biography. "Your request reminds me of the proposal to name a New York bridge in honor of General Douglas MacArthur while he was still fighting battles in the Pacific during World War II. Mayor La Guardia vetoed the idea until MacArthur was dead or retired."

Phyllis Schlafly was certainly not behaving as advertised. Any media hound worth her ego would have grabbed the chance to be the subject of a full-fledged biography published by a major New York house. I had promised Schlafly an objective book, but even if it were negative, it would still bring her loads of free publicity. Talk-show hosts, who knew that having Phyllis Schlafly as a guest guaranteed a lively show, would have been delighted to invite her back to respond. Here she was saying she would prefer to wait until she was dead or retired, and I knew she'd never retire.

So that was an answer I couldn't accept. For the next two months, I bombarded Phyllis and her husband, Fred, with letters and phone calls. (Phyllis was in Washington most of that summer fighting the proposed extension of time for ratifying ERA, and Fred was fielding some of the less routine press requests.) About all I knew of attorney Fred Schlafly was that he was reputed to be, if possible, even a stronger anti-Communist than his wife. Striving to get on his good side, I spent the first couple of phone calls roundly deploring the holes in the SALT II Treaty and the "betrayal" of Taiwan. Fred wasn't impressed. Then one morning, just as I was, in desperation, about to denounce the Panama Canal treaties, I recalled hearing that if there is one thing Fred feels stronger about than containing Communists, it's containing middle-age spread. "If I sound out of breath," I bragged to this avid jogger and general physical-fitness buff, "it's because I just finished running my usual eight miles." That did it. By the close of that conversation, he was enumerating "errors" he felt I had made in the magazine piece and "trusting" they would not be repeated in the book.

Even after I softened up Fred by promising to jog with him when I came to Alton, Phyllis continued to oppose my project. She argued against it, she pleaded with me not to write it, she ducked my phone calls. In the end, it was the fact that I already had a contract with Doubleday that changed Phyllis' mind. She knew there was no way she could stop me from writing her biography. Under First Amendment interpretations, she would be defined as a "public figure," and freedom of the press would inevitably win out over her right to privacy.

I gathered much of my material by spending days at the Schlafly home in Alton, Illinois, across the Mississippi from St. Louis. Besides talking to Phyllis, I combed several scrapbooks she diligently kept from the time she was in elementary school until 1949, when she married Fred. I interviewed several of her children, her sister, her best friend from elementary school, all but two of the members of her high-school graduating class of '41, cousins, nephews, nieces, aunts, uncles, and in-laws—close to a hundred people, all of whom had known Phyllis in the years when ERA still meant earned-run average.

My first trip to Alton was during the Christmas holidays in 1978, when the Schlafly children were home from school. Over lunch, they bantered with their mother, disagreed with her, teased her. Conversation was lively and natural even though my recorder and Schlafly's, who almost always tapes reporters taping her, were the table's centerpiece. Snow was falling, the foliage on the riverbluff looked storybook fluffy and white (the Schlaflys' home looks out over the Mississippi). The glittering Christmas tree was next to the glistening grand piano where, on Chrismas Eve, the family had gathered to sing carols. American eagles—Schlafly's trademark—

were perched everywhere, including the coffee mugs and even the powder-room toilet seat. That night, back in Chicago, I told my husband about lunch and the eagles and especially the six kids, the whole Norman Rockwell scene. The description must have sounded a bit too glowing. He listened, smiled slightly, and said, "Oh come now, Carol. Phyllis probably rented the kids for the day."

I was still so deep-down suspicious of Phyllis Schlafly that, for a moment, I entertained that possibility. In researching the *Chicago* article, I had tried tirelessly to get the goods on Schlafly. I had been assured by several sources that a reporter who "really investigates Phyllis Schlafly" would discover all sorts of scandal—that right-wing millionaires such as beer magnate Joseph Coors and oilman H. L. Hunt were picking up the tab for Schlafly's crusade against the ERA; that, without hefty contributions from the Ku Klux Klan and the John Birch Society and the American Nazi Party, Schlafly would go bankrupt; that executives of some of the country's largest insurance companies were secretly funding Schlafly (presumably, the companies were making money off policies that discriminate against women).

I spent a month investigating and came away with nothing. I felt defeated until I realized I wasn't the only one. In the course of my research, I also heard of several other reporters digging into Schlafly's finances. Louise Swartzwalder of the Des Moines *Register* and Carol Alexander of the Lindsay-Schaub News Service were two of many. Swartzwalder, who conducted the most extensive investigation, getting documents from the IRS and the SEC, inspecting financial records at the Secretary of State's office in both Illinois and Missouri, told me, "There are millions of rumors circulating and I examined all of them and came up with nothing."

Next I checked with ERA activists, hoping they'd have some leads. Grace Kaminkowitz, public-information chairperson of ERA Illinois, had, for the past several years, encouraged and cooperated with reporters investigating Schlafly. "We cannot find anything on funding," Kaminkowitz admitted. "We're completely stymied by it." Elly Peterson, former cochairperson of ERAmerica, said in exasperation, "I've had more reporters calling saying they're investigating where Phyllis gets her money. But that's the last I hear of it. They're not finding a thing and, as much as I hate to admit it, neither am I."

I was about to give up when Betty Friedan called a news conference to announce that, in conjunction with several "news organizations," she was investigating charges that Schlafly and STOP ERA received funds from the John Birch Society and the Ku Klux Klan. Schlafly denied that she had ever "received a dime" from either. "I hope Ms. Friedan spends her time investigating me. She won't find anything and it might keep her out of other mischief," Schlafly commented, as usual getting the last word. I had high hopes for Friedan's investigation, but, like mine and many others', it fizzled.

So maybe Schlafly *wasn't* getting money from the John Birch Society. That was no reason to dismiss rumors that she was a Bircher in good standing. In 1960 Birch Society founder Robert Welch called Schlafly "one of our most loyal members." Schlafly had immediately denied being a member. I was determined to prove she was lying. I must have called the John Birch Society headquarters in Belmont, Massachusetts twenty-five times trying in vain to coax secretaries and clerks and receptionists to peek at the top-secret membership rolls. It was Schlafly's word against her accusers'.

Then, when I had resigned myself to writing an article minus any shockers, a neighbor of Schlafly's called to tip me off that back in the early 1950s, Schlafly had tried to prevent integration of the Alton YWCA. As a board member, she was, according to my informant, unalterably opposed to allowing blacks to use the swimming pool and several other "Y" facilities, including the lobby. By this time, I was hungry for anything I could get. A stain on Schlafly's character would be just dandy. I began calling Schlafly's fellow board members. The three I tracked down, all ardent workers for ERA, had to admit, they said, that Schlafly had never shown herself to be a racist; had never tried to block or even stall integration.

When I started researching the book, I was still convinced there *had* to be some skeleton in Schlafly's closet. I searched and searched. I interviewed and interviewed, including scores of people who had worked hard for ERA—Martha Griffiths, Bella Abzug, Liz Carpenter, and loads of lesser lights. Looking for something, anything, in the winter of 1979, I ran a note in the New York *Times Book Review* asking for "information" on Schlafly. I received eighty-seven responses, all but two from dyed-in-the-wool Schlafly critics who mostly repeated the same gossip, out of which I could substantiate only one rumor—that neither Phyllis nor Fred had attended their daughter's piano recitals. And that I already knew. My source? The daughter in question, twenty-one-year-old Liza.

I did not change my mind about *The Power of the Positive Woman* or the ERA—although I find Schlafly's arguments against it convincing—but I did change my mind about Phyllis Schlafly. I now see her as a complex human being with some good qualities and some bad, whom, on balance, I came to admire. And that has been, at times, a most uncomfortable position for someone from my background (urban, liberal, Jewish). When colleagues, friends, and relatives, most of whom consider Schlafly downright dangerous, would ask me about the book, I'd launch into my litany: "No, I'm not writing a hatchet job." "No, I'm not writing an exposé." I might as well have admitted I was writing a balanced biography of Yasir Arafat or Adolf Hitler. Writing this book has often been difficult, but it has more often been challenging, stimulating, and satisfying.

For Phyllis Schlafly—love her or hate her—has made her mark. In fact, in an era of feminism, Phyllis Schlafly—the No. 1 enemy of women's liberation—may be the one contemporary woman who has truly changed the course of history.

CAROL FELSENTHAL
Chicago
April 1980

The Sweetheart of the Silent Majority

1

Love Her
or Loathe Her

On Pearl Harbor Day in 1977, Phyllis Schlafly and I lunched at Chicago's Bismarck Hotel—a hustling, masculine power center frequented by clout-heavy politicians, lawyers, and bankers. I was on assignment from *Chicago* magazine to interview the country's most controversial woman.

Schlafly's porcelain complexion was windburned around the edges and her unadorned hands, tipped by unpolished nails, were stiff from the cold. "I'll never be able to type again," she joked. She had just come from leading a rally against the Panama Canal treaties in the wind tunnel, also known as the Daley (Mayor Richard) Plaza, where twenty-mile-an-hour northerly gusts sent the wind-chill factor plunging to forty below.

In spite of the weather, a busload of Schlafly's "Chicago girls"—members of her Eagle Forum, "the alternative to women's lib"—braved the freeze to hear their leader denounce the treaties and announce, to their profound disappointment, that she would not challenge liberal Republican Senator Charles Percy in the 1978 Republican primary. They joined her for lunch afterward, but most were banished to distant tables in the crowded restaurant, where all they could do was gaze at their guru.

Suddenly, a group of the housewives, eagle pins perched on collars, rose, and, from across the room, offered a heartfelt toast to "Phyllis power." The then fifty-three-year-old, svelte, blue-eyed beauty, with impeccable posture, poise, and upswept streaked hair—who stood out among her disciples like Lauren Bacall at a Tupperware Party—saluted them with a glass of ice water.

Phyllis Schlafly's fans love her with an intensity, a spirit, a loyalty usually reserved for movie stars or members of the Royal Family. She has glamor and guts and intelligence and energy. She is awe-inspiring, a phenomenon, a heroine, a star, even, in her inimitable ramrod-straight way, a sort of sex symbol of the right wing. She is an authority—on the ERA, on the Panama Canal treaties, on SALT, on Medicare funding of abortions, on just about every major political issue. Her followers would as soon question her knowledge and commitment as they would question the Pope's.

A month earlier, I was with Schlafly at the Ramada Inn in Houston, where she led what she called a "pro-family alternative to the lesbian and libber-controlled" International Women's Year Conference. Several of her fans watched as she was interviewed in turn by correspondents from ABC, NBC, the BBC, the New York *Times*, and, finally, a correspondent from Swedish television. "Can you believe she has six kids?" asked one short, plump woman whose blouse was covered by red buttons bearing the STOP ERA, stop-sign-shaped logo. "Look at this one woman God raised up to teach us," gushed another.

As soon as the Swedish crew switched off its lights, the woman rushed up to Phyllis, grabbed her hand, and said, "I want to thank you for what you're doing for us." And they kept coming. "Bless your heart," said the next, and "We love you in Nashville" the next. Soon a long line of "Eagles" formed to get Phyllis Schlafly's autograph, but she had to cut the signing short and duck out. She was a featured speaker that afternoon at a "pro-family" rally in Houston's Astro Arena; a rally that would draw fifteen thousand people—mostly arriving on yellow school buses or CB-connected car caravans—from literally every state in the union, including Alaska.

Phyllis Schlafly's critics, on the other hand, detest her with an intensity usually reserved for history's full-fledged villains. There is no middle ground—love her or loathe her. But, unlike a movie star, Schlafly's enemies can't take her or leave her, can't turn her off—which makes them hate her all the more, especially when she appears not to care what they think. She evokes powerful, emotional reactions, but seems almost oblivious, occasionally even slightly amused, by her foes' fury. She is maddeningly cool.

Later that same day in Houston, the STOP ERA commander and I were eating a very late dinner at the Ramada Inn restaurant. The waitress had just brought two juicy filets, flanked by "Texas toast" dripping garlic and butter. Schlafly —whose last meal had been thirteen hours, four press conferences, and seventeen interviews earlier—gingerly transferred the toast to another plate, handed it to a busboy, cut a small piece of steak, and let it lie there as she continued her elaborate comparison of U.S. and Soviet weapons strength.

As she warmed to the subject and our steaks cooled, an elderly woman wearing pink polyester and sprayed hair approached the table. Interrupted again, I thought, by yet another fan paying homage to her leader—the sixth since we sat down.

Schlafly was still completing her case for the B-1 bomber when the woman barged in, not waiting to be acknowledged.

"I promised my friends," she said hurriedly, "that if I ran into you in Houston, I'd tell you what we think of you. You are a traitor to your sex. When you die, the women of this country will rejoice. And you don't have long, Phyllis, believe me." She rushed away, her face as pink as her pantsuit.

There wasn't a crack in Schlafly's composure. Smiling, she summoned the waitress, who, I assumed, would be directed to summon Schlafly's burly press secretary, or the armed sentry outside her suite, or perhaps the Texas Rangers.

"Please bring me some real milk for my coffee, instead of this fake stuff," she instructed the waitress. Then, without missing a beat, she continued her monologue on military budgets of the past five years—the statistics and weaponry jargon flowing smoothly and unstoppably from this self-styled "happy homemaker."

"How do you deal with the fact that so many people hate you?" I blurted.

"You know," she replied calmly, "when women say things like that to me, I just chalk it up to their frustration over the weakness of their arguments. We've beaten ERA in Illinois for six years straight. Last year, only one state ratified. In 1972, before we got organized, twenty-two states ratified. We're winning because we have the truth on our side. They're losing, so they're irrational and mad."

Schlafly had an arsenal of anecdotes to illustrate her point. Debating Betty Friedan in Bloomington, Illinois, in May 1973, seemed to be the encounter she relished most. That one ended when Friedan shrieked, "I'd like to burn you at the stake!"

A short time later, Schlafly debated Senator Birch Bayh (D., Ind.). He came so unstrung by the televised experience that he admitted to wanting "to commit mayhem live and in full color."

Schlafly's critics claim to ignore her. But it's obvious that they can no more ignore Phyllis Schlafly than anti-Vietnam War protesters could ignore Richard Nixon. In fact, feminists seem positively obsessed with her. She is a symbol.

Some ninety thousand ERA supporters gathered in Washington on a scorching day the next July to push for a three-year extension to the time allotted for passage of ERA—without which the Amendment would have died on March 22, 1979. President Carter's former women's adviser, Midge Costanza, had only to mention the words "Phyllis Schlafly" to bring the crowd to a frenzy.

National Organization for Women (NOW) President Ellie Smeal, heartened by the huge show of support for ERA, couldn't resist a sure-fire roar raiser: "Mrs. Schlafly, wherever you are, eat your heart out!" Nearby, a group of women burned Schlafly in effigy.

The next October, twenty-four hours after Congress passed the extension, Senator Ted Kennedy brought a crowd of two thousand women's-rights activists to their feet merely by asking, "Phyllis Schlafly, where are you now?" He chided her over and over again, sparking a roar of approval with every dig.

A year later—the extension having not yet produced a single new ratification—ERA supporters held a fund- and morale-raiser. They flew in Midge Costanza to galvanize the troops. The location was carefully chosen—at the home of Schlafly's Alton, Illinois, next-door neighbor Gladys Levis, an ardent ERA supporter. The crowd of women, many of whom liked to dismiss Schlafly as "just a nut, not nearly as important as she thinks she is," couldn't stop gossiping about her, denouncing her. In fact, they spent much more time exchanging rumors about Phyllis than discussing tactics for ratifying ERA.

Chicago *Tribune* reporter Dorothy Collin recorded snippets of conversation:

"There was a picture of her in the local paper taking a casserole out of the oven. She didn't have any mitts on. You could tell she really baked it."

"She has a staff. I bet she never washes her floor."

One woman captured the attention of the crowd in Levis's "great Gothic stone mansion" by announcing she had just seen Phyllis getting out of her car with an armload of groceries. Several women snorted that they doubted that Phyllis did any of her own cooking.

"That great female impersonator Phyllis Schlafly goes about the country telling women to stay in the kitchen," said Costanza, to thunderous cheers. (In June 1980, after the Illinois house defeated ERA for the ninth year, Costanza drew an even more spirited response by suggesting that Anita Bryant and Phyllis Schlafly would make "a fine set of bookends" for Hitler's *Mein Kampf.*)

Vice President Walter Mondale was only three minutes into his acceptance speech at the 1980 Democratic National Convention when he too drew massive applause by denouncing Phyllis Schlafly.

ERA backers—nearly every major newspaper and magazine, the White House, politicians of all stripes, the Republican and Democratic national committees,[1] Hollywood stars, talk-show hosts, organizations ranging from the American Bar Associ-

---

[1] During the 1980 Republican National Convention, following Schlafly's vigorous lobbying, Republicans dropped ERA from their party platform, ending a forty-year tradition of support for the Amendment. (During most of those years, however, the ERA that Republicans supported contained several exemptions—for example, a clause exempting women from the draft.) A month later, at their convention, the Democrats strengthened their already strong support for ERA by passing a platform plank denying campaign funds and assistance to candidates who oppose ERA.

ation to the AFL-CIO to the League of Women Voters—are baffled, frustrated, and infuriated by Schlafly's success.

And their attacks on her—more often than not personal attacks—show it. Gloria Steinem attacked Phyllis Schlafly for being rich. "Are you now or have you ever been a member of the John Birch Society?" was a question invariably asked at Schlafly's press conferences. The reporter asking the question was usually too young to remember Senator Joe McCarthy and too passionately pro-ERA to hide her contempt for Phyllis Schlafly. Schlafly answered "no" on both counts and the reporter's face showed she obviously didn't believe her. The McCarthyesque tactics only added the sympathy vote to an already huge following. And the ERA supporters got angrier and angrier.

"Women's liberationists have come to realize that in order to stop STOP ERA they must also stop Phyllis Schlafly," concluded Alton *Telegraph* reporter Mary Scarpinato, echoing a common theme of ERA analyses. Schlafly's family and friends fear that her opponents are beginning to take that conclusion literally. During her "pro-family alternative" to the International Women's Year Conference, her husband stationed a guard at her hotel-room door.

Most of the threats are probably harmless. A woman walked by Schlafly at a Missouri legislative hearing on ERA and hissed, "I'd like to kick you." Activist lawyer Flo Kennedy went on Florida radio and encouraged listeners to stop debating Phyllis and start slapping her. Yippie Aron Kay walked up to her at a Manhattan reception for the Women's National Republican Club and smashed an apple pie in her face, leaving Schlafly, who wears contact lenses, with a painfully scratched eye.

During her Washington "Gala," Schlafly was laughing heartily at her own creation—the *ERA Follies*—parodies she wrote herself, starring STOP ERAers impersonating Bella

Abzug and Gloria Steinem. Suddenly the lights came on. Schlafly was frowning, looking furious and a trifle frightened. A grim-faced emcee, Senator Orrin Hatch (R., Ut.), announced that the overstuffed Shoreham ballroom would have to be evacuated immediately. The hotel switchboard operator, he explained, had received an anonymous call warning that two bombs have been placed on the dais "under Phyllis' chair."

And so the "Follies" had an unplanned intermission while a bomb squad swept the room. Schlafly's eldest son, John, a then twenty-eight-year-old law student and talented pianist (the accompanist for the *Follies*), who normally shuns the press, leaned against a wall outside the ballroom talking to me. He seemed a bit shaken by the threat against his mother. "Of course, I'd like Mother to get out of this fight and get out of the headlines. She's already too controversial for her own safety. Too many people hate her for what she has done. I'm scared for her."

A week later, three assistant TV-talk-show producers were planning an end-of-the-decade wrapup. "Who is the most controversial male figure of the decade?" They couldn't agree. So they moved on to the female side. "Who is the most controversial female figure of the decade?" "Phyllis Schlafly," the three answered, almost in unison. A couple of minutes later one asked, "What about Bella [Abzug]?" "In comparison to Phyllis, Bella is about as controversial as Doris Day," answered her colleague. Case closed.

2

A Star Is Born

Phyllis MacAlpin Stewart was born on August 15, 1924, in Barnes Hospital, St. Louis, one ounce short of eight pounds and raring to go: "She was a peppy baby and she was never cross or had any fever," her mother wrote in reviewing Phyllis' first-year performance.

The baby's proud mother was 28-year-old Odile Dodge Stewart (nicknamed Dadie), now 84 and living with Phyllis in Alton. The father was 45-year-old John Bruce Stewart (called Bruce), who died in 1955 at age 76. This was the first marriage for both and the first child. (A second daughter, Odile, would be born 5½ years later.)

To say that Dadie was pleased with her new baby is a gross understatement. She was utterly euphoric. She noted—for posterity?—practically every move her beloved firstborn made, and went into great detail on the milestones.

"After coming home from the hospital, Phyllis' first outing was to the Cathedral (the St. Louis Cathedral) to be baptized —September 6, 1924, Feast of the Birthday of Our Lady. . . . The baptismal dress was made of real val lace from my sister Phyllis (for whom the baby was named) and my First Communion dress. She wore my baby gold medal and chain. The family all said the baby behaved beautifully."

"None of the relatives can believe it," wrote Dadie on her daughter's four-month birthday. "Phyllis smiles constantly."[1]

The baby, Dadie reported, was "indescribably precious." So she clipped poems—Alfred Lord Tennyson vying with anonymous doggerel—to express her joy with her blue-eyed, blond, curly-haired daughter:

> I've watched the gentle coming
> Of many a new-born spring.
> And England's sweetest sky-larks
> I've heard upon the wing.
> I've seen an Alpine sunrise
> And sunsets out at sea
> And nightingales in southern lands
> Have sung love songs to me.
> But sweeter than all song of birds
> And fairer than all skies
> Is a baby's first loud laughter
> And the sky blue in its eyes.

She saved every babyish Christmas and birthday card, painstakingly printed in a child's king-sized letters: "Love to dear daddy from your baby Phyllis" or "To Mother a kiss form [sic] Phyllis."

Every normal phase in a child's development was, in the Stewart home, an event: When Phyllis had her first picture

---

[1] And she never stopped smiling—a habit that years later would infuriate her opponents. "Phyllis Schlafly is such a fake," said Betty Friedan in 1977. "She's always smiling. Anyone who smiles that much has got to be a fraud. It's enough to make you want to punch her in the mouth."

taken; when Phyllis' first tooth appeared at seven months ("At twelve months she had twelve teeth!"); when she took her first step at age one; when she said her first word at thirteen months ("I was away at a party and Mother as usual was taking care of Phyllis," Dadie wrote breathlessly. "That afternoon, September 10, 1925, she said 'itta wag,' reaching for Mother's handkerchief."); when, at fourteen months, she "saw her reflection for the first time in the long glass."

Phyllis Schlafly today is a supremely confident woman; the product, obviously, of a secure and happy childhood.

Although Phyllis later married a successful man, and has been attacked by her opponents for not understanding the problems of the masses of her sisters, she grew up in very modest circumstances. Her father lost his job during the Depression and was never quite able to pull the family finances back together.

At the time of Phyllis' birth, Bruce Stewart, well into middle age, was a heavy-equipment sales engineer for Westinghouse. He did not have a degree in engineering, but he had a natural talent for it. His customers were chief engineers of factories, so he had to know his stuff. And, according to his younger daughter, Odile, he did. "He loved engineering and he loved his job and his company. He was just devoted to the company. Nothing was as good as a Westinghouse product."

The family rented a small house in the St. Louis suburb of Normandy, northwest of St. Louis. Bruce had just become a father for the second time and things were looking good.

Then the Depression hit. Westinghouse sent a man to St. Louis from the East to "run" the St. Louis office; in other words, to cut personnel and, wherever possible, to hire younger men at lower wages. In 1930, Bruce Stewart was fifty-one years old. He had been with Westinghouse for twenty-five years, but had no pension. His income simply stopped. "I always felt terrifically sorry for Bruce," said Carl

Pfeifer, also an engineer and Bruce's brother-in-law, "because he lost out when he was too old to go out and find something else."

The Stewarts, like millions of others, suffered during the Depression. Suffering, of course, is relative. They never wanted for food or a roof over their heads. But they were solidly middle-class people—Dadie was from an old, once socially prominent St. Louis family—in instantly and greatly reduced circumstances. Suddenly they had no income, and savings were dwindling rapidly.

Dadie's uncle, W. Pratte Layton, invited his niece and his grandnieces to his home in Los Angeles to spend the long, hard year of 1932–33. Bruce remained in St. Louis with Dadie's parents and embarked every morning, a sheaf of want ads stuck in his pocket, on a fruitless search for work.

Phyllis spent fourth grade in a Los Angeles public school (the Cahuenga, where she was already getting "exceptionals" in thrift, respect for private property, and recognition of the value of time). For eight-year-old Phyllis, the trip was a great adventure. "Mother, Odile, and I left St. Louis the night of June 7 for California," she wrote with flawless grammar and spelling. "Daddy put us on the train at the Delmar Station. We were on the train three days and nights before we pulled into Los Angeles. We stayed at Unkie's house and he took us many places. The most beautiful I thought was the San Fernando Gardens. It has a long pergola with a grape arbor over it. It also has all kinds of trees, plants, and flowers."

For Phyllis' mother, it was a trying time. She missed Bruce and she feared it was futile for a middle-aged man to go job hunting during the Depression. She worried the experience would scar, or perhaps even break, him.

She also worried about her parents, who, at this point, were nearly as hard up as their daughter and son-in-law. Ernest Dodge was a lawyer, an 1885 graduate of St. Louis Law

School, now known as Washington University Law School (from which his granddaughter Phyllis would graduate 93 years later). From 1894–99 he served as assistant city attorney. After leaving city government—he had run for office and lost—he opened a private law practice, practicing a total of 55 years. The Dodges were solid members of St. Louis Catholic society. But Ernest was ill for the last two decades of his life. Because he was in practice for himself, he had no pension to pay the hospital and household bills.

As an economy measure, the Dodges moved from their house in the city—on fashionable West Pine, where their daughters had grown up—into the Normandy house, with their daughter and son-in-law. When Ernest died in 1940, a year before Phyllis' graduation from high school, he and his wife were still, as an economy measure, living with the Stewarts.

Dadie was right about the dim job prospects for an out-of-work, middle-aged engineer without a college degree. "When she came back from California," her daughter Odile explained, "she knew what she had to do. She had to get a job. And she did." As Phyllis put it, "We had to eat."

Phyllis' mother went to work out of necessity, not for any reason as "frivolous" as personal fulfillment. Some of her daughter's impatience with women who glorify working and cheapen homemaking probably stems from this fundamental fact of her early life—her mother was forced to work at a time when women didn't; when she would have much preferred to keep house and work for good causes instead of wages.

What carried the family through those years was Mrs. Stewart's education. Both Dadie and her younger sister Lois (Phyllis' godmother) had been educated at a Sacred Heart convent and both had gone on to graduate from Washington University, making Dadie one of only two of her classmates to get a college degree. She had two degrees, in fact—a B.A. and a degree in library science.

But in those days, two college degrees were worth about as much as one college degree. Dadie needed a job immediately and so she took what she could get—she sold yard goods and then draperies for twelve dollars a week at Famous-Barr, a St. Louis department store. She spent nine hours on her feet and two hours traveling on streetcars between Normandy and downtown St. Louis.

Fortunately, she had a teaching certificate as well as a library degree. She applied to every school in the area and when nothing came of it, she reapplied. She kept at it until she was offered a job teaching English in a public elementary school. In 1937, when Phyllis was in eighth grade, Dadie landed a more challenging and slightly more lucrative job as librarian of the St. Louis Art Museum.

A year before, in the interests of saving money and being on a streetcar line, the Stewarts (and Dodges) moved from their suburban house into an apartment in St. Louis' Central West End.[2] Every morning, Dadie, who never owned or drove a car, took a streetcar, transferred to a bus, and then walked a hard half mile to the top of Art Hill in Forest Park, where the museum was located. Some of those years, there was no bus running into the park, which added another mile onto her daily hike.

Betsy Thomas Birmingham was Phyllis' neighbor, classmate, and probably her closest friend during school. She recalled Phyllis' mother as "strong, brilliant, and rather commanding. You wouldn't call her soft." "She had twice as much substance, presence, as anyone I knew," said Virginia Leyder, another classmate of Phyllis'. "She was serious, dedicated, of

[2] They moved frequently within the area—6105 Pershing, 4933 West Pine, finally 4961 McPherson, where they remained for many years—Phyllis' home during high school, in fact, until she married in 1949. Her wedding reception was held there on October 20, 1949.

the mind, completely of the mind," said Maie Kimball Schlafly, Phyllis' classmate and later her sister-in-law.

Dadie was, quite simply, a capable and qualified woman before it was thought necessary for women to be capable and qualified. "She took charge of that library like Napoleon at Austerlitz," said her brother-in-law Carl Pfeifer. The library had never been managed by a professional. Working on a very limited budget and starting practically from scratch, she turned it into a first-rate institution.

Sacred Heart nun Mother Richard, one of Phyllis' teachers, described Dadie as "the driving force in that family. She was a most determined woman. I don't always—or even usually—agree with Phyllis, but I knew way back then that Mrs. Stewart was going to raise a remarkable girl."

Dadie worked not only to feed her daughters, but also to educate them. She worked so her daughters could have a Sacred Heart education as she had—a private, Catholic, classical education, heavy on Latin, French, and Christian doctrine, that would require a hefty tuition payment.

Phyllis had started kindergarten in 1928, age four, at public school—the DeMun in University City, where her family then lived. In the third grade, the Stewarts painstakingly pinched pennies so Phyllis could go to a Sacred Heart school in St. Louis known as City House. Dadie considered that year of Catholic education essential because she wanted Phyllis to have the religious training she needed to prepare for making her First Communion (which she did in April 1932).

But that was the first and last year she would have of private education until the seventh grade. She spent the fourth in California, she spent the fifth and sixth at the Roosevelt Public School in Normandy. Times were so bad by then that no matter how assiduously they scrimped and scraped, City House tuition was as unreachable as membership in a country club.

But, as everyone said, Dadie was one determined woman.

She arranged with the Sacred Heart nuns to catalog and maintain the school's long-neglected library—in exchange for free tuition for her daughter.

It was, Mother Richard recalled, the kind of job that would have been full-time for most people. "Mrs. Stewart did what someone else would have done in five days, in one, and did it expertly." She worked Tuesdays through Sundays at the art museum and Monday—her one day off—at City House.

By the time she started working at the museum—her fourth year of full-time work—Dadie realized that working was not going to be temporary. She kept the museum job for twenty-five years, until her retirement.

Her husband eventually found work, but nothing that compared in pay or challenge to the Westinghouse job. He really didn't pull out of the slump until the country did, during World War II, when, suddenly, with all the young engineers being drafted, older men were at a premium. He landed a job as an electrical engineer with the War Production Board and later he joined the staff of the Reconstruction Finance Corporation, handling technical classification of government equipment and disposal of surplus equipment. He was already in his sixties, on the verge of forced retirement. And when he did retire, he didn't get a government pension because, two months before he became eligible, President Truman closed the St. Louis office and reopened it in Kansas City. Bruce's luck was not improving.

Bruce Stewart was the son of Andrew Frazer Stewart, who immigrated to the United States from Scotland at age ten (making him the only one of Phyllis' grandparents who did not have ancestors who fought in the American Revolution). Bruce was born in Jackson, Michigan, but lived much of his early life in Richmond, Virginia, where his father—a railroad worker—had been transferred. Bruce thought he was a confirmed bachelor when Westinghouse transferred him to St.

Louis. There he met and married Dadie. He was seventeen years her senior.

Friends of Phyllis' recalled her father as quiet—shy, not nearly as outgoing as his wife. (Phyllis' shyness—and she was, according to her Uncle Carl, very shy as a girl and young woman—came from the paternal side.) One classmate described Bruce Stewart as "mild."

But many of Phyllis' friends couldn't quite place him. "You know, I can't remember him. I just sort of vaguely see him. He was an engineer of some kind. I don't ever remember hearing him talk," said Maie Kimball Schlafly.

All those who knew him in the early years agreed that Bruce Stewart was a changed man—not a broken man, but a quiet one—after he lost his job with Westinghouse.

"He was a most loving man, a most considerate man," said Odile. "Of course, I don't know how his nature was affected. I know my mother told me that he was just almost destroyed when he was let go. . . . When this happened, something just closed in. He just couldn't believe this could happen after all the years that he had devoted to the company. He just never was able to have the zest that he had before. But he had a very good sense of humor. You'd never know that he felt bad about anything. He never quarreled. He never got excited about things. He read Shakespeare—he was thoroughly familiar with almost all the plays. He smoked a pipe. Those were about his only pleasures—and going to Richmond to visit his brother and sister." (He only went to Richmond about once every other year when his bachelor brother, a successful C.P.A., would send him money to come.)

Bruce Stewart was out of a job for many years, but he remained a Republican. He took special pride in saying he was born in Jackson, Michigan, "the birthplace of the Republican Party." A contradiction? Not in Odile's eyes. "Poor as we were, he was a Republican. Because I guess, I guess we're just individualists. We feel that people can do anything they want if they try, work at it, which is, I think, opposed to a philosophy that somebody will do it for you. He certainly didn't like [Franklin D.] Roosevelt. I can remember things he would not approve of. Welfare programs—he thought they were terrible." Bruce would have no sooner asked the government for help than he would have asked his daughters to quit school and go to work to help support the family.

"Bruce was one of the few people I knew in 1932 who did not vote for Roosevelt," said Carl Pfeifer. "He said the country was going broke with the election of Roosevelt, and we're sure getting there now. Bruce was in a position where maybe he could have benefited from Roosevelt's promises, but he knew Roosevelt's answers weren't the right answers. Bruce used to say that his grandchildren will be the ones who'll have to pay for Roosevelt's war on the free-enterprise system; for this planned economy and welfare state he was building."

Bruce, unemployed, let go without a pension, was nonetheless a true believer in free enterprise. For him, friends said, free enterprise was nothing less than an article of faith. He believed in it with a fervor that most people save for religion.

In 1955, when Bruce was ailing with what proved to be his terminal illness, Phyllis took him on his first and only trip that wasn't job- or family-related. They went to New York and took the boat ride around Manhattan Island to see the Statue of Liberty. "It was one of the biggest thrills of his life," Phyllis recalled. "To him the Statue of Liberty was like a holy shrine" —a symbol of a system in which a person could start at the bottom, and, with hard work, perseverance, and the bit of luck that eluded Bruce, climb to the top.

Bruce's passion for free enterprise was more than political in origin. He was what his daughter calls the most glorious product of the free-enterprise system—an inventor.

For seventeen years, in his spare time, Bruce worked on a plan for a rotary engine. He was granted a patent in 1944 and his spirits soared. He wrote to Phyllis, then at Radcliffe studying for her master's, "It is my hope that someday you may be able to realize something out of this." Like so many of his hopes, that one, too, was dashed. The invention was never sold. Although Bruce never made any money from it, he did make the papers—the New York *Herald Tribune,* the Chicago *Daily News,* the Seattle *Times,* the St. Louis papers and, the biggest thrill of all, the Richmond papers.

He was pleased that science editors considered his engine—which had only three moving parts—newsworthy. In an article in an influential trade journal, the "Stewart Rotary Engine" was described as embodying the "unconventional concepts typical of the kind of thinking that may bring needed changes in industrial procedures that have remained conventional too long. . . . For years, scientists and engineers have been trying to develop a satisfactory rotary, internal-combustion engine. Yet it has never been worked out on a practical basis. Now Stewart has invented a rotary engine incorporating principles which are entirely new."

Engineer Carl Pfeifer called the invention "way ahead of its time. I don't think at the time the auto companies were interested in rotary engines. But look at the Mazda—thirty years later they're coming out with that." But back then, no one thought much about a gas shortage. Unfortunately, Bruce was, again, at the wrong place at the wrong time.[3]

[3] Phyllis Schlafly's boundless—almost gushing—affection and respect for inventors undoubtedly reflected her affection and respect for her father. In her ninth book, *The Power of the Positive Woman,* she paid tribute to inventors (all male) as "the real liberators of women in America." The free-enterprise system, she wrote, "has produced remarkable inventors who have lifted the drudgery of housekeeping from women's shoulders. . . . The great heroes of woman's liberation are not the straggly-haired women of television talk shows and picket lines, but Thomas Edison, who brought the miracle of electricity to our homes to give light and to run all those labor-saving devices—the equivalent, perhaps, of a half-dozen household servants for every American woman."

"When you think about it," said Odile, "we got along very well. My mother was only earning about $150 a month [when she was librarian at the art museum]. And we lived on that for years. She was always able to stretch a dime into a dollar. She was extraordinary. She could walk into a department store and find the only bargain there. And so we had nice things. We lived like we had much more money than we did because my mother worked at it." Keeping up appearances was very important to Dadie.

Had Dadie married the man to whom she was practically engaged when she met Bruce (the man became a multimillionaire), she would have been very prominent in social work and volunteer work—the female occupation of the St. Louis aristocracy into which she was born.

Dadie Stewart was poor but blue-blooded. She was digging for her roots long before it became popular and had discovered that both sides—her father's English and her mother's French—were firmly implanted in U.S. soil at the time of the Revolution.[4]

Dadie's lineage was extraordinary. Her father, Ernest Dodge, was a descendant of General Henry Dodge, the Indian fighter. Fort Dodge, Iowa, and Dodge City, Kansas, were both named for him, the latter slipping into Wild West legend thanks to Marshalls Wyatt Earp and Bat Masterson, both of whom tried to tame the notoriously wild town.

Phyllis' mother's ancestor, Captain François Vallé, was the outstanding civil and military leader of Ste. Geneviève during the American Revolution. Another ancestor in 1818 gave hospitality to Mother Philippine Duchesne, who came to St. Charles, Missouri, to open the first Sacred Heart school in

---

[4] Phyllis, who inherited this fascination with her family tree, obviously had no trouble breaking into the DAR, which she served in both state and national offices—her most cherished, national defense chairman.

America. His daughters, the "two little Pratte girls," were Mother Duchesne's first pupils.

Dadie was determined to give her daughters the social graces that came with the genes. Phyllis was not quite twelve when she started going to Junior League dancing class in the ballroom of the St. Louis Woman's Club. Bids to the Cotillion came later.[5]

The Stewarts had no money to buy the proper gown, and not wearing the proper gown was, of course, unthinkable. So Dadie improvised. Dresses were homemade by Phyllis' grandmother from remnants Dadie bought, usually on sale, with her Famous-Barr employee's discount. Or gowns were hand-me-downs, donated by one of Dadie's still-prosperous childhood friends. Phyllis had as many dresses as the next little Junior Leaguer, but Phyllis did not have a store-bought dress until she was eighteen and earning her own money.

It was very important to Dadie that her daughters be exposed to, as she put it, "the finest things." Instead of getting perfume or some other frill for Christmas, the Stewart girls got balcony seats to the theater or the ballet. At the start of every school year, Mrs. Stewart directed Phyllis to write a letter to the manager of the St. Louis Symphony, telling him

[5] Phyllis even made a debut, although an unconventional one. The proper time for her to have "come out" would have been after her first year of college in 1942—but during World War II, very few people, and certainly not the Stewarts, thought of such frivolities. In 1946, after Phyllis had gotten her master's from Radcliffe and spent a year in Washington, many of her friends decided to give informal debutante parties. Phyllis, then earning her own money, happily participated.

The next year she was invited to become a provisional member of the Junior League. Provisionals had to attend lectures and pass a written examination before being admitted to full membership. Phyllis was one of two that year judged "outstanding." A paper she wrote, "St. Louis Slum Clearance," got quoted extensively on the front page of the St. Louis *Post-Dispatch*. She was, obviously, a debutante with a difference.

how much she wanted to attend the student concerts but that she couldn't afford the $2.50 for a season ticket. Phyllis wrote her first letter at age six, and for ten years straight, the manager sent her a complimentary season ticket.

How is a daughter shaped by her parents? The strongest features of Phyllis Schlafly's strong personality are traits she acquired from her parents.

Bruce Stewart may have been a mild man, but his opinions about politics and politicians were anything but. He couldn't, for example, find any redeeming quality in Franklin Roosevelt and his New Deal. And Bruce did not equivocate. People and trends and issues and policies were good or bad, black or white. Most things were as simple as that. He felt perfectly comfortable in speaking in absolutes.

The discussion around the Stewart dinner table was often about politics—even about the characters of politicians. "I would say that my father's politics had an enormous effect on Phyllis," said Odile, "because she admired and respected him very much. Phyllis wasn't very verbose, ever. She would just take it all in. She would always take things in, just listen very quietly to him—and remember."

"When she was convinced of something she held true," said Mother Richard, "she just wouldn't budge. She had her own opinions and she felt she had thought them out and she had a right to them."

"I know one thing for sure," said Carl Pfeifer, who had just watched his niece decimate ERA on "The Phil Donahue Show." ("There is *no* affirmative case for the ERA," she proclaimed. "There is *no* law that discriminates against women. ERA does not give women *any* rights, benefits, or opportunities that they do not now have.") "Whenever I see Phyllis on television, I always think, like father, like daughter."

But Phyllis got more than strong opinions from growing up in that household. She got a capacity for hard work that has turned one woman into the nemesis of an entire movement—a movement supported by practically everyone; by senators, Presidents, First Ladies, organizations ranging from Hadassah to Women in Communications.

When Bruce Stewart was disappointed in his job hunting or working at a job that didn't tax his considerable talent, loitering in a bar and ruing his fate with the boys would have been the last thing in the world he'd have done. He worked on his invention.

After five days and Sunday afternoon at her library job and the seventh day at City House working off her daughter's tuition, Dadie came home to her ongoing project—a book she was writing on the history of St. Louis.

Leisure time in the Stewart home did not mean what it meant for most families. "I think my sister thought studying was fun," recalled Odile. "She was a hard worker *always*. I suppose my best memories of her are just always studying. She'd come home from school and go into her room and sit at her desk and work." And when she wasn't studying, she was doing something constructive—always constructive; helping with the cooking, cleaning, shopping, ironing; writing a letter to her aunt in Richmond, working on her next merit badge for Girl Scouts. It was not a household in which one just sat and stared or moped. Wasting time was as *verboten* as wasting money.

Leisure time for Schlafly as an adult also did not mean what it meant for most people. Asked if she had any hobbies she answered, "Yes . . . nuclear strategy and Republican national conventions."

In Miami Beach in 1968, as a Nixon delegate to the Republican National Convention, Schlafly was interviewed on the convention floor by a St. Louis *Post-Dispatch* reporter.

"It's like being at a wonderful party," she bubbled. Of the 1964 convention in San Francisco that nominated Barry Goldwater, Schlafly recalled, ". . . that week has got to rate as one of the most happy, thrilling, exciting weeks of my life."

Phyllis Schlafly simply does not watch television or read novels or do her nails or go to lunch with the girls. Friends reported that her one unserious passion is for old movies (especially Nelson Eddy musicals), which usually air sometime after "The Late Show." So she goes to sleep, sets the alarm, watches the movie, and still gets up the next morning at her unvarying six-thirty. Fun to Phyllis Schlafly is reading the latest Heritage Foundation analysis of SALT II, and out-and-out frivolity is writing lyrics for a show spoofing the "libbers." Popular culture to Phyllis is a Gilbert and Sullivan operetta, which she considers clever and, best of all, useful—the political skits she writes are often parodies of Gilbert and Sullivan.

Former NOW President Karen DeCrow and Phyllis Schlafly were sitting on the stage of a high school gymnasium, waiting for the curtain to rise on a debate. DeCrow peered through the crack in the curtain and said to her opponent, "My God, all these people, Phyllis. I feel like Mick Jagger." "Who's Mick Jagger?" Phyllis asked. "He's the lead singer in the Rolling Stones." "What's the Rolling Stones?"

Most important, from growing up in that house, Phyllis and her sister developed a passion for achieving; for becoming strong and independent—a passion, in those years, found mainly in men.

Neither Phyllis nor Odile would ever forget the lesson, learned the hard way, that a good education is something no one—not a new district manager or politicians who lead the country into a Depression—can take away. "I felt a compulsion," Phyllis recalled of her teen-age years, "to get myself trained to support myself, which my mother had done before me and very fortunately."

Phyllis also felt a compulsion to make money; to prove to herself that she could, if necessary, take care of herself. And so, from a very early age, she kept meticulous lists of the money she earned and how she spent it. On her fifteenth birthday, she wrote, "By this time the money I had earned consisted of the following: When I was 10-years-old for selling the *American Girl* magazine subscription—$5 (money used to buy Girl Scout equipment); When I was 13-years-old for a joke sold to the *Post Dispatch* children's page—$1 (money used to go to a Nelson Eddy concert); When I was 15-years-old for three appearances in Dr. Patrick Gainer's Glee Club on KMOX radio station, 'The Land That We Live In'—$5 (money used to buy yarn for a sweater)," etc.

It has become almost a staple—a cliché—of pro-ERA editorials to note that Phyllis Schlafly's vehement opposition—indeed, aversion—to women's liberation and ERA just doesn't jibe with her achievements, which include a master's from Radcliffe, her races for Congress, her current, almost ubiquitous presence on television talk shows, her books, her syndicated column. "If I had a daughter, I'd want her to be a housewife just like Phyllis Schlafly," said Karen DeCrow.

"I don't see any contradiction," replied Schlafly with her best look of studied incredulousness. "You forgot to add my six children, this house, which is large and which I keep running smoothly." She was about to add another domestic virtue when she cut herself off.

"I'll tell you in one sentence what's wrong with ERA and women's lib. It's the libbers' dogma that there are no innate differences between men and women, that there are only 'stereotyped' differences that a sexist society imposes. That's rubbish.

"Perhaps because my mother provided a model of woman-hood, I've always known that there really are differences between the sexes—innate differences—which we ignore only at peril to the family and civilization as we now know it."

In her speech during the Washington "Gala" on March 22, 1979—the day, Schlafly claimed, ERA, long withering, finally fell from the constitutional vine—she offered some clues into "how we beat ERA." Surely she had her mother—who carried on so nobly, so efficiently, so cheerfully—in mind when she said: "It was first of all a battle that had to be fought and led by women. . . . The battle had to be fought by women because women brought something very special to this task. Women are like tea bags: You don't know their strength until they get into hot water. . . . Women have a very special quality of hope and of perseverance. It had to be somebody who laughs year in and year out. It had to be women who dared to hope that it could be won."

Surely she had her mother in mind when she wrote in *The Power of the Positive Woman:* "Women are different from men in dealing with the fundamentals of life itself. Men are philosophers, women are practical and 'twas ever thus. Men may philosophize about how life began and where we are heading; women are concerned about feeding the kids today. No woman would ever, as Karl Marx did, spend years reading political philosophy in the British Museum while her child starved to death. Women don't take naturally to a search for the intangible and the abstract. . . ."

In Schlafly's "God-given order of things," learned at her mother's knee, women are the weaker sex in only the most literal sense. (And no amount of Title IX-mandated coed football will ever change that.) This "fact," Schlafly argued with the confidence of one who claims "God is on our side," is the reason why society's premier job—bearing children, nurturing and holding the family together—has fallen on women's narrower but more resilient shoulders.[6]

Because they are special, women, Schlafly said, deserve "special" treatment, which may mean a bouquet of flowers, a door held open, an exemption from the draft—all external signs of man's respect for woman; respect that to Schlafly has a religious origin:

"American women are a privileged group . . . beneficiaries of a tradition of respect for women which dates from the Christian Age of Chivalry and the honor and respect paid to Mary, the Mother of Christ."

When women insist on acting like men, respect dissipates. And when men lose respect for women, they lose respect for the family, and society's edges and ultimately its core crumble (precisely, Schlafly claimed, one of the causes of the fall of the Roman Empire).

Incongruous, though, isn't it? Considering that Mrs. Stewart, Phyllis' "model of womanhood," was forced off the pedestal and into the bleak, cruel Depression-era job market. No, Schlafly replied, for to her the pedestal is not a perch for lounging around downing bonbons and receiving insipid callers. Women are special because they bear and raise children, make breakfast, keep the hearth burning, scrub the bathroom floor, nurse a sick child through the night—and also, perhaps, work a full-time job.

As a young woman, Phyllis Stewart got enough bouquets of

---

[6] The heroes that dot Schlafly's books and speeches are invariably sons and daughters of strong women—women who raised great children against staggering odds, often without the help of a husband. General Daniel James, Jr., the first black to be named a four-star general, started "in the ghetto with absolutely nothing"—except, of course, an invincible mother. In spite of the fact that she herself had only a limited education, she "taught Daniel at home until he entered high school."

flowers from suitors to stock a small florist's shop. She saved every card, often noting the exact number of roses, whether they were long-stemmed, whether they were yellow or red. To Phyllis, a dozen long-stemmed red roses were more than just a pleasant gesture; they symbolized something.

"When ERA first came up," said Odile, "I was a little confused as to what it was all about. Growing up, I never felt that I was a second-class citizen. I grew up to feel that women just have a superior life in this country. My father believed my mother was special—and he treated her as such."

Some years ago, NOW ran what has become a famous—in Schlafly's eyes an infamous—ad. A spirited, gorgeous baby sat atop the message, "This healthy, normal baby has a handicap. She was born female."

"When we were growing up," Odile continued, "I certainly never felt any tinge of prejudice or aspect of women being put down. I never did. I always felt that I could do what I wanted to do and I did."

"It's all in your outlook," her sister agreed. "I think women are superior human beings and in this country have every advantage. I agree with Eleanor Roosevelt, who said nobody can make you feel inferior without your own consent."

Schlafly thought so much of an address given to Radcliffe alumnae by Pulitzer Prize-winning historian Barbara Tuchman that Schlafly reprinted a portion in "The Gospel According to Phyllis" (that is, *The Power of the Positive Woman*). "I really identify with this," she said.

I had no idea that growing up female in America was a position of slavery. . . . I didn't know that to be a woman was really a very terrible fate. In fact, I thought we had an advantage. I thought that the capacity to re-create life, to create another life, which was what the Bible gave to God and Nature gave to women, gave us a superiority over men. . . . I didn't feel that anyone was repressing my potential. . . . I never asked for help; it just never occurred to me that someone ought to help me. . . . I always wonder when I read in the papers and magazines especially this year, International Women's Year, why young women feel their capacities have been repressed and that 'they,' some unnamed 'they,' have prevented them from fulfilling their potential. What's to prevent it? If you have energy and the drive, you're going to do something with it.

"I have three sons," said Carl Pfeifer, "and now that I look back on it—at that time, and even today, most men will say they won't be really happy until they have a son. As if a girl isn't quite good enough. Not Bruce, I never heard him say anything of the sort, ever. I think he was truly a liberated man in that sense. He didn't think a girl because she's a girl should be any less ambitious or serious—or taken any less seriously —than a boy. And Dadie certainly didn't think so.

"I remember how worried they were when Phyllis got the fellowship to Radcliffe, about her living away from home. But they certainly wouldn't have stood in a son's way and it would never have occurred to them to stand in a daughter's way. You know, Dadie and Bruce's college graduation gift to Phyllis was a Phi Beta Kappa key, which I think says a lot about the sort of family it was."

The prevailing stereotype of Phyllis Schlafly is as a cold, calculating woman, constitutionally incapable of warm relationships. Phyllis, from all accounts, did have a loving relationship with her parents. She saved one letter, from her father, dated June 1945 and sent to her in Cambridge. Above it she wrote, "The sweetest letter I ever received."

"My dear Baby, It seems such a long time since you went away and I have missed you so much. . . . The picture you sent us sits on the living room table and it is such a fine picture. I don't know how much time I have spent staring at it. . . . The picture looks so young that I cannot see how I ever let you go away from home [she was twenty]. I am always living in hopes that you will soon be back home again. I know I don't have to tell you to take advantage of the wonderful opportunity. It is unique and so are you."

3

The Education of a Conservative

"Phyllis took to school like most children take to the circus," said her Uncle Carl Pfeifer.

September 4, 1928: Phyllis Stewart had barely turned four, and already she was in kindergarten—a year earlier than normal, her mother eager to launch her daughter's academic career.

"Her first day at kindergarten was a very momentous event," wrote Dadie at the time. "She wasn't too thrilled about going because one of her little friends knew what it meant. . . . But the stimulus of the other baby playmates has made her breathless to return." The shine never wore off. "All my school years were most happy and most full," wrote sixteen-year-old Phyllis Stewart, revealing not a hint of the turmoil that torments most adolescents.

The major influence, certainly, on Phyllis Stewart Schlafly's intellectual and spiritual development was City House, the all-girls Sacred Heart school she attended four years of high school and in third, seventh and eighth grades of elementary.

City House was a Catholic school, but very definitely not a parish school. It commanded three times the prestige, tuition, and respect for tradition.

Mother Madeleine Sophie Barat founded the Society of the Sacred Heart in France in 1800. Five years later, Napoleon Bonaparte dispatched the "Ladies of Christian Instruction" to the colonies, and in 1818 Mother Rose Philippine Duchesne arrived in the primitive Louisiana Territory, three years before Missouri joined the Union. In 1827, the Religious of the Sacred Heart built a school in St. Louis, down by the Mississippi, where it remained until 1893, when they moved City House to Taylor and Maryland avenues in the city's Central West End.

City House always had a certain snob appeal, perhaps because the Sacred Heart order was patterned after the Jesuits and, by tradition, taught Latin, French, and other classical subjects to girls of good family. Also, in France, after the Revolution, the only people who could afford to send their daughters to a Sacred Heart convent were the monied classes.

"I've been very lucky in being in such a class at such a school," sixteen-year-old Phyllis wrote. "The girls were not only versatile, did fine and were really nice, but also came from the good, long-standing St. Louis families whose homes I was always proud to visit."

Mother Doyle, a City House graduate and teacher during Phyllis' time, claimed that the snooty reputation might have fit in France but didn't really in the United States. "You had children of all kinds of people. We had Kit Carson's daughter going to City House. She was a half-breed. It's a mixture. You will have plenty of wealthy people but not all."

By Phyllis' day, the "monied classes" requirement *had* loosened considerably. Many of the children, as Phyllis noted with such satisfaction, were "from good, long-standing St.

Louis families," but many were, like Phyllis, from families that were long on lineage and short on cold cash.

Current finances aside, the school did attract daughters of a certain kind of old-line Catholic family, with certain kinds of goals and values, which City House nuns taught and reinforced. It was more an atmosphere than a statement, a feeling than a policy. City House girls came away believing they were somehow special, blessed. Phyllis Stewart came away sure of her family, her religion, her teachers, her friends—and, most of all, sure of herself. She came away knowing who she was and where she was going.

Devotion, stability, continuity, direction were at City House's core. It was the sort of place where generation after generation of a family's daughters got educated. The nuns would stretch the rules and shrink the tuition to keep a Sacred Heart education in the family. (Phyllis' Aunt Lois graduated from City House and her mother graduated from the original Sacred Heart convent in St. Charles, Missouri.)

As an adult, Phyllis Schlafly oozed self-confidence—in 1975 taking on law school, for example, in the midst of an already insanely busy schedule, and telling a reporter she planned to get her degree in her spare time. Confidence of that magnitude just doesn't happen. It's bred early on—stimulated by the sort of unstinting personal attention a girl got at City House.

The nuns knew every student personally. If they didn't teach her, they probably taught her mother or sister. They knew each girl's strengths and weaknesses. Students were not here this year and gone the next. "Today I could tell you the married name of every one of the girls in Phyllis' graduating class," said Mother Doyle. "I could probably even tell you what her rank in class was and whether she had an aptitude for mathematics or Latin."

Which is not to say that City House was all warmth and personal concern. Phyllis Stewart left that school so disciplined that she was convinced that anyone could do anything if he or she was willing to work and work and work. Society's failures were not failures because they were deprived or because they were victims of racism or sexism. They were failures because they were lazy and undisciplined.

City House standards were as rigid as they were exalted. The student who failed to meet them or flouted them was likely to bring down upon herself, if not the wrath of God, then, at the very least, the wrath of the Reverend Mother. Strict discipline was considered a prerequisite, not an inhibitor of creativity. A girl stood up when the nun entered the classroom. A girl curtsied when she passed Reverend Mother in the hall. If a girl slipped up, she came in on Saturday and polished the giant brass doorknobs on the massive oak doors. There were history medals and English medals and Latin medals for outstanding academic achievement, but there was also an equally coveted politeness medal.

During classes, except when a student was reciting, the rule was silence—no exceptions. When the nun dismissed them, students marched to their next class in ranks and, of course, in silence. After an opening prayer, more silence. The girls were required to wear uniforms, of course, and also gloves, every day; black normally, white for special occasions.

One of many French traditions that Mother Duchesne brought over from France was this equal emphasis on literature and discipline, on mathematics and manners. Anyone who has watched Phyllis Schlafly "present" herself to a state legislature during an ERA hearing can see evidence galore of this early training.

Every week, the girls gathered for awesome, sometimes terrifying conduct-rating sessions called Primes. They formed a semicircle and on signal fell into a deep curtsy to the Reverend Mother. *Faux pas* were invariably committed—a girl would stumble or forget her gloves or have a torn glove—

which meant instant mortification. The purpose, according to Mother Doyle, was to "train girls how to present themselves."

The Reverend Mother would then call up each student individually. The usually trembling girl would fall into another deep curtsy, at which point the Reverend Mother handed her a card on which was printed one of three conduct ratings (determined by weekly meetings of the faculty): *très bien* (very good), *bien* (good), or *assez bien* (which literally translates as "good enough," but psychologically translated as poor). As the girl looked at her rating, the Reverend Mother announced the "judgment" to the entire class. If a girl had committed some dreadful infraction of the rules—such as whispering in study hall—she "lost her notes," which meant she got no card at all—a horrendous disgrace.

"Primes were a very significant thing for these girls," Mother Doyle emphasized, "because they would know every week—and their parents and peers would know—just how they stood in relationship to everybody else." Phyllis Stewart not only almost always got the highest rating, she also regularly won the special ribbon of merit at year's end for the student who had accumulated the most *très biens*.

The City House curriculum was rigorous and rigid. There was no such thing as an elective. Students took French and Latin and they took them simultaneously and they took them in addition to all their other academic courses. A girl could take typing but she'd get no credit for it. "The only practical thing we learned was hem stitching," recalled Mary Hauldren Proctor, a classmate of Phyllis'.

The school day lasted from nine in the morning to five in the afternoon. There was no leaving for lunch and there were few breaks during the day. In the course of the morning it would be typical for a girl to go from English to history to geography to religion to math—all before lunch.

Phyllis flourished under the regimentation. In her class was one other girl of comparable intelligence against whom Phyllis competed with great spirit and success. At the close of every quarter, Phyllis Stewart was the first honor winner, with Jean Fahey a close second—except on one occasion. In a scrapbook Phyllis kept of those years, she explained the lapse. "The highest average was won by Jean Fahey—the first time I lost it. It was because of the absence caused by my having the measles."

"Graduation was all I could have hoped for," Phyllis the sixteen-year-old valedictorian wrote in June 1941. "I won the highest average in classical diploma with gold and blue ribbons for maintaining a ninety-three average over four years."

Asked to describe Phyllis as a schoolgirl, classmates invariably chose the same word: "brilliant." "Her intelligence was extraordinary," said Jean Fahey Eberle. "I certainly wasn't surprised that she went out into the wide world. Simply because it would have been a shame to waste that kind of mind."

A second adjective classmates as frequently used was "serious." Mary Hauldren Proctor recalled a year when the two tied for an essay prize. "We both had to read our essays in front of the class. Hers was very cerebral and mine was kind of silly. I remember a couple of the girls saying they thought Phyllis was hurt because people laughed at me and they just clapped for her."

"She never went through that silly, giddy stage as a teenager," Mary added. "She was never silly. She was always sort of seventeen going on thirty-five."

"She always, always, had her work done. She was never behind—never," recalled Betsy Thomas Birmingham, Phyllis' closest friend. "Two of us had a running four-year bet," said another classmate. "The bet was, would Phyllis ever deviate from being perfect—perfect, I mean *always* knowing the answer, *never* looking out the window or daydreaming when the nun called on her. Even stuff like never looking sick or being the one whose stomach growled so loudly the nun looked annoyed enough to revoke your *très bien*. I bet Phyllis would maintain perfection. I won a Tommy Dorsey album."

Phyllis, Mother Doyle recalled, always had the capacity to concentrate, not to succumb to that irresistible adolescent urge—that strikes girls particularly hard—to pass notes or to send secret signals. "In the study hall she was one of my best students because she wanted to get her work done. She wanted to use every minute of that time. She would work the whole time, never looking around and apparently never daydreaming. She was just a disciplined person. I myself sometimes felt slightly lazy in her presence."

Early on, said Phyllis' teachers, they realized that this was not an ordinary student destined for an ordinary life. Mother Dugas, who taught her Latin, described Phyllis as "a go-getter all along; obviously preparing herself for something big." Mother Doyle agreed: "From her very early years she was definitely there to make her way and that's in the best sense of the word. We admire girls like that and we encourage them." Mother Richard, who was principal during Phyllis' years there, recalled, "You could see that she would amount to something. She was a leader—very, very serious, very determined, very ambitious."

Phyllis Stewart schoolgirl and Phyllis Schlafly political activist were not, friends say, all that different. The traits that have made her what one reporter called "the great white knightess of the anti-ERA movement" were firmly entrenched in her adolescent personality.

Any day of the week, Phyllis Schlafly can keep tabs on ERA hearings in two states and a vote in another and rallies in three others because she is organized, exceptionally organized and efficient. Her life is outlined, she says. That's the way she thinks and writes. Every detail has its place, every task gets added to a list, every item on every list gets completed and deleted. Phyllis is never caught unprepared or unaware. In school, Phyllis Stewart was not only winning the prize for the best average, she was also winning the prize for order, "for having the best-organized school life."

One year, Jean Fahey took biology a semester after Phyllis and borrowed her notes, which turned out to be a perfect outline of a fat, complicated textbook. "I remember her telling me," Jean said, "that she had determined, definitely, that this was the *right* way to handle course material."

Back then, Phyllis displayed an ability to persevere, an uncanny tenacity that later would win her victory after STOP ERA victory. Mother Doyle called this tireless dedication "unmatched in my several decades of teaching experience." If Phyllis didn't know the answer to something, she would have been insulted if the teacher gave it to her. She insisted on figuring things out for herself and she wouldn't rest until she did.

She also developed a meticulousness, an attention to detail that later would flabbergast and frustrate her opponents, but then won her the dubious honor of being spoofed in a satiric newspaper, written by the junior class for the graduating seniors of 1941: "Mrs. Phyllis Stewart, 1941 president of the National Prehistoric Society, discovered a mistake in Webster's Dictionary." As Barry Goldwater wrote in a fund-raising letter for her 1970 race for Congress: "Phyllis is the kind of woman who leaves little to chance."

Her penchant and talent for research—another key to her success in the anti-ERA fight—were, classmates said, also fully formed, and, as one put it, "mind-boggling." When the class was given an assignment, say, to compare one writer to another, she would delve much deeper than the primary works. She'd read criticism and reference works and come up with comparisons that no one, not even her teachers, had thought of. By the time she was through, she had enough background to anticipate any question anyone might ask.

Phyllis Schlafly's most potent weapon in the fight against ERA was, friends and foes agreed, her typewriter—her ability to motivate, some say scare, people into action. She had a knack for words that her teacher praised as early as the sixth grade, when she edited *The Roosevelt Rocket* and posed "The Big Question: Shall we have a Valentine Party?" Editor-in-Chief Phyllis Stewart was squarely on the affirmative side and made her case in a recognizably detailed and impassioned fashion.

In high school, she was one of only two people in the class sufficiently serious about writing to enter what was called the Vicariate Essay Contest (in which Sacred Heart students from Missouri, Louisiana, Illinois, and Ohio competed).

The manner in which Phyllis tackled the assigned topic was radically different from the way, years later, she would tackle FDR or LBJ or ERA or just about anything or anyone smacking of "big government." The essay that won her first prize back in 1940 was excessively romantic, flowery, and breathless—nothing like her succinct, studded-with-sensational-charges style of the 1950s, '60s, and '70s. The similarity, of course, was that in both cases she knew her audience and she knew what style was likely to get her first prize.

The assignment was to write a letter to a friend, describing a third person whom the friend had never met. The woman fifteen-year-old Phyllis described was her Aunt Rebecca, "a fantasy of my own imagination." She wrote to "Judith Darling: . . . I woke under a dry wintry sky, my whole spirit pregnant with the expectant thrill of a new figure about to cross the canvas of my life. She's like the queenly full moon striking only her classic simplicity. . . . To say she is beautiful seems trite when compared with her infinite loveliness. . . . To attempt to analyse her features seems sacrilegious. . . . Everything about her builds up to the climax of those two deep, dark pools of loveliness [her eyes]. . . . I confess I don't understand Rebecca, perhaps no one does. But then if there were no women like Rebecca there would be no need of philosophy."

She won first prize again the next year—graduation year, 1941, when a war raged in Europe and an argument raged at home about whether the United States should come to England's aid. The subject was "Our World Today," and again, the Phyllis writing at sixteen, not yet disillusioned by World War II's aftermath, bore faint resemblance to the adult who often seemed to spot evil lurking around every corner, behind every intention, and in every heart.

". . . to others surveying the unrest and war of today what has been a night of terror has been for me the dawn of a calm, fair day. For I have a rock to stand on—the world itself: a goal to win—success, and a means to my end, a love of beauty. . . . It is a wonderful faculty to be able to look at the world and see only symmetry, to have it shadow everything ugly and sordid. . . . There's war in Europe and blood and hatred and only one nation which still reveres the things I love —England [in the 1940 prize letter to Judith, she signed herself Sylvia Windsor, obviously a teen-aged Anglophile], the citadel of civilization. Tales of her suffering and fortitude flow across the ocean to us until, what can I do, but ache and long that our country peaceful and rich, will come to her aid. . . . I can't believe and I don't believe that the world as I know it is going down. As for the war: I am no voice of experience, nor can I propose any wise or philosophical solution. . . . Only this do I know. But I know it as surely as I live. As long as men and women do not lose that simple refinement of soul which is the key to happiness, the flame of culture and right thinking will never go out. I am not a victim of optimism but I have faith in the integrity of mankind. . . . My only preconceived ideas are unalterable faith in human nature and a fierce determination to always look forward to adventure. . . . Understand our world today? No. But as it is my heritage, I promise to see in it only beauty and truth and to accept it as a thing of elegance and grace."

Just a few months later (unknown to Phyllis), Colonel Charles Lindbergh and General Robert E. Wood addressed fifteen thousand people at an "America First" rally in the St. Louis Arena. They begged the United States not to enter World War II on the side of the Communists, but to let Hitler and Stalin destroy each other and thereby save American and English lives—a view that Phyllis later came to share. (When she became the mother of four sons, she bestowed on General Wood, who was one of the builders of the Panama Canal and the principal builder of Sears, Roebuck, her highest praise: "If I were to name one American whose career I hope my four sons might emulate, that man would be General Robert E. Wood.")

As for her Anglophilia, to Phyllis Schlafly, England came to symbolize socialism run rampant—a once-glorious economy choked, perhaps beyond resuscitation, by government controls.

"I am not a victim of optimism, but I have faith in the integrity of mankind," Phyllis wrote in that prize-winning essay in 1941, a year after Franklin Roosevelt trounced Wendell Willkie. "My only preconceived ideas are unalterable faith in human nature." In her high-school scrapbook, Phyllis Stewart pinned anti-FDR buttons ("No Third Term" and "I Don't Want Eleanor Either") under an election post-mortem that was not intended to win her any prizes, and, perhaps consequently, sounds much more like the adult Phyllis: "The events of the 1940 election have occupied most of the interest from August to Christmas. It was a great surprise to me as well as a disappointment and a loss of faith in the integrity of the American people to see Roosevelt win a third term. Wendell Willkie with his mussed hair and his gallant sincerity won everyone's heart as well as Mrs. Willkie with her simple, lady-like manner. Here's hope for '44."[1]

Phyllis Stewart was certainly not spending all her time fretting about whom the Republicans would put up in '44. She had a fairly normal social life for a Catholic high-school girl of those years.

Already, though, she had acquired the impenetrable, per-fection-personified image that, as Mary Hauldren Proctor remarked, "makes mere mortals shrink or almost want to genuflect in her presence"—the sort of image that would, many years later, prompt George Shipley, her opponent in the 1970 congressional race, to admit his penchant for ignoring the issues in favor of belittling his opponent. "I like to do it. You know how she is. She thinks she is perfect."

Several classmates said, though, that this regal, remote, holier-than-thou image was simple, garden-variety shyness. Phyllis, they agreed, was much too interested in ideas to be a snob of the sort sometimes found at City House—girls who, in the words of Virginia Leyder, "would cut you because your parents couldn't afford to throw a dance at the country club. I always had the impression Phyllis would rather have been home reading than at the country club anyway." What Virginia forgot is that the Stewarts couldn't even afford City House tuition much less country-club dues. People often for-

[1] Twenty-four years later, purged of all vestiges of romanticism, Phyllis Schlafly denounced Willkie as a tool of the "New York king-makers whose long fingers of money and propaganda reached into every state." She also labeled him a "phony Republican" (as a regis-tered Democrat in 1935, he'd been elected by Tammany Hall to the New York County Democratic Committee); a socialist (he'd been a member of the Socialist Club at Indiana University), and a Commu-nist sympathizer ("He hired an identified Soviet agent to ghost-write his book *One World,* and he donated his legal services to defend a top Communist and take his case to the U. S. Supreme Court.").

got that because Phyllis looked like someone whose parents could.

Mary Proctor, then the class's lonely Democrat and today its lonely ERA supporter, described Phyllis' teen-aged appearance in awesome terms: "She had beautiful hair, lovely golden hair. It was sort of like—I've never seen Queen Elizabeth but I imagine her hair is much like that. It had a natural curl to it—perfect. She had a lovely clear complexion like alabaster, when all the rest of us had blemishes."

Phyllis' one physical flaw was nearsightedness. But she hated wearing glasses—perhaps to her a sign of weakness. "Sometimes when she acted like she didn't see you," said Mary Proctor, "she probably didn't." (Phyllis got contact lenses in 1946, when they were as thick and hard as a circle cut from a Coca-Cola bottle. "It's all strictly vanity," she admitted. "I'm the oldest living artifact ever to have contacts.")

Classmates, in fact, recalled supercompetitive, superstudent Phyllis Stewart as being very generous about helping others solve a trick math problem or Latin translation. "Phyllis was fantastic at Latin. She probably speaks Latin," said another member of the class of '41, Dottie Manewal Stephens. "I was not that great. One of the things we used to do on Saturdays was walk over to Forest Park and study. There was a fountain and we'd bring lunch. Phyllis was very, very super at tutoring anybody who needed help."

She was also, classmates said, not a showoff. When called on to recite, she could, undoubtedly, have marshaled her facts, figures, backup research, and made the rest of the class look hopelessly unprepared. She didn't. "She wasn't one to make herself shine at someone else's expense," said Jean Eberle.

Was Phyllis one of the crowd? Yes, although classmates remembered her as being a bit of a loner, very self-sufficient and self-assured. "She wanted friends and she wanted friendship," said Virginia Leyder, "but it wasn't necessary. She could get along on her own. She was more independent than many of the others, who had to travel in groups."

"I think for our age group, she was more dignified, not quite so giggly as the rest of us," said Jean Eberle. "Probably we held her in a bit of awe if the truth came out. She was probably seriously interested in a lot of things that the rest of us didn't get interested in for another ten years—if ever."

A classmate recalled one incident in particular—a fashion show at Vandervoort's Department Store, featuring the collections of and an appearance by Russian exile Grand Duchess Maria. Everyone was interested in two things: one, seeing the majestic, gaudy, wonderful clothes, and two, getting an ice-cream soda afterward—everyone, that is, but Phyllis, who was interested in only one thing—the Russian exile and her treatment by the Communists. "I went to see this famous Russian exile, niece of the Czar killed in the World War," Phyllis wrote at the time. "I talked to her and she was one of the most charming and heroic women I have ever met."

Phyllis had her lighter moments, friends maintained. Betsy Thomas used to spend the night with her at the Stewart apartment. "We'd gossip and giggle. We never went out and painted windows or turned over garbage cans, but she was lighthearted. We collected records and Phyllis liked Glenn Miller and Tommy Dorsey just like everyone else." When Dottie Stephens went away to summer camp, she wrote Phyllis that she couldn't stand it another minute without a hamburger from the neighborhood greasy stand. Phyllis sent her one in the mail.

Fifteen-year-old Anne Schlafly, Phyllis' youngest, was driving with her mother when "Mother pointed out a place where she and her friends used to hang out when she was a teenager. So it wasn't all work and no play," Anne concluded, still sounding somewhat skeptical.

When asked if Phyllis ever got in trouble in high school, Mary Hauldren Proctor replied, "No, never. Wouldn't it be nice to discover something really naughty." From all reports, the naughtiest Phyllis got was smoking, a habit she picked up just out of high school and renounced forever the night before her wedding. The January following graduation, Mother Richard held an informal reunion in her office. Seventeen-year-old Phyllis wrote, "Our first reunion for the ten who graduated last June. All were present and we hadn't changed at all. Five were at college, five working, but we were just as congenial as ever. Mother Richard was so glad to see us and served us tea. Besides, it was the first time we could smoke at the old school."

If her fellow students held her in awe, Phyllis' indifference to sports may have been part of the reason. "Some people might have interpreted it to mean that she thought she was so far above them she didn't need to play sports," explained Virginia Leyder. Phyllis was tall, slender, coordinated, healthy, and, obviously, energetic. She played field hockey and basketball, but really felt they were wastes of time—a tough position to take in a school that required daily athletics and maintained a feverish competition with its suburban counterpart, the Villa Duchesne. "They were kind of disappointed in those who didn't make it athletically," recalled Mary Proctor. Girls' basketball had six players to a side and, in a class of ten, Phyllis didn't make the team.

Given the choice of practicing her French pronunciation or her basketball dribble, Phyllis would always choose the former—and so she got a ninety-five in French and a mere eighty in physical education. "Oh how I used to hate playing that game," she wrote at the time about soccer.

One year, responding to peer pressure, she took a few horseback-riding lessons. When her classmates entered an annual horse show, she borrowed the gear and entered too. To everyone's surprise, she won a ribbon—surely due to her erect posture and the cheering of her friends rather than to any riding skill. She was scared to death. A week later, she was talked into taking a horse named Steamboat for a ride in Forest Park. He threw his nervous rider, and Phyllis never got on a horse again.

The class of '41 remained close, if not geographically, then at least spiritually. Gerry Gipson, now the mother of seven, sees Phyllis the same way many of Phyllis' friends "see" her. "I make it a point to go to hear her speak periodically, and, of course, I see her on TV.

"I must admit I couldn't keep up with her," Gerry said, remembering the years after graduation when she was already married and Phyllis was putting herself through college. Gerry's husband, an army sergeant stationed at a barracks near St. Louis, had a friend who was a crack bridge player. The four would get together for bridge. "But we finally had to stop it," Gerry explained, "because we couldn't hold our own. My husband's friend was a tournament player and Phyllis was right on his par, if not better. Everything she did, she did so well. It was hard to compete with her."

After college, Betsy Thomas went to Ireland to work for the American embassy. She married an Irishman and later came back with him to live in the old neighborhood around City House. When Phyllis announced her marriage, Betsy wrote her best friend from London. "Of course you know how thrilled I am. It's much too marvelous to talk about. All I can do is sit and squeal. I think it's the happiest and best thing in the whole world. I hope Fred realizes what a wonderful girl he is marrying. . . . I want you to know I'm so happy for you I could squeeze you to pieces." She didn't make it back for the wedding, but three years later Phyllis and Fred Schlafly were members of Betsy's wedding party and Phyllis became godmother to Betsy's first child.

The friendship lasted. "Phyllis is probably my closest friend, always will be," said Betsy, even though their friendship is not the conventional kind. Betsy would not call Phyllis just to gossip. Phyllis has neither the time nor the inclination.

Betsy would not call Phyllis to discuss the latest best seller. Phyllis doesn't read novels.

What do they talk about? "Phyllis likes to give advice," said Betsy. "When the children were little, we'd discuss diapers or formula. She'd always be advising me on the correct way to do things. 'You're not feeding the kid that, are you? Why don't you feed it this?' she'd say. I never minded because that's just Phyllis and besides, she doesn't offer advice unless she knows what she's talking about."

In general, her classmates agree with her stand against ERA. Betsy, who recently became advertising director of a legal newspaper, agrees wholeheartedly. Jean Fahey Eberle, a free-lance writer whose first book was recently published, said she's certainly not as anti-ERA as Phyllis but "I do think ERA's a big waste of time. I think the legislation is already on the books, so why bother? I think she has a very valid position. It may not be the popular one, but there is a rationale behind it and somebody has to take it."

As to the frequent criticism that Phyllis is riding ERA into the limelight, Jean commented, "If Phyllis wanted to be in the national limelight, I'm sure she could arrange to get there. I think she feels this is an unnecessary piece of legislation and possibly mischievous in the sense that you don't know what will come out of it. . . . She's not one to mess around. Or to be just so interested in prominence she would take a position she really didn't hold. I mean she's smart enough, God knows, that she could take any position and hold it very well, but I think she's sincere in this."

Even the Democrat, Mary Hauldren Proctor, a former newspaper reporter, now a free-lance writer, pronounced Phyllis "sincere." She remarked with awe that Phyllis, whom she hadn't seen since high school, appeared to have defeated ERA single-handedly.

"You've got to hand it to her. That's an achievement. Not one I admire, but what a feat! If only I could have converted

Phyllis back then when she was young and impressionable, although I must say I don't think of her as ever having been either young or impressionable. If you had asked me back then what Phyllis would be doing forty years from now, I really think I might have guessed she'd be leading the bandwagon on some hot national issue. Quite an extraordinary person. Too bad she's on the wrong side."

"The Sacred Heart education—its values and lessons," Phyllis wrote shortly before graduation, "is something that will stay with me always. I never," she pledged, "as long as I live, shall forget the things I learned here. They are etched indelibly on my soul."

A maudlin statement from a young girl, perhaps slightly saddened by her approaching graduation. But, it is fair to say, this early education did mold her; made an impression more profound than a public-school education ever could; in fact, made Phyllis Schlafly what she is today.

Common threads—religious, moral values, a conviction (to Phyllis utterly indisputable) that there *is* a right and a wrong, that everything is *not* relative—tie together, permeate, often stimulate the positions she has taken in over three decades of political activism. They tie SALT to ERA to communism to abortion to the size of the defense budget.

At City House, students were taught morals in the morning just as they were taught geography in the afternoon. The Sacred Heart nuns approached both as distinct bodies of knowledge to be digested—learned. Phyllis Schlafly declared herself so pleased with her "moral education" that she went one big step farther: Public-school teachers should be required to teach what she called the "4th R" (that is, right and wrong). It mattered not if the classroom was populated by Hindus, Unitarians, Jews, or children of agnostics. It mattered not that the First Amendment separates church and state. "I'm not advocating teaching one particular religion. I'm suggesting that the schools—the public schools—had better start teaching a general code of conduct; yes, a moral code, so that young children know that it is wrong to shoplift; it is wrong to have premarital sex; it is wrong to spread their graffiti over the side of someone else's private property."

She mourns the fall from fashion of the concept of sin ("The World Book Encyclopedia does not even list an entry for sin."). The result, she said, "has been a shift of blame for misdeeds away from the individual to the entire society."

"Time is running out on America as an orderly and safe society," she wrote in *The Power of the Positive Woman*, "if we continue to permit our schools and colleges to be citadels of atheism and moral neutralism. It is more important for our schools and colleges . . . to teach and train students to obey the laws of God and Country than it is to impart any other knowledge. . . ."

The way to turn things around, she advised, is for "the people" to "undo the mischief the Supreme Court has wrought." Lobby your congressmen, she urged. Demand a constitutional amendment to restore prayer to the public schools. Not only would she like to see public-school children praying, she'd also like to see them studying the "theory" that man was directly created by God. She would like to see schools forced to balance the teaching of evolution with the teaching that a "divine engineer" laid out the universe.

When twenty inches of snow fell on Baltimore in 1978, looters raided more than a thousand stores. "Who were the looters?" Schlafly asked. "Mostly young people whose years in school came after the U. S. Supreme Court banished prayer and moral training from public schools. Probably nobody ever taught them that it is morally and legally wrong to take property that belongs to somebody else." To Schlafly, the trampling deaths in 1979 of eleven persons at a Cincinnati rock concert proved again that "some young people haven't been taught enough basic morality to stay alive in a civilized society."

In a recent speech, Schlafly recalled her early education; how she was taught that there is as surely good and bad, right and wrong as there is night and day. And there is indubitably a God up there who knows the difference.

At a "Pro-Family Rally"—a protest to the International Women's Year Conference in November 1977—Schlafly told an audience of fifteen thousand, without a bit of face-tiousness, that, in the ERA battle, "God is on our side. We have somebody on our side who is more powerful than the President of the United States," referring to the fact that Jimmy Carter is a strong ERA backer. "Pray every day," Schlafly urged women attending her 1979 Eagle Forum Leadership Conference, for the success of lawsuits challenging the extension of time for ERA.

Having gone to a school where she studied American history at 11:00 and Christian Doctrine at noon, Phyllis inter-weaves religion with history, morality with political science. Explaining the philosophy of the Eagle Forum, the organization she founded and heads, she wrote: "We support the Declaration of Independence and its fundamental doctrine that we owe our existence to a Creator who has endowed each of us with inalienable rights; and we support the U. S. Constitution as the instrument of securing those God-given rights. We support the Holy Scriptures as providing the best code of moral conduct yet devised."

In *The Power of the Positive Woman,* she called the Declaration of Independence "the official and unequivocal recognition by the American people of their belief and faith in God. It is a religious document from its first sentence to its last. It affirms God's existence as a self-evident truth that requires no further discussion or debate."

Schlafly's judgment (in the religious, legal, secular senses of

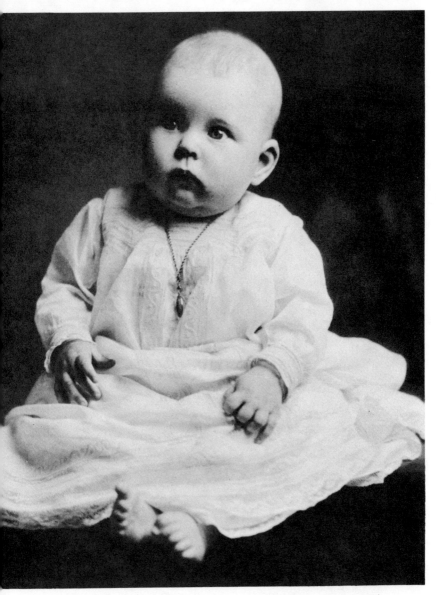

Phyllis Stewart on September 6, 1924, in a baptismal dress made from her mother's first communion dress. She was baptized at the St. Louis Cathedral where, twenty-five years later, she would be married. (Schlafly collection)

For seventeen years Phyllis' father, John Bruce Stewart, worked on a plan for a rotary engine. He was granted a patent for it in 1944. "It is my hope that someday you may be able to realize something out of this," he wrote to his daughter, then at Radcliffe College. The invention, although received enthusiastically by engineers, was never sold. (Credit: Lloyd Spainhower, *St. Louis Post-Dispatch*)

Phyllis Stewart in the first grade at DeMun School just outside St. Louis. Phyllis is the girl who obviously didn't like the high-laced shoes her mother insisted she wear. (Schlafly collection)

Phyllis Stewart's high school graduation class from the Academy of the Sacred Heart in St. Louis. Phyllis was valedictorian. (Credit: Jules Pierlow)

The month before she left for Radcliffe, twenty-year-old Phyllis Stewart worked in the darkroom of Todd Studios in St. Louis. To earn a bit of extra money, she modeled dresses, making a grand total of $12. (Credit: Todd Studios)

Phyllis met Fred Schlafly in March 1949 and was married the next October. Their courtship consisted of one date per week—a Sunday afternoon swim at the Naval Air Station or a Saturday evening visit to the St. Louis Law Library. Between dates were letters discussing the '48 party platform, the upcoming Communist trials, and the mistakes of the New Dealers. (Credit: Julies Pierlow)

From a long line of strong women. Four generations: Phyllis' grandmother (far right); Phyllis' mother (far left); in center, Phyllis and her firstborn, John. (Schlafly collection)

The Schlaflys in Miami Beach, 1968, during the Republican National Convention. Phyllis, a Nixon delegate, considers nominating conventions more fun than just about anything, so she turned this trip into a family vacation. From left: John, Bruce, Phyllis holding Anne, Fred holding hands with Liza, Andy (directly in front of Fred) and Roger. (Credit: Mort Kaye Studios, Inc.)

The Schlaflys consult on the draft of "P.S. to the News," Phyllis' semiweekly column. They stand at the entrance to her office in their Alton, Illinois home. (Credit: *Alton Telegraph* photo)

the word) of a public servant's performance depends equally on an assessment of the quality of his soul as on the quality of his mind. She wrote in 1964 that such men as Senator J. William Fulbright and Secretary of Defense Robert McNamara made the "wrong" decisions about national defense because they "have no real faith in the American people, in the U. S. Constitution, or in God." In 1979, calling it essential that the United States remain the number one nuclear power, she described the atomic bomb as "a marvelous gift that was given to our country by a wise God."

She even explained the failure of the Susan B. Anthony dollar to catch on as precisely what Carter and the Congress should have expected for "selecting a militant atheist as the first woman to be honored on a U.S. coin." (Schlafly's choice would have been St. Elizabeth Seton, founder of the Sisters of Charity, or Clara Barton, founder of the American Red Cross.)

Eleanor Schlafly—Fred Schlafly's sister—recently accompanied her sister-in-law to a speech at a small women's college. A student read the introductory biographical blurb. "Mrs. Schlafly is the wife of attorney Fred Schlafly and the mother of six children." The last two words provoked an audible hiss.

"Phyllis was shocked, hurt because her education, everything that means anything in her life, teaches the sanctity of the family," Eleanor explained. "Phyllis was taught reverence for the family, and these girls thought that babies were pollution. These girls weren't born with the notion that having six children is wrong; they learned it."

Phyllis learned exactly the opposite. The City House curriculum was college preparatory, but it was also, more so, wife/mother preparatory—not in the sense that girls were taught home economics, but in the sense that they were taught ("brainwashed," according to Mary Hauldren Proctor) what their life's role must be.

Proctor, who is more cynical about her education than any of her classmates, explained: "Sacred Heart girls were expected to marry well, be supportive of their husbands, and raise as many children as God chose to send them. ('The more He sends you the more He loves you.') One of us had twelve; I had nine, but I think the class average is about six or seven."

"I just finished law school, but I have seen enough of the law to know that I would much rather be a lawyer's wife and a mother than be a successful lawyer," fifty-five-year-old Phyllis Schlafly said in 1979. "And I will never be in the rank of top lawyers because I spent twenty years raising children, but I don't see that as oppression. It's not my loss. It's my gain." Her critics groaned when they heard that statement. Her classmates, to a person, insisted she really meant it.

"Women's liberation teaches women to put their own goals above every other and therefore is destructive of the family," Schlafly argues. In a column she bemoaned the fact that 85 percent of the married graduates of a recent Radcliffe class are childless.

And so Schlafly's issues link and coalesce, creating this religious framework within which she has, perhaps, dealt the death-blow to ERA.

"Look," said Shirley Spellerberg, STOP ERA Florida chairman, "Phyllis is a religious leader—perhaps the most powerful in the country today. Because it's women who generally keep the family's faith and it's women who support Phyllis.

"Make no mistake about it. This is a religious war. Do you think women would drop everything to run to Springfield or up to Tallahassee to fight for a politician or a political issue?

"Our women figure that the politicians and bureaucrats have had their turn and they've botched it. They've managed to turn the United States from a country with a mission, with standards and moral values, into a moral pygmy—the laughingstock of the world.

"ERA is a religious issue and that's why we're winning. There's nobody—nobody—on the other side who inspires an eighth of the loyalty and zeal—the reverence these women give Phyllis. They'd do anything for her. To quote Phyllis, 'We're the most powerful positive force in the country today.' Believe me, that's putting it real mildly."

The nuns closed City House in 1968. Today, all that's left is a fenced-in marble pedestal from an old statue, shrouded by a development of nondescript townhouses. When the wrecking ball hit, Phyllis Schlafly was upset, hurt; for the leveling of City House represented far more than the death of a building. City House represented a whole set of values and goals, which in her mind were "right" and "moral"—words that Phyllis Stewart grew up with, and, at a time when most people eschew absolutes, she uses without a trace of embarrassment or doubt. She has, after all, concluded that "God is on our side."

4

A Liberated Woman

Phyllis Schlafly may call herself a "traditional" woman, but few times in her life has she ever taken a traditional route.

A few months before high-school graduation, she wrote of her "fierce determination to always look forward to adventure"—bombastic, high-school-style writing, to be sure, which contained, nonetheless, a nugget or two of truth.

It didn't take Phyllis Stewart too many months to decide that the college that had given her a full scholarship—the college that good Sacred Heart girls were expected to attend—was simply not for her. Three years later, when most of her high-school classmates were either getting married or getting pregnant, Phyllis, clutching her Phi Beta Kappa key and her briefcase full of plans and ambition, headed for graduate school.

"Twelve-forty p.m. on the Jeffersonian to arrive at New York 10:35 a.m. Tuesday and then on four hours to Boston and across the Charles River to Cambridge to begin my graduate work in political science at Radcliffe. Good-by St. Louis, Hello Harvard!!!!"

After breezing through the master's program in seven months, she decided in September 1945 to complete her political education with a year in Washington. The Japanese had just surrendered. Washington was in a state of pandemonium. She had no relatives there, no job, no place to live. She was just twenty-one years old. It was, as her mother said at the time, "a great experiment." Her Radcliffe roommate, who had recently married, wrote Phyllis in Washington: "You are now a career woman and earning your own living. What a wonderful, independent life. I envy you."

In 1979, *Newsweek* editor Diane Weathers dubbed Phyllis Schlafly "the first lady of anti-feminism." But this "anti-feminist" was obviously "liberated" decades before the word got hackneyed. She was liberated in the sense that she never, ever allowed her sex to stand between her and her goal. And that, perhaps, is one reason for her unrelenting disdain for "libbers." "Is there anything valuable about the women's movement?" Schlafly is often asked. "Nothing," she answers, without a moment's hesitation. "The claim that American women are downtrodden and unfairly treated is the fraud of the century."

She has "never" been discriminated against, she says. Women who blame sexism for their failures are just looking for an excuse, she adds. Some of these women, she elaborates, are lazy, others have been "brainwashed" into thinking there is something wrong with being "just a housewife," so they try to achieve in areas in which they have no aptitude, no qualifications. When they fail, as they're bound to, instead of staying home and caring for their families or getting a job suited to their abilities, they make a job of running around the country "wailing" about discrimination. "If you're willing to work hard, there's no barrier you can't jump."

In 1977, when Schlafly was riding the publicity circuit to promote her just-published *The Power of the Positive*

Woman, she appeared on "The Merv Griffin Show." The orchestra had barely finished its flourish when Schlafly and another guest, psychologist Dr. Joyce Brothers, clashed.

BROTHERS: Are you an attorney?

SCHLAFLY: No, I'm not.

BROTHERS: Are you studying to be an attorney?

SCHLAFLY: Yes, I am.

BROTHERS: [with trembling voice] My mother is an attorney. And when she became an attorney it was only possible for her to practice with my father. My sister now is an attorney and the world is open to her. The reason you are able to study to be an attorney and to get into schools is because of all of the change that has taken place.[1]

SCHLAFLY: That's absolutely false. I was invited to attend the Harvard Law School in 1945 and there was absolutely no discrimination then.

BROTHERS: There is for a lot of other women. You may be different.

(What Brothers didn't know is that if Phyllis was invited to attend Harvard Law School in 1945, she was invited five years before the law school changed its rigid policy against admitting women. On the other hand, it appeared from correspondence with her constitutional-law professor—who taught in the graduate government department at Harvard and called her "brilliant"—that the law school, if she had pushed it, might have made an exception for Phyllis Stewart.)

Phyllis gave no sign, ever, of worrying about the limitations

---

[1] Dr. Brothers was referring to the fact that in 1979, 30 percent of all law students were women (45 percent of Schlafly's Washington University graduating class), but back in 1945 a woman in law school was a rarity—a curiosity.

—legal or psychological—that society imposed on women. It never occurred to her that there was any reason why a woman who had the motivation couldn't make it in a "man's world." In her own case, she no more feared that her sex would hold her back than she hoped that it would reap her special treatment. It was simply irrelevant.[2]

If a woman had the brains to play by the rules that men had set up, fine. If she didn't, too bad. She couldn't change the fact that the "man's game" was the only game in town. That was just the way society evolved. And that was just fine with Phyllis. She considered men a source of lively competition, not oppression. She was proud of herself for competing against them so brilliantly, and she had no compunction about telling the world.

She boasted in a 1970 campaign brochure that she was "the only woman invited by the Senate Foreign Relations Committee to testify on the U.S.-Soviet Nuclear Test-ban Treaty." She considers herself an expert on nuclear strategy, calling it "a very specialized career. There are very few men in it. For a woman, it is almost unique."

"Oh I never get bored," Schlafly told a reporter covering the 1968 Republican National Convention—a year when she was the only woman elected delegate in Illinois to the Republican Convention. "This is fun. I don't think there are more than a half-dozen women in the country who have been a delegate as many times as I have. I've been on the credentials committee twice." Later that day, she told another reporter that in 1956 she beat four men for the delegate post.

Schlafly has won many more than her share of "most admired woman" and "most influential woman" polls, but the

[2] In later years, she came to consider "making it" and "affirmative action" to be a contradiction in terms. A woman should be allowed to compete equally with a man, but a woman should never be given a job over a more qualified man, simply because she is a woman.

poll that is first in her heart and on her publicity releases is an Associated Press poll that named her one of the ten most powerful people in Illinois—and the *only* woman.

Schlafly believes that any woman with talent, energy, and ambition could be a Barbara Walters or a Barbara Jordan or a Phyllis Schlafly (that is, make it in a "man's world"). The difference between Barbara Walters and the "average late-'70s libber," Schlafly said, is that Walters made it to the top through hard work—not as a token; not as just another affirmative-action statistic collected to placate the government. And so did Ann Landers, whom Schlafly likes to quote as saying, "Opportunities are usually disguised as hard work, so most people don't recognize them."

Commenting on *Ms.* magazine, Schlafly made the movement's monthly manifesto sound about as substantial as *Hustler.* "All it is is a bunch of gripes and complaints. . . . They had one article about some woman's supposed great act of courage—she refused to carry the laundry up from the basement anymore. Another one's great act of courage was she wasn't going to wear underwear anymore. Ugh . . ."

"The Positive Woman," Schlafly wrote, "spends her time, ingenuity, and efforts seizing her opportunities—not whining about past injustices." Schlafly simply can't stomach, much less understand, women who have to depend on a constitutional amendment to make it. If a woman blamed discrimination for her failures, Schlafly blamed her for not trying harder. "I've achieved my goals in life and I did it without sex-neutral laws." Glaring at a pair of disheveled delegates to the International Women's Year conference, she said, "ERA supporters aren't seeking a more just society. They're seeking a constitutional cure for their laziness and personal problems."

As feminists groan and grind their teeth, Schlafly repeats these statements and repeats them, with more conviction each time—for she has, indeed, practiced what she preached. She got where she is through four decades of hard work; through seeming, since age seventeen when she started college, to know at all times what she wanted and working until she got it.

Before graduating from City House in 1941, Phyllis Stewart took an exam for a scholarship to Maryville College, an all-girls school in South St. Louis, run by the same order of nuns who ran City House. She won a four-year scholarship—very fortunately, because her parents could not afford to send her to college.

She had her heart set on going much farther than South St. Louis, to Massachusetts and Wellesley College. She had even paid the ten-dollar application fee. "This was ten dollars thrown after a dream when money was far too scarce," she wrote philosophically at the time. "Now I know it will never come true. But the hope was happier than its fulfillment could have ever been."

So Maryville it was, and at 7:00 A.M. on September 23, 1941, she left her parents' apartment to wait for the Maryville bus that would pick her up and take her to her first day of college. She must have felt a bit like the kid who waits breathlessly for the big yellow bus to pick him up and take him to his very first morning of day camp. Almost immediately, she knew something was wrong.

The first Friday night of the term she went to a candlelight dance given for freshmen by seniors. "Had a hell of a bad time," she noted at the time, sounding quite unlike the Phyllis who usually limited her on-the-record comments to "grand times" or "wonderful times" or "exciting times."

Then came October and "Formal Initiation" and Phyllis had to board the bus dressed in baby clothes and wear them all day. Of the secret nighttime initiation, she wrote, "I was scared, but it wasn't so bad. Then ice cream and sandwiches on the hockey field"—certainly not Phyllis' idea of an evening productively spent.

"It just wasn't everything I wanted out of college," she concluded. So she made the hard decision to leave Maryville and give up the scholarship—the only reason she was going to school instead of work. The decision was tough too because Phyllis was steeped in Sacred Heart traditions and friendships. Some classmates and teachers reacted as if, having accepted an invitation to their homes for dinner, she left after sampling the appetizer, explaining that neither the food nor the company were quite what she expected.

"What I did was bad enough," said Mary Hauldren Proctor, Phyllis' City House classmate who went straight to journalism school at the University of Missouri. "What Phyllis did really took courage. I had the devil's own time getting permission from the Reverend Mother, who finally called in the Archbishop himself to try to prevent me from going to Missouri. But Phyllis spent a year at Maryville and then rejected it. There must have been a big pressure campaign to make her change her mind." There was.

"Mother Odile was grand when I went to tell her," Phyllis noted. "But the City House girls gave me the cold shoulder when I went to their graduation." The City House nuns also took it personally—as a betrayal. She went to say good-bye to a former teacher who was leaving St. Louis for a Sacred Heart school in New Orleans. "My last friend at City House . . . how sorry I am to see her go as she liked me better than any other nun and she stood by me longer than any other."

Maryville was a cozy and secure environment, but it wasn't a challenging one. Phyllis easily got A's in everything (except a C in health, which she felt was a waste of time; she had learned what she needed to know at home). City House classmate Dottie Manewal Stephens, who was at Maryville with Phyllis that year, explained, "Well, she was just so brilliant.

Face it, intellectually, at that time, Maryville wasn't that stimulating."

Phyllis' last day at Maryville was June 1, 1942. Two weeks later, she was up at 6:00 A.M. to make an 8:00 A.M. English literature course at Washington University, a private school—a streetcar ride away from home—with a national, coed, and top-notch student body and faculty. In other words, the competition promised to be a lot stiffer. "It will be great fun competing with the men!" she exclaimed.

The challenge was sharpened by the biting put-down hurled at her when she presented her transcript of credits to Washington University. Looking down her nose at Phyllis' A's from Maryville and City House, Assistant Dean Winifred K. Magdsick, Ph.D., assured her, "You'll find you won't get nearly as good grades here."

Two months later, Phyllis started working a 48-hour-a-week night job to pay the college bills. Her starting salary was $1,260 per year, enough to cover her tuition and expenses and save for graduate school. She continued living at home.

The schedule—school full-time and work full-time—was ridiculously hectic. "The world is upside down this year," Phyllis wrote in October 1942, "and I am too, but I hope this is worth something." For the school year 1942–43, she noted that her entertainment was limited to a "poor *Faust*" and one movie—the latter, one of the very few dates she had in college —a breakfast/movie date sandwiched between the end of the night shift and the start of her first morning class. Things didn't get any better. The next school year "The only college activity I had time to attend all year was *The Women* by Clare Boothe Luce. Took Mother to see it and it was wonderful."

Why did she do it? "Phyllis knew she was going to do something with her life," Betsy Thomas Birmingham explained, "and she didn't think she'd get the proper preparation at Maryville. It was obvious her parents couldn't afford to send her to college and if it had been me I would have figured, 'Well, maybe if they can't send me I won't go.' But that never occurred to Phyllis. She would go. I think she always had goals whereas the rest of us may have thought maybe the goal is to get married and that's all you'll do. Play bridge. Her goal was never just to get married and play bridge. Being from a conservative family, she would never have thought of asking the government for help. She was going to get a job and put herself through."

Finding a job, or rather finding the right job, was not easy. Phyllis was determined to work nights so she could go to school days. Night school, of course, would have been the perfect solution—for most people. But not for Phyllis, who quickly decided that night school would provide about a third the challenge, and, besides, was not the route to acquiring a set of sterling academic credentials.

On August 26, 1942, she worked her first night as a gunner at the St. Louis Ordnance Plant, firing rifles and machine guns to test the ammunition the plant manufactured. Half the time she worked from midnight to 8:00 A.M., and then rushed to a 9:00 A.M. class, then home to study, then to sleep and up at 11:00 P.M. and back to work. The other half she worked from 4:00 P.M. to midnight, went home, studied, then slept and made a 9:00 A.M. class, and then studied before reporting back to her job.

One term she had to take two courses that met at the same time (alternating cuts) in order to squeeze in a full course load. Her job required concentration, making it impossible to sneak study time. The schedule was positively grueling—a tough school day and a tougher work night. She fired as many as five thousand rounds in one eight-hour shift. There was nothing glamorous about it. Her work uniform consisted of navy blue slacks and light blue blouses. She was able, she brags today, to use all her old City House uniform blouses, which she wore out, along with a dozen others donated by her classmates.

"That was a man's job in those days," Phyllis said proudly (apparently missing the irony that she got the job only because able-bodied men were off fighting the war). She worked as a gunner and as a ballistics technician, testing .30- and .50-caliber ammunition in the various tests required before government acceptance: accuracy, penetration, velocity, rifle function, machine-gun function, aircraft function. She was required to duplicate as nearly as possible every condition of actual use of the cartridge and then figure out why misfires didn't work. She also photographed incendiary bullets (tracers) in flight and developed her own film.

The work was dirty and noisy, but for Phyllis, even though there were very few young men to add romantic interest, it had its charms. She was already beginning to see a certain beauty in the weapons of war. One young man gave her a cherished souvenir before "greetings" from his draft board sent him, too, off to the war. At the time, Phyllis described the memento as "a beautiful piece of jewelry"—a pin made of a polished .30-caliber cartridge on which were soldered two extra bullets in a V, from which came two pieces of chain leading to another bullet two inches higher. "Rather gaudy," she admitted later, "but I wore it for several years and I still have it somewhere."

The job was also not particularly safe. One night she was working alone in the lab completing a test that required baking twenty empty cartridges in the oven (to see if they could stand the heat) and dipping twenty full rounds (with powder and bullets) in a solution that coated them with silver. As she was standing at the sink inspecting the silver cartridges, she suddenly had one empty shell in her hand, and so knew that a loaded bullet had to be in the oven. Instead of running out of the lab, she rushed to the oven to take it out. Just as she opened the door, the round exploded with a frightful noise, but fortunately did no damage to anything except the oven.

Phyllis worked there just short of two years, until late June 1944, when production was cut back (the plant, the largest in the world, produced more than six billion cartridges during the war). She had been promoted five times, with salary increases from $105 per month to $182.50.[3] "I am my own boss and delightfully free and important," she wrote.

Most women would have been relieved at the reprieve from manual labor. Not Phyllis. On her last day she bid *adieu* to "Dear old proof house building No. 207" and called the job "the most wonderful two years of my life—a unique experience."

Although she was the first to admit that money, not patriotism, was her motive in taking the job, she credited the experience with sparking her interest in defense. It also gave her the perfect answer to the question reporters, in later years, inevitably asked, "Mrs. Schlafly, how did a housewife from Alton become so interested in national defense and nuclear warfare? These are subjects that even most men don't understand."

In spite of the rigors of the job, Phyllis, who majored in political science, managed to graduate with a full set of honors —Phi Beta Kappa, Pi Sigma Alpha (the political-science honorary), a fellowship to Radcliffe. And she graduated almost a year earlier (in September 1944) than she would have had she taken it easy and remained at Maryville, where she would have been a member of the class of June 1945. She turned twenty just two weeks before graduation. She was still twenty when she got her master's in government from Radcliffe.

[3] Men doing similar work started at $125 a month. Although she often says she believes in equal pay for equal work, in her own case, she claimed not to mind a bit. At least once a week, the men were required to lift armor plates weighing at least a hundred pounds. "They deserved to be paid more."

When Phyllis Stewart started college she had no more natural inclination to political science than to English literature. In fact, were it not for her frantic schedule, she might never have taken a political-science course. She didn't have the luxury of spreading her classes through the day. She needed a course that met at 10:00 A.M., and a political-science course just happened to fit that slot.

By the next semester, she was loading her schedule with political-science courses and she was getting A's in all of them. The semester ending January 1944 was typical. She took five courses, four in political science and got A's in all those, and chemistry, and got an A in that.[4]

"Political science really turned out to be my chosen field," she wrote shortly before graduation. Her professors agreed. Arnold Lien, then head of Washington University's Political Science Department, was so impressed that, years after graduation, he was still urging her to come back to get her Ph.D.

When she was applying for a graduate fellowship, another Washington University professor, O. E. Norton, wrote a glowing letter of recommendation. He was obviously not accustomed to heaping such praise upon a woman.

"Miss Stewart is a person of very unusual attainments. Her intellectual capacity is extraordinary and her analytical ability is distinctly remarkable. . . . I have no hesitation whatsoever in saying that Miss Stewart is the most capable woman student we have had in this department in ten years."

On March 31, 1944, an envelope from the dean's office at

---

[4] As usual, her only B was in physical education. In those years, Washington University required students to pass a swimming test before graduation. Phyllis was afraid of the water, couldn't swim and, above all, couldn't face the community showers (all female, of course). So she didn't, and, lucky for her, through an oversight, university officials never discovered that she graduated without knowing how to swim. (Several years later, she realized her mistake and joined a swim class at the YWCA until she learned how.)

Radcliffe arrived at the Stewart apartment. Good news. The fellowship committee had awarded her a Whitney fellowship of five hundred dollars for two terms—in those days a goodly sum, which, added to money she'd saved from the ammunition-plant job, would be enough to finance the year at Radcliffe.

The next day, the frustrating news arrived from Columbia: She had been chosen a graduate resident scholar. Phyllis had her heart set on Radcliffe, but Columbia offered a better deal —seven hundred dollars. "It was a hard decision," she wrote at the time, "but Harvard won."

Radcliffe's term started in November. In the meantime, Phyllis was not catching up on her sleep or shopping for her graduate-school wardrobe. She was working. (She'd turned down several offers for permanent jobs, including a job as a photographer for Washington University and a reporter for United Press.) To make some extra money, she worked in the darkroom of Todd Studios and, between mid-September and mid-October, she dutifully recorded earnings of $134.55, plus $12 in modeling (for Todd Studios) fees.

The Radcliffe program was run jointly with Harvard, which meant that Harvard supplied all the faculty and the majority of the students. She had no trouble competing with Harvard men, making an A in constitutional law, an A— in modern political theory, an A in public administration, and an A— in international law. She called her master's orals "that gruesome affair with four of my professors," but she passed it effortlessly, getting her master's in short order—in June 1945.

"I just loved that year," Schlafly recalled. "It was a very happy year." She lived at 55 Brattle Street—a then 250-year-old landmark named Reed House, which housed nine female graduate students, a housemother, and a housekeeper. For the first time, she had a social life. "I never really had any dates until I went to Radcliffe, but I made up for lost time that year." She went with various Harvard men to the Brattle Theater in Cambridge, to Symphony Hall in Boston to hear the Boston Symphony perform Beethoven's Ninth under the baton of Serge Koussevitzky, to Sander's Theater at Harvard for harpsichord concerts, to the Harvard Chapel for Glee Club Christmas carols. She went sight-seeing around Boston and took side trips to Concord to see Emerson's house and the North Bridge and to New Haven to see Yale. Over Christmas, lacking the money to go home, she moved into a student cooperative that she pronounced "rather bohemian."

Her Harvard professors tried to convince her to stay on for a doctorate, but she could no more afford that than she could have afforded law school. And while law school sounded appealing (constitutional law, which would figure so largely in her fight against ERA, had been her favorite course in the master's program), she was tired of academia.

"It was a pleasure to have you around last year," wrote Professor Benjamin Wright the summer after her Radcliffe graduation, "and I'm sorry you won't be there in September even though I agree that you aren't cast for the role of female professor." One last try: "If you should change your mind and decide that a research assistantship looks attractive, I'm sure that something can be found."

On June 27, 1945, commencement day, Phyllis received her master's in the early afternoon and left immediately for her first trip to New York. Carrying all her luggage, she took the subway from the train station to the Barbizon Plaza, a proper hotel for women, where a telegram from her parents awaited her: "Be vigilant. Keep us advised."

Phyllis even worked hard at sight-seeing. She noted at the time: "I did a tremendous job of sight-seeing all over the city, into the harbor, the Statue of Liberty, and around the islands. Everything there was to see except the nightclubs."

The Harvard commencement speaker that year was David E. Lilienthal, chairman of the Tennessee Valley Authority. He so inspired Phyllis—here, perhaps, was one worthy New

Deal project—that she stopped in Knoxville en route back home to St. Louis. "Had a grand time talking with all the important men," she wrote. At that time, there was much talk of a Missouri Valley Authority modeled on the TVA, and Phyllis was preparing herself to apply for a position with the projected MVA.

That summer of 1945 Phyllis' mother was still working seven days a week—six days at the St. Louis Art Museum and the seventh at City House, where Phyllis' sister was a student. Her father recently had been granted a patent for his rotary engine, but it still hadn't been sold.

Phyllis knew she had to get a full-time job, but, having studied government for the past four years, she was determined to see it in action. She decided not to wait around for the MVA, but to go to Washington to look for a job.

5

The Life
of a Working Girl

Phyllis Stewart arrived in Washington to search for a job on
V-J Day, September 2, 1945. "It had been announced that
the government was closing up, so who was going to hire me?
But I decided that's what I wanted, so I got on a train and I
went."

By November, when she had long since landed a job with a
congressional research organization dedicated to boosting the
free-enterprise system, she got a letter from Dr. Arnold Lien,
her Washington University professor. "It was amazingly courageous and wonderful on your part to set out into the unknown and uncharted and pick a good position. The work
should prove very interesting and valuable."

Dr. Pendleton Herring, one of her Harvard professors, had
offered to help her get a job in the budget bureau or some

other public agency. He wrote a letter describing her as a "very able and highly personable young woman who did excellent work with us here last year." By then, however, Phyllis already suspected the government had grown too big for the public's good.

She explained her feelings to her school friend Betsy Thomas: Collecting a salary from the taxpayers is fine if the employee produces an honest day's work. But if the bloated bureaucracy blocks him at every turn, making him just a cog in a clumsy, broken machine, he has no right to accept a salary. He is "cheating" the "overburdened" taxpayer. He is as "immoral" as the high federal officials responsible for creating this "monster" that is Washington.

Working for the government by test-firing ammunition during a war was one thing; pushing papers was another. She opted for the private sector.

The interview at the congressional research firm ended with a snag. "I got an ultimatum," she recalled. " 'Fine, we'll hire you, but you'll have to know how to type.' They made me go to typing school. And that was the worst punishment I ever had." No, she said, it had nothing to do with her sex. It was simply a tool she needed to do the job. "And I certainly thank them for it because there's absolutely no way I could turn out the volume of work I turn out today if I couldn't type. My work pattern is thinking to the typewriter."

So she started work at the then two-year-old American Enterprise Association (since 1962 known as the American Enterprise Institute), a small, private group that did bill analyses and speechwriting for congressmen—mainly conservative congressmen. Philosophically, she was right at home in this industry-supported organization dedicated to "educating" congressmen on the "virtues of free enterprise." (Congressmen paid nothing for the service. The supporting industries—a Who's Who of the *Fortune* 500—paid the salaries and bills;

well worth the price, they figured, for generating congressional sympathy for a free market.)

AEA offered congressmen two services: first, analyses of legislation, prepared with the help of experts in academia, law, and government; second, spot research, supplying congressmen with summaries and data on pending legislation. If a congressman wanted to give a speech or issue a press release on a particular piece of legislation, an AEA staffer would write it.

The AEA president in 1945 was Lewis Brown, head of Johns Manville. Phyllis saved a speech he gave during her time there, a speech she might have written herself. "I wouldn't be able to work for an organization whose goals I did not admire," Phyllis said at the time—certainly no problem at AEA.

"We are still searching for shortcuts to Utopia," Brown wrote, "financed through public spending. . . . We must recognize that a wide gulf exists between a free economy under which a self-reliant citizen asks only a minimum of assistance from government and the sinister menace of the Welfare State with its tireless effort to bring all economic groups into complete dependence upon its vast bureaucracy and numberless regulatory agencies."

Phyllis was surely never a fan of Roosevelt's "planned economy," but living in Washington, where the postwar regulators ran wild, "regulating everything you eat, everything you wear, everything you earn," as she put it, horrified her.

While working for AEA, she wrote an article entitled "Not Enough Tires in 1946" and sent it to, of all places, *Cosmopolitan*. In short order a polite rejection arrived: "Our staff doesn't feel this article is quite right for *Cosmopolitan*." Obviously, Phyllis didn't realize that government "overregulation" might not be as compelling a subject to the *Cosmo* girl as it was to her.

The subject was to remain compelling to Phyllis—thirty years later still the focus of a good deal of her writing. The title of one of her syndicated columns in 1978 was "All Americans Benefit from Business Profits." In 1977, she devoted another column to venting her outrage at the results of a poll of recent high-school graduates showing that 61 percent did not believe in the profit system and 55 percent believed that the government should own all banks, railroads, and steel companies. "Students are not born with these ideas. . . . These fallacies are what they have been taught in the schools deliberately, systematically, and pervasively."

That same year, she wrote in *The Power of the Positive Woman,* "Progress has been the greatest in those areas where there has been private enterprise without government interference, such as automobiles, airplanes, and computers. There is no ceiling on man's ingenuity and resourcefulness to cope with problems—so long as we operate in the American climate of freedom. . . . Progress has been the least in those areas where government has traditionally undertaken the job, namely the postal service, public schools, and garbage collection."

Perhaps her most famous plug for free enterprise came, again in 1977, when Schlafly was a commentator for CBS radio's "Spectrum" series. She criticized the police for arresting a poor St. Louis couple who sold their well-cared-for baby to an undercover policeman. While agreeing that adoption agencies provide "the better way," she said it would be "ridiculous to send that pathetic couple to jail for a year"—the punishment for that offense. "Where the baby moves from an unwanted environment into a home with loving adoptive parents, where's the crime? If I hadn't been blessed with babies of my own, I would have been happy to have paid thousands of dollars for a baby." (Schlafly's critics saw that broadcast as a pitch for unfettered free enterprise without any government regulation. It is more likely that her concern was moral, not economic. "I would, naturally, support any life-saving method of coping with the problem of unwanted babies rather than death by abortion.")

Later, of course, Schlafly became much better known as an enemy of women's liberation than as a champion of free enterprise, although she often managed to link the two. She came, in fact, to see free enterprise as a sort of panacea for some strains of discrimination. "It was not the strident demands of the women's libbers," she argued, "that brought high prizes to women's tennis, but the discovery by sports promoters that beautiful female legs gracefully moving around the court made women's tennis a highly marketable television production to delight male audiences."

Many of ERA's most vociferous supporters, Schlafly claimed, put the family and the corporation in the same category and damn them both. In *The Power of the Positive Woman,* she quoted from an April 1975 interview with Gloria Steinem: "We seek the elimination of the caste system and the overthrow of the patriarchal values that underpin a wide variety of social systems. That would mean the abandonment of hierarchical, authority-based organizations of which the corporation is a prime example."

"I enjoyed that year in Washington," Schlafly recalled. But at the end of it, she had "had enough of the single woman's life in Washington" and came back to St. Louis. Besides, as she so often said, "Washington is a nice place to visit but I wouldn't want to live there." In Schlafly's scheme of things, Washington remained an unreconstructed and unreconstructable villain.

In 1977, release of the headline-making social statistic that in Washington abortions and illegitimate births now outnumber legitimate births made Phyllis Schlafly say, "I told you so." The statistic, to her, was concrete proof that "Big Brother" was terminally ill, economically and morally bankrupt.

As she so often does in her column, she managed to hit several favorite targets, all within her eight-hundred-word limit, starting with a denunciation of college-campus immorality and ending with, "If the best and the brightest refuse to respect any objective standards of morality, then our nation will decline as rapidly as has Washington, D.C." Note the implication that Washington has so decayed that it has dropped from the Union like a rotten apple from a tree. She wrote of it as if it were a foreign country.

When Schlafly put aside her consuming interest in defense and nuclear strategy and took on the ERA, the motivating factor was her inbred fear and suspicion of this hulking bureaucracy. ("One of five Americans is now working for the government. The other four out of five Americans are working hard to support the new affluent privileged class of Washington bureaucrats.") The hazy language of ERA's Section I was bad enough, but Section II, in Schlafly's mind, was just awful.

"Many people think that the ERA is not a question of 'rights' at all," she said, "but a question of power. Section II would transfer to the federal politicians, bureaucrats, and judges the last remaining jurisdiction that now lies exclusively in the state legislatures—including marriage, divorce, child custody, adoption, prison regulations, protective labor laws, and insurance rates." Section II, she concluded, means "total federal control."

Schlafly's relationship with Washington has something of the love-hate aspect to it. She did, after all, run twice for Congress, and congressmen do live in or near Washington. On the other hand, if Schlafly really wanted to get to Washington she would have moderated her positions, cooled her criticism years ago. People with opinions as strong as hers usually don't get appointed and often don't get elected to federal jobs.

When St. Louis television personality Dick Keefe profiled Schlafly on KMOX-TV he asked, "Have you ever been disappointed . . . that you haven't received any kind of federal and national appointments by Presidents when the Republicans were in?" She answered, without a moment's hesitation, "Well, the last thing in the world I want is a Washington job. I've got a nice home in Alton. Why in the world would I want to move to Washington?"

Keefe persisted, unconvinced that Schlafly wasn't really pining away for an offer: "There are very few women who have the background you have in foreign policy and foreign relations. It would seem to me that you would be a natural."

"You understand with the firing of General Singlaub," she answered, "that you have to go along with the Administration or you get fired. I think I've been more useful in not being beholden to the government in any way. I'm able to analyze the strategy and speak the truth about it."[1]

When Richard Nixon became President, Senator Everett Dirksen (R., Ill.) recommended Schlafly for appointment to the prestigious (but unpaid) Foreign Intelligence Advisory Board, telling her, "I think that's the least the Republican Party should do for all your volunteer efforts." But Nixon, for whom Schlafly had been both a convention delegate and, on

[1] When it became obvious that Ronald Reagan would be the 1980 Republican candidate for President, several of Schlafly's supporters started promoting her as an ideal Supreme Court nominee in a Reagan administration. Schlafly, however, told a reporter that the job she'd want is Secretary of Defense, "so I could do whatever is necessary to give us superiority over the Russians. . . . I don't want just any job in Washington."

several occasions, a painful thorn in his side, did not take Dirksen's suggestion.

The closest she ever came to a Washington job was when President Eisenhower appointed her Secretary of the Treasury in his "Kitchen Kabinet." Along with such "Kabinet" members as Hedda Hopper, Schlafly's charge was to "share GOP recipes on GOP accomplishments with the housewives of the nation" by issuing monthly summaries of "What's Cooking in Washington."

In September 1946, Phyllis Stewart was back in St. Louis living in the McPherson Avenue apartment with her parents, sister, and grandmother. She was looking for another job.

She had been reading about a young Republican lawyer from her district who was challenging the Democratic incumbent for a seat in the U. S. House of Representatives in the November election. Claude Bakewell was a tough anti-Communist and a champion of free enterprise. He sounded, to Phyllis, like a good man.

Although Bakewell had picked a propitious year to run— President Truman was extremely unpopular and, in any case, the party out of power usually did better in midterm elections —the race was by no means a shoo-in. Bakewell's opponent, John Sullivan, was not only an incumbent, but also a very popular incumbent.

The district, then the 11th, which lay entirely within the city, was slowly but surely becoming a Democratic stronghold. In 1944, the Democrats had easily carried it. In 1946, with Roosevelt and his coattails gone, the CIO-PAC (political action committee) and the AFL were working overtime to keep the district in the Democratic column and their man— Sullivan—in Congress.

Bakewell was in the market for a combat-tested campaign manager—a savvy precinct impresario who could mastermind a victory over his formidable opponent. The would-be congressman had never even considered hiring a woman.

He changed his mind when he met Phyllis Stewart—only twenty-two years old and with no campaign experience. Somehow, she convinced him to hire her.

"I was impressed," Bakewell recalled, "by her incredible knowledge of the most nitty-gritty details of St. Louis ward politics. Here was this beautiful young girl sitting in my living room analyzing what I had to do to win, and she had so much plain good political sense, I had to keep looking at her to remind myself I wasn't talking to a fat, old cigar-chomping ward heeler."

"I was the general jack-of-all-trades," Phyllis recalled. "Campaigns were very unsophisticated in 1946. I did everything. I was his appointment secretary, his press secretary, his speech researcher, everything. He didn't have any other campaign employees."

Bakewell described Phyllis as "very effective"—an "immensely hard worker" who had a natural feel for politics and, best of all, an inexhaustible fund of energy.

She worked in a tiny windowless office typing on an antique Underwood someone had donated to the campaign. (The typewriter's distinguishing feature was that two or three keys, in various combinations, were always broken.) She wrote reams of press releases, making seven or eight onion-skin carbons, which she hand-delivered, traveling by streetcar, to each of the newspapers. She would almost always get past the guard and hand the release in person to the city editor. "I don't know how she did it," recalled Bakewell, "but the papers always printed our stuff."

The Sullivan/Bakewell race was a clear-cut contest between a liberal and a conservative and it was just the sort of battle to rouse Phyllis Stewart. (The absence of an out-and-out liberal opponent would stymie Schlafly in her own races for Congress in 1952 and 1970.)

Sullivan was a fervent New Dealer who voted the labor line religiously; who voted for FDR's foreign policy, including large doses of foreign aid ("foreign giveaways," as Phyllis labeled them); who voted for Truman's policy of, in speechwriter Phyllis Stewart's words, "spend and spend, tax and tax. Direct taxes now consume a staggering sum of $260 a year out of the pocket of each resident of this country."

In another speech she wrote for Bakewell, she charged that under successive Democratic administrations, Communists "had wormed their way into positions of power" where they could "disrupt a nation's economic foundation and destroy the people's confidence in their government. It is because of this technique that today, with more beef cattle on the ranges than ever before, there is still no meat on American dinner tables."

Price controls—Communist-inspired or not—were a hot issue that year and Bakewell's campaign was designed to milk the public's disgust with this legacy of the New Deal. Veterans who had fought for their country returned home to find no place to live. "The slogan of the present Administration with respect to veterans' housing," Phyllis wrote, "is two families in every garage."

By October, Bakewell had come so far so fast that the political prognosticators declined to prognosticate, calling the race a tossup.

"In politics as in war there is no substitute for victory," said Phyllis Stewart at the time. So she worked even harder. During the last, most hectic month of the campaign, she was also working full-time as a researcher, speechwriter, and librarian for a St. Louis bank. (She needed the money and the permanent job, so when the bank insisted she start immediately, she did.)

Bakewell won—41,202 to 39,879, undoubtedly helped by a nationwide surge of resentment of and impatience with the Democrats—and the Republicans won control of both houses of Congress for the first time since 1930. The newspapers, however, still called Bakewell's victory an "upset" and attributed it to a "smooth, organized, tireless campaign."[2]

There was no time off for Phyllis after election day. She was already immersed in her new job, an unusually challenging one that she would keep for three years, until her marriage in October 1949, when, in her words, "Fred rescued me from the life of a working girl."

The First National Bank in St. Louis paid half her salary and the St. Louis Union Trust Company paid the other half. She divided her time between the two affiliated organizations, half the time serving as librarian of the bank, cataloging and managing its library ("I had no training in that, but I knew enough about libraries that, with a little coaching from Mother, I managed.") and writing speeches for bank officers. The other half, she worked for Towner Phelan, a trust company vice president in charge of advertising, who produced a monthly newsletter called *The St. Louis Union Trust Company Letter*.

The four-page *Letter* focused on government, foreign policy, economics, politics in the larger sense—"nothing partisan about it," said Phyllis. She did the research, editing, proofreading, production, layout. Soon she was doing much of the writing too. "It was a very interesting time. I loved every minute of it."

The newsletter might not have been partisan, but it was

[2] When Bakewell ran again in 1948, Phyllis, still working at the bank, did not get involved. (During his first term, the freshman congressman had shifted his positions from the hard line of his campaign.) This time Bakewell lost, and, after a couple more losses, the last to John Sullivan's widow, he retired from politics, eventually becoming St. Louis postmaster. As it turned out, Sullivan's widow, Leonor, who was still serving in Congress in 1971 and still a staunch liberal, was the only congresswoman to vote against ERA. She charged that ERA would mean the "breakup of family life."

every bit as enamored of the free-enterprise system as were the AEA and Phyllis Stewart. The titles of several of the *Letters* during her tenure included "The Social Welfare State," "Profits and Economic Progress," "The Left Wing and The Bill of Rights," "The Significance of Our Defeat in China." Obviously politics and economics were closely linked.

Describing the *Letter's* purpose, she wrote at the time, "We believe that the people we serve are basically anti-New Deal. . . . The continued success of the St. Louis Union Trust Company is obviously dependent on the continued prosperity of its customers. We believe that the continued prosperity of our customers is dependent on the preservation of a society which exalts personal integrity and freedom, rather than a society which idealizes the all-powerful state. . . . Of this belief was born our newsletter." Phyllis had found her niche.

She so enjoyed what was to be the last salaried job she would hold to date that when the Association of Bank Women invited her to speak—just a few days before her wedding—about what she had been doing for the past three years, she opened by saying: "I have decided to forsake the financial world in favor of a much more complicated career." But she closed by saying: "I had not been hired to take anybody's place. It was a job that I created and built from nothing. . . . Friday was my last day. And I feel as though I were walking away and leaving my three-year-old child in the hands of strangers."

The bank experience honed two sets of skills that Schlafly was to exploit brilliantly in the ERA battle. Many ERA backers blamed her extraordinary skills as a speaker and debater for seriously, perhaps fatally, wounding ERA. One of her bank responsibilities was to address women's groups and urge them to handle their own financial affairs, explaining how the trust company could help them.

The year before, while working in Washington, Phyllis—

who was dreadfully shy of speaking before groups—forced herself to conquer her nervousness by taking a public-speaking course from the UN Club Academy of Languages. Apparently incapable of ever coming out second best in a classroom situation, she got a letter from the Club president: "You have done such excellent work in the UN Club speaking class that it is a pleasure to award you first prize for the course just finished." (Little did the letter writer know that the first-prize winner would later become one of the most strident and spirited speakers against the UN. At that point, Phyllis thought the UN was "the last best hope on earth.")

A news story from the St. Louis *Globe-Democrat* of March 6, 1949, gave an account of a speech she delivered to the Zonta Club of St. Louis. Calling her a "blond banking expert," a "financial authority," and a "forceful speaker," the reporter quoted her as saying, "When women have been able to get adequate information and experience in investing, they have done as well as men."

In addressing such diverse groups as the Scottish Rite Women's Club and the Radcliffe Club, the Soroptimist Club and the American Association of University Women, Phyllis got on-the-job, on-her-feet training in taking a very complicated subject—particularly for women—and making it understandable, even interesting.

One trick she learned early was to enliven her material by mixing her philosophy of life with her philosophy of financial planning, or whatever the subject, no matter how dry. "Most of us recognize the importance of a plan in our daily lives. As I have learned, success is usually the reward, not of effort alone, but of effort combined with the strictest organization and planning."

More important, though, she learned how to research, edit, lay out, and write an advocacy "message" newsletter. (Many ERA supporters pointed to the monthly *Phyllis Schlafly Report*—certainly a newsletter with a message; since 1972, a relentlessly anti-ERA message—as the single most important reason for ERA's unexpected misfortunes.) The message went to some six thousand "important" people, a good many of them financial, political, and community leaders.

"Before the meaning of freedom was debased by neoliberals," wrote twenty-four-year-old Phyllis Stewart in one issue, "freedom and responsibility went hand in hand. . . . The man of modest means who sends his children to college chooses to skimp and save and sacrifice to do so. The left wing rejects responsibility . . . as too harsh. . . . Freedom under this definition is the freedom to gratify one's desires without making the slightest sacrifice or suffering the slightest inconvenience. Again and again we are told by the left wing that our people are not free; that they are subject to the compulsion of their environment and the circumstances under which they live; that they do not have a chance in life; that they are wage slaves and that they will only be free when the state will give them all that they want without effort and without limit."

One of those six thousand "important" people who got the message was thirty-nine-year-old confirmed bachelor and successful lawyer Fred Schlafly of Alton. After reading a particularly intriguing item in the March 1949 issue, he drove down to St. Louis to meet what he assumed was the "guy" who wrote it.

6

A Serious Courtship

In 1973, a few months after Phyllis Schlafly took on ERA, she explained her reason for switching fronts from battling Communists to battling women's liberationists. ERA, she said, would chip away at and eventually shatter the institution of marriage, and marriage "is the best deal for women the world has yet devised." For Phyllis, marriage has, indeed, been a very good deal.

In September 1949, Fred Schlafly announced to his law partners his plans to shed his long-standing bachelorhood. "The undersigned is pleased to announce that effective October 20, 1949, a new partnership is being formed to be known as Schlafly and Schlafly with offices at 620 Union Street (the newlyweds' rented home), Alton, Illinois. The senior partner —not in years—in this firm is now research director for the St. Louis Union Trust Company and the First National Bank in St. Louis, and is now known as Miss Phyllis B. Stewart."

The Schlafly marriage has remained a partnership between two highly intelligent, highly opinionated people who genuinely like, respect, and—perhaps most important considering their strong personalities—agree with each other.

Their sharing of a conservative, individualistic philosophy, in fact, was what brought Phyllis and Fred together. Ironically, the unwitting matchmaker was a liberal Democrat—former Illinois Senator Paul Douglas.

Fred was preparing to debate the senator on the subject of free enterprise vs. a planned economy when Fred received an issue of *The St. Louis Union Trust Company Letter*. It carried an obscure quote from Senator Douglas' early writings that, Fred decided, "showed that Douglas was a Socialist."

Fred dropped by the bank to find out "if the guy who had dug up that intriguing quote had anything else on Senator Douglas." The "guy" turned out to be pretty, curly-haired, blue-eyed, twenty-four-year-old Phyllis Stewart. Fred asked her to dinner that day in March, proposed in August, and married her seven months after their first date.[1]

When Fred proposed, he was thirty-nine and Phyllis was twenty-four. Both his younger brothers, Robert and Dan, were already married. With the exception of his Georgetown classmates who chose the Church instead of a wife, so were most of his college and law-school friends. But if the prospect of marrying one so young and—devout Catholics that they were, the large brood that would probably result—worried Fred, he didn't show it. Mostly he joked about the fifteen-year difference in their ages.

He wrote one married friend: "As I approach this event, I can't help but ruminate a little bit because I find that, as I am

[1] Thirty years later, Phyllis debated ERA at the University of Tulsa. One student asked her a question obviously calculated to embarrass what he had sized up as a very traditional matron from a very proper generation. "Mrs. Schlafly, do you think a girl should let a guy kiss her on their first date?" Without the least embarrassment or hesitation, she replied, "I did. It was love at first sight. And we lived happily ever after."

getting along in years, things do change. Not me, of course, but other people and things. Recently I went back to an alumni reunion at Georgetown (Class of '30) . . . and I was more than a bit shocked to see the mere tots they are admitting as students. . . . Several called me 'sir' and one asked if he could help me across the street. . . . The other day when I was calling Phyllis I had to back halfway out of the telephone booth in order to read the number on the coin box. It is obviously ridiculous to suggest that a person of my age needs glasses, but the only way I can find out what is going on is to have people read out loud to me, which is not very satisfactory because people have such low voices these days that I can't hear them very well. You wouldn't believe it but the hills in Alton are growing too. Some of them are a lot steeper than when I moved here."

As for Phyllis' feelings on the age gap, marrying older men was becoming a tradition in her family. Both her mother and grandmother married men who were at least twelve years their seniors. One of Phyllis' boyfriends, whom she described as a "college Joe," had bestowed upon her his highest praise: "Dating you has been like having a new car." She was ready for someone more substantial.

But Fred was a self-described "confirmed bachelor." "Marriage," as he wrote at the time, "is a fine institution but I'm not ready for an institution." A couple of weeks before the wedding, a Harvard Law School classmate of Fred's and one of his groomsmen wrote the bride-to-be: "Every time I think of meeting you it scares me right down to my sacroiliac. It isn't just what I've heard about you. After all, you're probably not the only extremely beautiful girl in the world. . . . Nor are you in all likelihood the only feminine bag of brains. . . . But you are the only girl to be wooed and won by John Fred II. In all my too many years of friendship with the subject, I must admit that none other ever even came close."

Fred had acquired the reputation as an immovable, imperturbable, unimpressible hulk, nicknamed "the Alton Bluff" after the steep rock formations that tower above the Mississippi. At a prenuptial party, friends wrote and performed a skit set on board the U.S.S. *Sumaria*. The *homme fatal* was Fred Schlafly.

GIRL: There's only one way for you to make an impression on that Schlafly dreamboat. That's to bowl him over as he gets off the boat.

ELEANOR: Do you think he would respond?

GIRL: Bowl him over with your looks, your personality, your, mmm, everything. But wait, here he comes now. Just as he starts down the gangplank, you rush up to him and throw your arms round his neck and say, "Welcome love" and get ready to kiss him.

FRED: Hello girls, hello Eleanor. Gosh it's tough the voyage is over.

GIRL: Go ahead Eleanor. That's it. That's it.

ELEANOR: Oh how wonderful to have my arms around you, Fred. Kiss me, big boy.

FRED: Why Eleanor, I don't know. Nope. Spreads disease. Spreads disease. Kissing spreads disease. But it's nice to see you.

A friend of Phyllis' wrote her after the engagement was announced, "I met Fred twice at the Schlaflys' and couldn't imagine why he was still single, but Charlie said it would take someone really sharp to interest him!!!"

When he found Phyllis, Fred became very interested. As he wrote at the time, "Not only was I a bashful bachelor, but I was also a lawyer bachelor, which made me even more cautious. Then I met THE GIRL. I didn't believe in love at first sight so I took a second look. I gave her a look that you could have poured on a waffle. I fell for her so hard and fast that I didn't have time to pull the ripcord on the emergency chute before she landed me."

A friend joked:

> It has been obvious for ages that poor old Fred,
> Was giggly and giddy and clear out of his head.
> Shaving on Sundays in midafternoon,
> Deserting the golf course three holes too soon.
> Attending three Masses when one is enough,
> M'God, could this be the old Alton Bluff?

Eleanor Schlafly, the youngest of Fred's three siblings, described her brother in the years before his marriage as "a terribly hard-working lawyer who did not socialize a great deal." He had a lot of friends, and when he was asked out, he went. Otherwise he worked. "After he met Phyllis, he was taking her out about once a week, which was very exciting at our end." But Eleanor and her mother were worried that Phyllis wouldn't realize that, for Fred, this was a very serious courtship. Apparently she caught on.

Fred and Phyllis' children find it difficult to understand their parents' pattern of courtship: only one date per week until marriage. The dates were most frequently a Sunday-afternoon swim at the Naval Air Station near Lambert Airport (Fred was in the Naval Reserve), or a Saturday-evening visit to the St. Louis Law Library on the top floor of the Civil Courts Building in downtown St. Louis (which Frank Lloyd Wright called the ugliest building ever built because it is a modern office building with a Greek temple on top of it, and an Egyptian pyramid on top of that).

Midway in their courtship, Phyllis tried to vary the entertainment and speed the tempo by buying tickets to *Lucia di Lammermoor,* and asking Fred to escort her. "I almost lost him over that blunder," she recalled. "I learned afterward that he hates grand opera, and besides, the performance was in the middle of the week."

Those seven months before the wedding bounced over a few bumps like *Lucia,* but mostly they brought Romance with a capital "R" in the high style of Phyllis' favorite Nelson Eddy-Jeanette MacDonald operettas. Fred often brought her flowers for just an ordinary date. Almost every date included dinner at a coat-and-tie restaurant. (Fred always ordered chicken livers.) But, in addition, there was much, much more —an intellectual courtship. Fred's hobby was current affairs and conservative politics, and in Phyllis he had found his match.

When the Schlaflys appeared on "Good Morning America" in the summer of 1978, host David Hartman asked Fred to recall his first date with Phyllis and what about her attracted him most. "Of course I thought she was very beautiful. But also she was extremely well-informed. Better than I was on many subjects and it made a very interesting courtship and marriage." Obviously, brains were as important to Fred as beauty.

Instead of a love letter, Phyllis sent him an essay entitled "The Meaning of Liberalism." Fred responded in verse:

> My goodness gracious,
> What an essay sagacious
> From one so young and pretty.
> To dispute it,
> Even to refute it,
> Is really a great pity. . . .
> A liberal's such a generous paw,
> He'll spill YOUR blood to have his wah.
> He's liberal with YOUR money and life,
> He will even expropriate YOUR wife.

Is this too strong?
Well read the list,
Of liberals who will never be missed.
Draft-dodger Wallace, rich marrier Ick,
Tightwad C. Chaplin—take your pick.
Scratch a liberal and you'll find a man,
Panting to get and keep all that he can.
Pursuing riches and spouses with crude élan,
Take not my word,
Look at the Roosevelt clan.

Phyllis responded in kind and in accord:

Mr. Schlafly,
You thus deny that you are a liberal,
Pleading you don't belong in that wastrel group.
For the "liberals" have borrowed and stolen a line,
Lied and cheated the people and made them a dupe . . .
Crying "progressive democracy" and "freedom from want,"
They've corrupted our language in line with the Red,
But they are not descended from Jefferson and Locke,
To whom freedom meant more than state-issued bread. . . .

As lovers are wont to do, they played guessing games, but
not of the conventional kind. Fred challenged Phyllis to pick
the outcome of the Communist trials. "In the last few months,"
Phyllis replied, "other matters have interested me somewhat
more than the Communist trials, but I'll play your game anyway: Judith Coplon—guilty; Alger Hiss—not guilty. (The
above are not to be confused with what I personally think
about their guilt.)"

For Phyllis and Fred an exciting evening meant a heated
discussion of the '48 Republican Party platform. "Charissima
Phyllis: Thanks for your splendid outline of the 1948 party

platform. . . . Please send me an analysis of the defects of this speech." A letter from Phyllis a couple of weeks later bemoaned the fact that "there hasn't been time for you to give me the blow-by-blow account of the Republican conference as you promised."[2]

Fred was more interested in politicking than partying; in debating than dancing. He simply loved to debate, driving even polemical Phyllis to desperation:

[2] The Schlaflys' idea of a good time hasn't changed much. In August 1967 Representative John Ashbrook placed in the *Congressional Record* a parody of Gilbert and Sullivan's "When I Was A Lad," written for fun by Fred and Phyllis. "When the Gravediggers Were Lads" attacked, among others, then Defense Secretary Robert McNamara and then Air Force Secretary Harold Brown, later Secretary of Defense under Jimmy Carter.

Robert McNamara

When Mac was a lad he served a term,
As whiz kid in Ford's auto firm.
He supported the left like ACLU,
And promoted the Edsel which wouldn't do.
And promoted the Edsel which wouldn't do.
He promoted the Edsel that's failed and gone,
And now he is the ruler of the Pentagon.
He promoted the Edsel that's failed and gone,
And now he is the ruler of the Pentagon.

Harold Brown

Since Harold was a lad he's never flown,
An airplane or worked on his own.
He stayed at a desk and avoided every war,
And scrapped new weapons for men fighting over thar.
He scrapped new weapons for men fighting over thar.
He canceled the B-70 and big missiles of course,
And now he is the ruler of our air force.
He canceled the B-70 and big missiles of course,
And now he is the ruler of our air force.

I don't know why I ever try,
To argue intellectual.
My every point you fast destroy,
And make it ineffectual.
I stand corrected, my pride subjected,
So you can have your way.
I'll let you win, without chagrin,
My principles betray.
Eternal male, to what avail,
Do you flaunt your erudition.
It was my hope,
That I could cope,
Were love your mission.

Even when they got down to basics, there was always a puzzle, a trick; always a mental challenge.

In Los Angeles visiting her great-uncle in July 1949, Phyllis received a letter from Fred; well, not exactly a letter— a sheet of music paper, notes penciled in, *sans* lyrics. The challenge to Phyllis was to tell Fred if she agreed with the sentiment expressed in the "mystery tune's" first eight measures. "No help allowed on reading the above music," Fred instructed. The tune, she guessed correctly, was "Why Do I Love You?"

In the meantime, Phyllis left for points north. Awaiting her in San Francisco was an envelope from Fred. She ripped it open. A marriage proposal? No, a graph with X indicating the time in days and Y "the amount I miss you."

"California seems to have much to recommend it," she wrote him, "but I definitely think you gave me that picture of you (in hunting gear holding a dead pheasant by the feathers) with malice aforethought, so I could look at it and remember there's someplace else that is a great deal more attractive than anything the local talent has to offer here."

To leave on vacation during the heat of the romance had

been a big gamble. "I'll never forget the look on Eleanor's face," Phyllis recalled, "the evening I told her I was leaving town for two weeks of vacation. Fred and I and Eleanor and her beau were double dating. When she and I went to the ladies' room, I casually mentioned that I'd be gone for a couple of weeks. She was speechless, but her face spoke a volume: How dare you take a chance of leaving town when you are just on the verge of catching my wonderful brother!"

By the time Phyllis was bouncing home on the two-day train ride from San Francisco to St. Louis, she was beginning to think that perhaps the vacation had been a fatal mistake. To be fresh and ready for Fred to meet her on her arrival at Union Station, she washed her hair in the Pullman lavatory. Her two weeks' absence, however, proved to be just what was needed to advance the cautious bachelor from square one to square two. "That was the first time," Phyllis recalled, "that Fred actually said, 'Angel, I love you.'"

But still no proposal. On August 1, long back from California, she was beginning to sound, for Phyllis, rather desperate. "I'm returning your very fine speech on 'Fooling the People.' . . . I cannot point out defects which aren't there. . . . The speech is really very good, interesting, logical and original. Take a bow. . . . Boy, do you have a good paragraph about Yalta, Teheran, etc. It is a most remarkable phenomenon that defects of that magnitude were ballyhooed by the Administration and by the press as great diplomatic victories for Roosevelt and we're still paying the price of those blunders. You also have an excellent paragraph on the United Nations which I think has been nothing but a fraud and a racket from the beginning. . . . Now if you want to say that Roosevelt deliberately led us into war and deliberately precipitated Pearl Harbor, I think you have a valid, logical case. That argument is much more convincing in revealing Roosevelt's treachery, dishonesty and deception of the public."

Then she gets down to downright flattery: "The only way I

can improve on your speech is in the typing. You definitely
need a new secretary. May I apply for the job? If you sounded
as good when you gave this speech as you did on the radio
yesterday, I'm sure that you must have won first prize. I expect to hear shortly that you and your 'welfare state' ideas are
going on the national hookup. . . . You are not going to get
any well-deserved fan mail if you hide these distinguished accomplishments from your public. If you would hire me as
your press agent I think that you would find me very useful."
(Phyllis' letter continued on and on, including several pages
of a complex analysis of Fort Knox and an argument for returning to the gold standard.)

Phyllis' City House friend Betsy Thomas Birmingham recalled those courtship days: "Phyllis told me she'd just be des-
olate if he didn't ask her to marry him." "Phyllis had a lot of
boyfriends," recalled her sister, Odile, "She just had flocks of
them coming over to the house all the time. . . . When she
met Fred, however, I think he just swept her off her feet. She
never was seriously in love with anybody until she met him."

On their first anniversary, Phyllis—eight months pregnant
with their first child—wrote her new husband:

> My darling,
> A year ago I loved you so,
> I thought that I would die
> If I should lose, and
> You should choose,
> Another wife than I.
> But now my dear,
> After a year,
> I love you more than ever.
> And every day,
> In my own way,
> To please you I'll endeavor.
> So if you think,

I'm on the brink,
Of letting myself bore you,
Why please don't mind,
For you may find,
It's just that I adore you.
My only prayer,
On this day fair,
Is make the years go slower;
So there will be,
Enough time for me,
To learn to love you more,
And give you children four.

In July 1949, a month before he proposed, Fred presented Phyllis with a poem, perhaps half in fun and half in fear:

Cover girl with executive know how,
You don't desire a home now.
For Kuche, Kirche, and Kinder,
Will surely a career hinder.
Career girl happy without spouse,
She'll dance to waltzes by Johann Strauss.
But despite all efforts she's shown,
She'll not march to music by Mendelssohn.

Nevertheless, Fred decided to pop the question. As he later joked at their wedding rehearsal, "Nineteen forty-nine was a year when a good many bachelors older than I gave up their freedom. I thought of forty-two-year-old Jimmy Stewart's marriage and forty-eight-year-old Clark Gable's elopement, and I took courage. It's true that they were handsome movie heroes, but 1949 seemed to be an especially romantic year, and that was only the beginning. When fifty-five-year-old Mayor O'Dwyer became engaged to a beautiful girl half his age, and seventy-two-year-old Alben Barkley [then Truman's

Vice President] started courting that St. Louis widow, I realized that I had a chance, too. Finally, when Dick Tracy decided to really marry Tess Trueheart, to whom he had been engaged ever since 1931, I knew that it is never too late."

Ever true to form, Fred didn't simply propose. "I had tried for several months," he explained, "a carefully calculated strategy of waiting until Phyllis proposed to me. But that plan had failed miserably and, bashful bachelor that I was, I was getting impatient. I considered asking her if she would make it possible for me to give up poor quarters for a better half, but that didn't seem quite romantic enough. Then I considered offering Phyllis a sixty-four-dollar ring if she would give the correct answer to a certain question. But I finally hit on the perfect proposal. I decided to invoke Holy Writ. The girl was a Scottish lassie. So I asked her to listen carefully to the next Sunday's gospel and then give me an answer."

On that Sunday, August 14, the eve of Phyllis' 25th birthday, the gospel told the parable of the unjust steward who was called in before the master and fired from his job. When the priest read the words of the master, "For thou canst be steward no longer," Phyllis rushed out of church and phoned Fred, "Will trade Stewart for Schlafly as soon as you can teach me how to spell it."

Both knew Phyllis was a quick study, so they dispensed with the long engagement typical of their social circle, and set the date for Thursday, October 20, 1949, at noon in the Blessed Sacrament Chapel, St. Louis Cathedral, a block east of Phyllis' City House.

Obviously thrilled with the right-angle turn his life was about to take, Fred sent his own announcements to friends. "The potential Mrs. Schlafly is a beautiful nearsighted blond. If she learns to spell my name and becomes the Mrs., I will attribute my success to keeping my distance. You may address your condolences to 4961 McPherson."

Meanwhile Phyllis was sending out her own personal announcements. Her Aunt Jessie (Bruce's sister) from Richmond responded: "So you are in love with a 'wonderful guy' and you're going to marry him too. This is interesting news but not too surprising since we have known all along that the time would come when you would find that someone with the intelligence and the superlative graces to match or supplement your own. With the many suitors you've had since a little girl it was hard to avoid being pushed into marriage before you had met the one person whose qualifications would measure up to the standard of perfection that your intellect and character require for satisfactory marriage." Bruce's brother Frank, a bachelor C.P.A., wrote: "I am very happy for you. I had thought that you were to be a career woman consisting of statistics and sourpuss with any thoughts of marriage being abstract and devoted only to community property, marital exemptions, new wills and all the other irritations that spring out of Washington. I'm glad I was mistaken."

Then started the rounds of dinner parties and kitchen showers. The Friday before the wedding, Fred's younger brother Dan Schlafly and his wife, Adelaide, threw a "Fish Fry for Red Eye," another nickname for Fred, whose eyes turned bloodshot from swimming.

That and several of the prewedding parties featured toasts, parodies, and jokes, as Fred and Phyllis' families and close friends used their talents to celebrate the coming event in word and song. Phyllis responded with a parody of the then-popular show tune from *South Pacific*, "A Wonderful Guy" (a skill she used later in political rallies, and most extensively in writing the lyrics for the *ERA Follies*, performed on March 22, 1979).

> I've traveled from Boston to Agua.
> I've searched both lowlands and high.
> Life may be rough,

When you wed Alton's Bluff.
But I'm in love with the one called "Red Eye."
I attended some City House classes.
Later at Radcliffe a Master was I.
You'll pardon my droop,
If I marry that stoop,
Known to the world as Red Eye.
My *summa cum laude* means never brain cloudy.
There's nothing in brilliance I lacked.
Your explanation dismisses this minus equation,
Is a doctrine that opposites attract.
I'm thinking the future looks pleasant.
Scarcely a fuss or a feud in the sky.
You'll never show strain,
When you wed a lame-brain.
I'm in love, I'm in love, I'm in love, I'm in love,
I'm in love with that wondrous Red Eye.

After meeting Phyllis at a party some weeks before the proposal, a friend of Fred's had warned him, "I congratulate you on your improving taste in pulchritude. You had better be very careful, or you are not going to be able to maintain your bacherlorhood status if you continue consorting with such charming lovely ladies." Fred had been getting such rave reviews of Phyllis that he began warning his friends, "I know you will think Phyllis is a wonderful girl but well, you know, don't overdo it when you meet her." After the wedding a friend from New York wrote, "It is impossible to tell you how much I enjoyed and appreciated being a member of your wedding party. After all the wonderful advance notices about Phyllis, all I can say is that she exceeds every one of them. She is superb!"

The night before the wedding, Fred and Phyllis exchanged presents. Fred gave her a Ford—the most exciting gift he could have given his twenty-five-year-old bride, who had never had a family car to drive. (The Stewarts had sold their car before Phyllis reached driving age.) Phyllis' wedding present to Fred was her promise to stop smoking—immediately. She had picked up the habit in the smokers' room at Maryville College when she was seventeen and eventually smoked between a half and a full pack per day (except during Lent each year). "I had my last cigarette about midnight the night before we were married."

The ceremony was performed in the St. Louis Cathedral's Blessed Sacrament Chapel, its gold mosaic altar ablaze with candles and awash with white chrysanthemums and white snapdragons. Officiating was Fred's cousin, Father James Schlafly, of Immaculate Conception Cathedral in Kansas City. Phyllis' maid of honor was her sister, Odile; the groom's best man his brother Dan. Phyllis wore an ivory satin wedding gown (borrowed from Adelaide Schlafly), and her three attendants wore gold-tone floor-length gowns with bustle backs. The groomsmen wore gray gloves, ascot ties, and silk hats. It was a Thursday noon formal affair.

Did Phyllis promise to obey? As she recalled three years later on her husband's birthday and in the midst of her campaign for Congress:

> Columnists prattle and pundits prate,
> How we lost the election in '48.
> They warn of hard work for me and for you,
> If we are to win in '52.
> My campaign is hopeless they all opine,
> But my prospects are brighter than in '49.
> Three years ago it was uphill all the way,
> In order to win I had to promise to "obey."

Friends say, though, that no, Phyllis didn't promise to obey Fred. She promised instead to cherish him—at a time when practically nobody realized there was anything wrong with promising to obey.

Fred's friends had obviously recognized an independent streak in his fiancée. A priest had warned Fred a month before the wedding, "It'll be difficult for a Radcliffe, Junior Leaguer to be obedient." An Alton judge before whom Fred frequently argued reminded him of the lines from Longfellow's "Song of Hiawatha": "As unto the bow, the cords, so unto the man is woman. Though she bends him, she obeys him; though she draws him, yet she follows; useless each without the other."

After the ceremony, family and friends gathered at the Stewarts' apartment for refreshments (the sit-down breakfast was held upstairs in a neighbor's apartment), and a host of toasts—most funny, but one serious from Fred.

> To an angel my golden dear,
> Sent from heaven to me here.
> Please be always at my side,
> My precious, beautiful bride.
> Here's to the bride,
> The loveliest ever,
> Talented, charming, pretty, and clever. . . .

Earlier a toast from Fred's brother Dan:

> A toast to my last bachelor brother,
> Whose prowess in legal and muscular battles,
> Was known by us well, and of some good use,
> But who could suspect of prowess another,
> In gaining the hand of one Phyllis Bruce.
> A toast to my latest sister-in-law,
> Whose A.B. and M.A. should certainly suffice,
> For one LL.B known as an old iron jaw.

Another toast described Fred at the altar:

> I thought that I should never see,
> A man as nerveless as a tree.
> Until this noon the Red Eye knelt,
> As placid as a hunk of smelt.
> His collar wilted, his knees they pumped,
> I almost called the city dump,
> To take this piece of man away,
> And spare the bride on her wedding day.

There were also gag telegrams: "Congratulations to our charter member of the last-man club," from the Alton Post, Veterans of the Spanish-American War. And there was also a telegram from a friend of Fred's and, later, "a great hero" of Phyllis'—Senator Robert Taft: "If you can't raise more dough, you can at least raise Republicans."

At a prenuptial party, Adelaide and Maie Kimball Schlafly —Phyllis' former classmate and later her sister-in-law, married to Fred's youngest brother, also a lawyer—composed *A Lament for a Lawyer's Wife:*

> There was a young bride named Phyllis,
> Who perhaps dreams of connubial bliss.
> But after a brief jaunt,
> She will be faced with a haunt,
> Of being lost in a legal abyss.
> She may plan on dinners and dances,
> She may look for a life of romances.
> But take it from me,
> Who learned to my misery,
> He'll be too exhausted from chasing ambulances.
> He will talk of Latin maxims,
> And mumble learned writs,
> While you wonder where his hat is,

And why his suit no longer fits.
Listen to me poor victim-in-law,
And ponder on your fate.
You'll soon find that as a lawyer's squaw,
Libraries and juries will share your mate.
Instead of acquiring a husband named Red Eye,
All you are getting is a corpus delicti.
Sooner or later you will discover,
You have a briefcase instead of a lover.

Late that afternoon the newlyweds left for a seventeen-day honeymoon, spending their wedding night at the Shamrock Hotel in Houston, and arriving in Mexico City the next evening. They spent half their honeymoon in Mexico City at the Del Prado Hotel and half in Acapulco at the Hotel Las Americanas, in a cottage overlooking the harbor. The cottage's previous occupants had been Rita Hayworth and Ali Khan (before they were married). There, in the now-famous words of Jimmy Carter, the Schlaflys were stricken with "Montezuma's revenge." "It was awful," recalled Phyllis. "We spent our honeymoon in the bathroom."

As life turned out for the Schlaflys, someone should have written *A Lament for an Achiever's Husband* for Fred. Eleanor Schlafly recalled what happened on the honeymoon:

"A day or so before the honeymoon Fred was packing his suitcase. And I saw he had put in a couple of books on mathematics, which is a hobby of his, and I said, 'Fred, you're taking math books on your honeymoon? Oh Fred, how insulting to Phyllis!' I should have minded my own business."

When Fred first lifted Phyllis' suitcase, he wondered why it was so heavy and then remembered, "Well, she is a woman. It must be stuffed with more clothes than she could wear in two months and more cosmetics than she could use in two years." When they got to the hotel and she opened her suitcase, he saw that she had brought less to wear than he had. But there were some very thick books on politics and economics in there. "Well, he just couldn't wait to call me when they got back and tell me," Eleanor said. "I knew it was going to be a very harmonious marriage."

7

"Mr. Phyllis?"

In late December 1977, papers all over the country carried an AP story headlined, "Fred Schlafly Underdog of the Year." The Underdog Club of Clio, Michigan, conferred its 1978 award to "the man behind Phyllis Schlafly" for being "one of the No. 2 persons who contributed so much to one of the No. 1 persons we've heard so much about."

The prize was a black-and-red-striped jersey—black for depression and red for frustration. (Second place went to the Tampa Bay Buccaneers, the National Football League team that had lost twenty-six games before its first victory. ABC anchorman Harry Reasoner won the award the year before, soon after teaming up with Barbara Walters.

To add insult to injury, the Schlaflys' hometown Alton *Telegraph* ran the story beneath a headline, "Mr. Phyllis Gets Recognition."

Just two days later, Mrs. Phyllis made her own headlines when the World Almanac selected her as among the nation's most influential women. Earlier in the year, the AP named her one of the ten most powerful people in Illinois—and the only woman named. *Good Housekeeping* then chose her as one of the ten most admired women in the world.

Fred Schlafly accepted his one award of the year in good humor. "I find this a good year-end joke," he remarked to reporters. "He is a very good-humored, cheerful, kind man," said his daughter Liza, a law student at the University of Virginia. "He believes 100 percent in what Mother is doing and so he's willing to put up with reporters calling and insults."

Professionally and personally, Fred Schlafly is anything but an underdog. Just the opposite. He is a man of such supreme self-confidence, so directed, so sure of himself (and his wife) that, except for reporters calling for comments, the "underdog" headline might have passed barely noticed in the rush of a long workweek. Fred Schlafly is the third generation of very successful Schlafly men, and he has done more than his share to continue the family tradition, in spite of having two very hard acts to follow.

August Schlafly, Fred's grandfather, came to America with his parents in 1855 when he was four years old. After ninety days at sea, the family, natives of Bern, Switzerland, landed in New Orleans, traveling up the Mississippi to the Swiss settlement of New Helvetia (now Highland, Illinois, in the same county as Alton). The Schlaflys were poor, and August left school at age ten to go to work making bricks—for fifty cents a day. August was the classic American Horatio Alger success story—a rugged individualist, a shrewd, tireless businessman, he started with nothing and ended a millionaire.

The name "Schlafly" is Swiss from the German root *schlafen,* which means to sleep (literally, to nap)—a ridiculously inaccurate word for this indefatigable, enterprising clan.

When August was still a young man, he began acquiring local banks with such speed and spunk one would have thought he was acquiring hot-dog stands. He became the first president of the Citizens National Depository in Alton, which later became the First National Bank of Alton. He founded and controlled the Union Trust and Savings Bank of East St. Louis, the First National Bank of Edwardsville, the Belleville Bank and Trust Company, the First National Bank of Breese, the Farmers' and Merchants' State Bank of New Baden, the First National Bank of Granite City.

When August died on March 3, 1934, aged eighty-four, he was also retired president of several flourishing businesses, among them the Mountain Valley Spring Company. He founded that one when, while vacationing ("taking the waters") at the Mountain Valley Hotel in Hot Springs, Arkansas, he recognized the potential of that untapped natural resource and bought the hotel, lock, stock, and spring. Ultimately Mountain Valley became—and still is—the nation's best-selling domestic spring water.[1]

August's son Fred inherited a good deal of his father's business acumen and luck. When Fred, Sr., died in 1967 at age eighty-seven, he was retired head, not only of the Mountain Valley Spring Company, but also of the Arkansas Beverage Company. In the 1930s, when Pepsi-Cola was little more than a weird-sounding and weirder-tasting drink, Fred, Sr., set up Arkansas Beverage, whose main asset was the exclusive Pepsi-Cola franchise for the major part of the state.

---

[1] Tradition has it that the Mountain Valley Spring at Hot Springs (known in the family as the "Schlafly Shrine") was actually the Fountain of Youth for which Ponce de Leon was searching but never found. Fountain of Youth or not, it has quite a following, including Frank Sinatra, Dean Martin, and the U. S. Senate (it is on every table in the Senate dining room). In 1957, after his heart attack, Dwight Eisenhower announced that he was drinking the water on advice of his physicians. President Nixon took it with him to China on Air Force One. Anwar Sadat brings his own to dinner parties. Racehorses Nashua, Secretariat, and Kelso were watered on it. William Randolph Hearst and Elvis Presley insisted on it. Oh, and Fred and Phyllis Schlafly also drink Mountain Valley exclusively, even though the family no longer owns the spring.

Fred, Sr.'s son, Fred, Jr., decided he wanted to go into law instead of the family business. (His younger brother Dan took over the reins of Mountain Valley and Arkansas Beverage.) In 1933, in the depths of the Depression, Fred graduated from Harvard Law School. He returned to his native St. Louis —August ultimately had settled there—to find a nonexistent market for young lawyers.

Through an uncle who lived in Alton, Fred met a local lawyer named Emil J. Verlie. Verlie was looking for a young associate who would do as he had done—devote his life, his evenings and weekends, to the law. He found him in Fred Schlafly, who, during the 1930s, did little else but work. Before he left, at age thirty-two, for a four-year tour of duty in the Navy, Fred already had his name on the door. Today, he is the senior partner of Schlafly, Godfrey, and Fitzgerald. For more than thirty years, Fred has held the "av" rating, the top rating for lawyers in the Martindale-Hubbell national legal directory. In the highly industrialized city of Alton, his clients include major oil companies and other big corporations.

Fred's practice, not the family business, provides most of his considerable income. When the Schlafly family recently sold Arkansas Beverage (they sold Mountain Valley in 1966), Fred got very little of the proceeds.

Fred is a shy man and a busy one—apparently not attracted to the limelight in which his wife basks. In addition to his law practice and athletics—he was a champion handball player and, at age seventy, still chins himself twenty-five times each morning—[2] he devotes himself to civic

[2] He takes physical fitness very seriously. When Navy officials informed Fred—a lieutenant commander in the reserves—that he had reached retirement age, he made his case for an extension by offering to wrestle any of his fellow officers. The extension was granted.

When Fred was in his mid-50s, the decaying rectory of the Schlaflys' parish church was demolished. John Schlafly persuaded his mother that

affairs, having served as president of nearly every organization in Alton, from the local bar association to the Community Chest. Economic development of the Alton area has been Fred's longtime interest. Appointed by Democratic Governor Adlai Stevenson, he was a charter member of the Bi-State Development Agency, a Missouri/Illinois group that plans development of bridges, roads, and recreational facilities. He has often combined his civic dedication with his legal skills, whether battling in the courts for a new bridge over the Mississippi or for an end to the federal government's freeze on highway funds for the Alton area.

The other major—consuming, even—interest in Fred Schlafly's life has been his forty-year crusade against communism. In 1957, as a member of the American Bar Association's Committee on Communist Tactics, Strategy, and Objectives, Fred wrote the Committee's detailed report—released at the ABA convention in London—criticizing a string of U. S. Supreme Court decisions that "threaten the right of the United States to protect itself against Communist subversion." Earl Warren, then Chief Justice, was incensed by the criticism of his Court—he was in London for the convention—particularly when it became the meeting's hottest news story and the subject of several favorable editorials. In the New York *Daily News,* under a picture of the Chief Justice, ran the lead:

---

the one thing the family needed to make their home perfect was the clock from the rectory steeple. The clock was a huge four-faced monster with a clanging bell. The church held an auction and Phyllis was the high bidder at $75.

Then came the problem of how to get it down. The company hired to level the rectory refused to send a man up because the steeple was too high and too wobbly. The Schlaflys' yard man, who had washed windows on the outside of the Chrysler Building (then the third tallest building in the world), also refused. When the demolition company set its final deadline, Fred made the climb—alone—unscrewed and dismantled the clock and bell, which had been bolted up there a half century earlier, and carried it all down.

"At the ABA's big London get-together yesterday, an important ABA committee got up in public and kicked the Earl Warren Supreme Court right in the teeth." The Chief Justice resigned from the ABA.

The ABA's new president, embarrassed that the highest legal official in the United States had broken with the bar association, pleaded with Warren to reconsider and promised he would never be similarly embarrassed. The ABA president quickly dropped the chairman of the offending committee, but left Fred, about whose role as chief draftsman he was apparently unaware. The Chief Justice then rejoined the ABA.

But not for long. The next year, another committee report —again written by Fred Schlafly and again critical of Supreme Court decisions on communism—was released. Efforts of ABA leaders to squelch or at least to delay it proved fruitless because Fred, anticipating that move, had given a copy to Senator Styles Bridges, who immediately placed the report in the *Congressional Record*. This time the Chief Justice resigned for good.

This time, also, Fred Schlafly was not reappointed to the committee. But he continued to devote a good portion of his life to debating, lecturing (several times for Dr. Fred Schwarz's Christian Anti-Communism Crusade schools), filing lawsuits, and heading organizations (among them the World Anti-Communist League)—all dedicated to "exposing and meeting the Communist threat."

"I think that if you look at the world situation," Fred explained, "the biggest threat to us is from communism. If we just pretend it doesn't exist as we sometimes do, we're setting ourselves up for the slaughter."

So absorbed is Fred in this crusade that, for him, social conversation often means discussing the U.S. "betrayal" of Taiwan. Fred's sister Eleanor recalled a phone call from her brother in late 1978, just after President Carter announced

U.S. recognition of mainland China. "He greeted me by saying, 'I guess you've heard the terrible news?' "—a question guaranteed to strike fear in the hearts of most doting aunts. Not in Eleanor Schlafly's. "And then we discussed Taiwan and Red China."

An article on Phyllis in the *National NOW Times* (National Organization for Women) described Fred as "so dedicated to combating Communism that he makes the late Senator Joe McCarthy sound mellow and Senator Barry Goldwater look pink." Fred indeed is a man of very strong opinions. And, friends say, many of Phyllis' strong opinions— her frame of reference—were molded by her husband.

Paul Weyrich, head of the Committee for the Survival of a Free Congress, credited Fred with the formation of Phyllis as a political being. "He was older and already active. She picked it up from him. He was sort of a teacher."

"Teacher" is a word used frequently when friends describe the Schlafly marriage. "She calls him her No. 1 adviser," said Kathleen Teague, co-chairman of Virginia STOP ERA. "Every once in a while she'll call me up—oh, say when NOW announced its boycott (of unratified states)—and I'd say, 'Phyllis, you've got to do a press release.' She'd call me back and say, 'Well, I've been talking to some of my advisers about that.' Eventually I figured out—I kept thinking, 'advisers? How many people does she talk to?'—and I finally figured out it was Fred, only she wouldn't want to say, 'Fred thinks that we should reconsider this whole thing.' "

Phyllis' goddaughter, Claire Birmingham Hanlon, who lived with the Schlaflys one summer, recalled that after dinner Phyllis would frequently turn to her husband: "Fred, I'd like to see you in my office." The tone, Claire said, was slightly imperious; it reminded her of a superior commanding a subordinate, "but I think that's just Phyllis' style. What she was doing was seeking his help; his input into a column or a newsletter or his assistance with legal interpretations or research. Clearly, she depended on him a lot."

Take the ERA fight, for example. Fred has done more than supply his wife with the endless array of constitutional arguments and legal precedents with which she clobbers debating opponents and impresses legislators. He has done more than serve as an unpaid legal counsel to STOP ERA, filing several suits on its behalf. Fred has also helped build for his wife the religious backdrop against which this battle has been waged —and which, probably more than anything else, has brought STOP ERA an incredibly large number of supporters and successes.

Fred is as devout about his Catholicism as he is about his anti-communism. His religious beliefs are, of course, the basis for his anti-communist ones: Communism is atheistic, therefore godless and therefore evil.

When Phyllis Schlafly speaks against ERA, it is as impossible to separate the issue from her religion as it would be if the speaker were Billy Graham.[3] Religion permeates nearly every speech and column, whether the subject is ERA or the United States' plunging prestige, defense capabilities, birthrate, or SAT scores. Fred Schlafly, friends said, was very definitely the catalyst for this all-pervasive piety.

"Our mother was very loyal to her religion," said Phyllis' sister, Odile. "We went to church every Sunday. But she wasn't obsessed with it. Phyllis is very influenced by Fred in this regard. He has had a much more serious influence on her than our family."

Kathleen Teague recalled the first time she shared a hotel room with Phyllis. "Before she goes to bed she kneels down.

---

[3] In a revised version of "The Impossible Dream"—the only serious number in Phyllis' *ERA Follies*—she called the battle against ERA "a heavenly cause."

Honest to God, the first time I saw her do it I couldn't believe it. She kneels down and says her prayers."

When Phyllis Schlafly attacked ERA on religious grounds, she was, regardless of her arguments' merits, at least being consistent. From the start of her public career, three years after her marriage, it was on religious grounds that she attacked everything from permissive education to bloated bureaucracies. Her arguments that ERA is anti-family and will encourage abortion, homosexuality, and divorce are arguments that one would expect Fred Schlafly to mobilize if he were on the front lines fighting ERA.

"She wouldn't be where she is today without my father and they both know it," said their daughter Liza. Fred Schlafly is, quite simply, a very supportive husband—in anyone's terms. If *Ms.* magazine gave a "Man of the Year" award, Fred Schlafly could definitely qualify.

Fred has been the perfect political husband since back when the phrase was a contradiction in terms. In 1952 he campaigned enthusiastically for his wife for Congress. In 1967, when Phyllis ran for the presidency of the National Federation of Republican Women, he spent the week in Washington with her; at a preconvention debate he grabbed a front-row seat and clapped loudly whenever his wife scored a point or even when she didn't; when her jokes were funny and even when they weren't. During the heat of the convention, while his wife relaxed in their hotel suite, Fred presided over an angry swarm of delegates who'd gathered to complain of the "Gestapo tactics" of the opposition.

When Phyllis travels, which she does weekly, she calls Fred every night—be it 11:00 P.M. or 1:00 A.M.—to get the messages that her secretary has taken during the day and that Fred has continued taking at night. "It'll be 1:00 A.M.," said STOP ERA leader Shirley Spellerberg, "and she'll be calling him from Florida. Fred is on the line for thirty minutes like a loyal secretary relating to Phyllis the messages that have come in."

Which raises a question that is frequently asked about the Schlaflys—here by David Hartman, when Fred and Phyllis appeared together on "Good Morning America" in the summer of 1978:

"Your wife . . . she has a very strong, dominant kind of style. . . . Is she the same way at home? Does she wear the pants in the family?"

"No, she doesn't. I'm obviously physically larger than she is," answered a serious-looking, six-one, broad-shouldered Fred. "She's very, ah, ah, submissive."

David Hartman, his eyebrows nearly meeting his hairline in amazement, responded, "Submissive? Phyllis Schlafly, submissive? Is that right?" looking to Phyllis for refutation.

"Weeell, uh, Fred is the boss of the family and that's the way it is."

The traditional marriage roles—the man as head of the house—are God-given fundamentals, Phyllis Schlafly contends, essential for Western civilization's survival. "The 'liberated' Roman matron," she wrote in *The Power of the Positive Woman,* "who is most similar to the present-day feminists, helped bring about the fall of Rome through her unnatural emulation of masculine qualities, which resulted in a large-scale breakdown of the family and ultimately of the empire."

Phyllis favors a sharp division of labor in marriage—his job, her children. Nature has determined that "women have babies and men provide the support. If you don't like the way we're made you've got to take it up with God."

In Phyllis' scheme of things, not only are there physical differences between men and women (men have more muscle; women, fat), there are also emotional and psychological differences. For example, Schlafly advises "positive women" to "appreciate and admire" their husbands. Whereas a woman's chief emotional need is active (that is, to love), a man's prime emotional need is passive (that is, to be appreciated or admired).

When, in December 1977, Phyllis announced that she would not challenge incumbent Charles Percy for the Republican Senate nomination, she gave as one of her reasons: "I was afraid that Fred would think I didn't need him anymore. [If she had been elected, Fred would not have left his law practice and moved to Washington.] A man needs to feel psychologically needed as well as financially needed, and it causes problems if the wife is financially and emotionally so self-sufficient that he feels unnecessary."

"I want to thank my husband, Fred, for letting me come here," is one of Phyllis' favorite out-of-town speech openers. "I like to say that," she explained, "because I know it irritates the women's libbers more than anything else."

Anne, the Schlaflys' youngest child, claimed that there is some truth in it. "If Dad thinks she's spending too much time away from home, he'll just insist that she cancel some speaking engagements. They may discuss it for awhile, but then she'll say, 'Well, if that's what you want, then I'll do that.' Of course, my father does that only very rarely. He respects Mother's judgment."

"I never get the feeling at family gatherings that she's calling the shots," said Shannon Schlafly, a professor at Washington University, a niece through marriage, and an ERA supporter. "He's a very successful lawyer. He doesn't just sit home and clip coupons."

A nephew, Tom Schlafly, pointed out the irony in the whole question—the sexism inherent in the assumption that Fred's just the man behind the woman. "She's obviously more prominent than he is and so I guess it's sort of a stereotype that any man who has a more famous wife is dominated by her and henpecked by her, but I don't think that's true. He has certainly achieved pretty well independently. He hasn't simply gone around tugging at her skirts."

"Before I went up there," said Claire Birmingham Hanlon, "my impression had always been that Phyllis sort of ran things. I found out quickly that's not true. Fred is nobody's fool." However, he did do something regularly that made Claire suspect that Fred saw some threat—rather he recognized the possibility of being dominated by such a strong personality as Phyllis'. Dinner at the Schlaflys' is always at six on the dot. Phyllis likes everyone to be on schedule and on time —no exceptions. Fred used to come five or ten minutes late every night, which Claire decided he did on purpose to remind Phyllis that she couldn't control him.

Much about the Schlafly marriage was revealed in the latest of Phyllis' accomplishments—getting her law degree.

Phyllis claimed to have had two reasons for starting law school at age fifty-one, while already a radio commentator, a syndicated columnist, and the only nationally recognized leader of a movement against one of the decade's most popular social issues. "I had been trying to convince my second son, Bruce, to go to law school. John [the eldest] hadn't gone [he did later], and Roger [the mathematician] certainly wasn't going to go, and I wanted Bruce to go. And he didn't want to. [He went to medical school instead.] It was kind of a dare. 'Well, if none of my sons will go to law school, Mother will go to law school,' and so in trying to bait them into it, I took the LSAT [a standardized admissions test] and got admitted."

Second, and surely the key reason, was that Schlafly frequently found her authority and facts challenged during ERA debates and testimony because she wasn't a lawyer. (Her first ERA-related trip to the Illinois Capitol was as a companion to Fred the lawyer, who testified before the House Judiciary Committee.)

A couple of years later, she was in the midst of testifying before an Illinois House committee when a legislator interrupted and asked belligerently, "Mrs. Schlafly, are you an attorney?"

"No, I am not, but I'm quoting some of the most respected constitutional authorities, including Professor Thomas Emerson of Yale Law School, who favors the amendment."

"Well, I am an attorney," he snapped, "and I know better."

In July 1974, Schlafly debated Congresswoman and lawyer and chief pro-ERA strategist Martha Griffiths at a "National Town Meeting" in Washington. Toward the end of the debate Griffiths groaned loudly and complained, "It would be simpler to argue with you if you were a lawyer. . . . Then you would have to account for what you say."

After the debate, Schlafly complained to Washington *Post* reporter Sally Quinn, "She pulled rank on me. I used to be intimidated by these people because I'm not a lawyer, but I'm not anymore."

Intimidated, perhaps not. Angry, definitely. "I had debated some of these women lawyers and I found it so easy to beat them in debate," she said a few weeks after being admitted to the Illinois bar. "They would say they're lawyers, and people are impressed by that, so I figured, 'Well, I can do that in my spare time.'"

Fred knew nothing about her taking the law boards, applying or getting admitted. One night at the dinner table in April 1975, "I dropped the bombshell. Fred first thought I was joking. Then he got kind of mad and said, 'That's the craziest thing I ever heard! How are you going to have time to do that? It's ridiculous for you to go to law school.' Since he was angry, I thought, 'Well, if Fred doesn't want me to go to law school, I'm certainly not going to do it.' So I wrote the law school on May 4 and I said, thank you very much, but I'm not coming because of personal considerations. I didn't say anything to Fred. I just figured if he didn't want me to go to law school, I was not going to oppose him on that.[4]

About three weeks passed and one night Fred said, "That was a great idea for you to go to law school. It would help you in your ERA work." "It's out of my life," Phyllis replied. "I wrote the law school and told them I'm not coming." "No," he said, "I think you ought to go." And then, recalled Phyllis, "he turned on a whole campaign to get me to go. Meanwhile, the children assured me it was far too late to reapply since it was already the end of May. But I figured I'd just write the law school and say I'd changed my mind (just like a woman, she laughed), and they would tell me it was too late. To my great surprise, I got a letter back the first week of June accepting me." (She entered the law school in August 1975 in a class of 204 students, and graduated in December 1978, with the rank of 27.)

Anne Schlafly explained why her father was so upset by the prospect of her mother going to law school that, in her words, "When she announced it at dinner he blew up and stormed out of the room. My brother John explained that Mother was trying to move in on the one thing that he had that was his very own—his law practice." As it turned out, Anne added,

---

[4] She should have been the first to understand Fred's reaction, considering her past comments on the subject: "A man who fights the competitive battle every day does not want to compete with his wife on the same terms that he competes with other men and women in the business world. However, he is perfectly happy to have her compete against others . . . so long as he knows that she admires and needs him." "You don't seem to have a clash of wills. There's not a lot of competitiveness in your home," David Hartman remarked to his guests, Fred and Phyllis Schlafly. "No one feels threatened. Politically, can you understand those marriages where that is not the case?" The question was beside any point Phyllis wanted to make, so she simply ignored it: "You see, I'm not competing with Fred in his career. He has a wonderful, successful legal career and I don't compete with him in that. . . ."

"He made her go. He now wants to make her a member of his firm. [Phyllis serves Fred's firm as "of counsel."] What happened, I think, is that he thought it through and decided he was being silly. He's really a very secure man. I mean, I sure wouldn't want to compete with Mother."

8

The Famous Six Kids

Nothing is more certain to spark feminist groans and teeth gnashing than hearing Phyllis Schlafly expound on her six children.

"If someone were to ask you what was your greatest contribution up to now, what would you say?" asked St. Louis TV personality Dick Keefe, obviously expecting an answer that had something to do with ERA or Barry Goldwater or guided missiles.

"I'd say my six children, of whom I'm so proud," replied Phyllis, smiling, of course. "I just don't think that for most women a career success is enough," she added for good measure.

In 1975, Schlafly told a reporter from *People* that nothing pleases her more than fixing buckwheat cakes for Sunday breakfast. "I think of my marriage and family as my No. 1 career. When I fill out applications, I put down 'Mother' as my occupation.

"Those fifteen years between 1949 and 1964 were happy ones," Schlafly assured another reporter. "I don't think there's

anything as much fun as taking care of a baby. When I had
three in diapers and was doing the laundry and cooking, I was
very happy. Oh yes; as happy as now." She deplored the fact
that women—particularly the most educated women—were
having careers instead of babies: "Myself?" she said, "I'd
rather scrub bathroom floors than write the newsletter that I
write for the organization [Eagle Forum]."

The choruses of "Oh sure's" and "Right on, Phyllis's"
spring automatically to mind and mouth. "Phyllis would
much rather be eating airplane food than preparing buckwheat pancakes or, for that matter, plain old eggs for her
loved ones," said Susan Catania, a state legislator from Illinois.

Most reporters, ERA activists, and assorted critics simply
don't believe her. Schlafly's devotion to diapers, they said,
started years after the last of her children was toilet trained—
at precisely the time she became the nationwide spokesman
against ERA. Obviously, they explained, someone who was
hopping from talk show to talk show warning that ERA
meant the destruction of the family found it to her advantage
to act like she was running for mother of the year.

Schlafly, on the other hand, complained that her critics deliberately painted her as a woman who deserved to become
mother of the year about as much as Joan Crawford. In
Omaha, a newswoman interviewed Schlafly, asking her many
personal questions about her family. "I tried to answer,"
Schlafly recalled, "although it was obvious she didn't believe
anything I said." In the course of the interview Schlafly volunteered that she had nursed all her children for at least six
months. The next day Omaha readers read that Phyllis
Schlafly had a nurse for all her children.

In Alton, a contingent of local women toil for ERA with
unrivaled dedication—perhaps to offset the ignominy of hailing from the same town as the woman who has stalled and,
perhaps, stopped ERA. A young ERA devotee assured a re-

porter that Schlafly's six children were forced to live in the servants' quarters.[1] Dorothy Haegele, the woman who founded Alton's ERA Center, wrote a letter to the editor of *Chicago* magazine after a profile of Schlafly appeared there in June 1978. "Residents of this area know that Phyllis has never been a homemaker, is a tyrant in her own home, and that her children are looked upon with pity." Still another Alton resident has a friend who goes to the same beauty shop as Phyllis. "She said those kids would come there with their faces dirty dressed in rags. She said they did everything but hang on the chandeliers."

Undoubtedly, Phyllis Schlafly is grist for one of the country's busiest gossip mills. Normally, Schlafly responds to personal attacks with an imperturbability that further infuriates her attackers. But charges that she ignored her children leave her livid. A reporter repeated some of this gossip to Schlafly and got, as expected, a blanket denial. But the reporter did not expect a phone call that night at home from an obviously distressed Phyllis Schlafly. "People making nasty remarks about my abilities as a mother really bother me. I spent a good part of one summer taking my Roger to learn ice hockey at a rink in St. Louis County. Now he's captain of the ice-hockey team at the University of California [Berkeley]."

Schlafly, no doubt, deserved what she got. She set herself up as the queen of motherhood and it should have come as no surprise that her critics would try tirelessly to knock her off the throne.

But her critics were wrong when they claimed that adver-

---

[1] The Schlaflys have no servants' quarters. The previous owner of their house, the Spencer Olins (of Olin Industries), had a housekeeper who lived on the third floor. The week after the Schlaflys moved in, in 1962, they put a wall-to-wall wrestling mat in that room, where all the boys practiced wrestling. The family's domestic help consists of one housekeeper who comes in on weekdays to clean and cook. They never had overnight help.

tising herself as supermom is new—of the same vintage as ERA. Her children have always figured prominently in her politics.

"I appear here as a mother who is eager that her five small children have the opportunity to grow up in a free and independent America and because I do not want my children to suffer the fate of children in Cuba, China, and the twenty captive nations," she said in 1963 during testimony before the Senate Foreign Relations Committee against the nuclear-test-ban treaty.

On a press release promoting her 1967 book, *Safe—Not Sorry,* was a photo of all six children wearing matching red vests, above the caption: "Will your future Christmases be as happy as this picture of Phyllis Schlafly's children?"

When Phyllis Schlafly ran for Congress in 1952, her eldest son, John, was just a year and a half old. When she ran for Congress in 1970, her youngest daughter, Anne, was five. Schlafly, obviously, has never been "just your average housewife." "Just your average housewife" does not run for Congress and testify before Senate committees and study nuclear strategy and write an eight-hundred-page book on Henry Kissinger. But having done these things does not mean that she neglected her children or banished them to the servants' quarters or dressed them in rags.

In fact, relatives said that if Phyllis Schlafly's six suffered from anything, it was from a little too much maternal attention.

"Perhaps she spent too much time with them and attempted to mold and teach them too much without letting them get into the flow of society on a more normal basis," said cousin Joe Schlafly, a young lawyer and contemporary of the Schlafly children. "It wasn't a question of her writing all these books at her family's expense. She gave them an enormous amount of time and devotion."

At the banquet in Washington on March 22, 1979, celebrating the "End of an ERA," the audience of Phyllis fans went wild over the six Schlafly children, all in attendance. "Just let me take one minute to reassure you," Schlafly told the crowd, "that when the ERAers put up reporters to ask me, 'Mrs. Schlafly, who's taking care of your children?' you don't need to worry about my children. So if you'll allow me one minute to present them to you, you'll know that you can cross that off your worry list. I feel a little like the Roman woman Cornelia Gracchus who visited with a friend who proudly displayed her box of jewels. When she finished, Cornelia said, 'I will show you my jewels—my two sons'—and they later became Tribunes of the Roman Republic. So give me one minute to present to you my six jewels." And then she introduced her embarrassed but smiling offspring (in order of birth): John, a law student; Bruce, a medical student; Roger, a doctoral student in mathematics; Liza, a student at Princeton; Andy, a student at Princeton; and Anne, a ninth-grader.

"I have heard many women say that the happiest day of their lives was the day their kids started school," Schlafly said during the Christmas holidays when all but her eldest son were home. "I don't feel that way. I loved having them home and I get along fine with the little baby—the preschool child. I hated to see them go to school."

Talk is cheap, of course, but in Schlafly's case backed up by a rather extraordinary action, even for the most doting of mothers. "It was one of the most rewarding and successful and exciting things I've ever done," Schlafly said about teaching each and every one of her children how to read. And not only teaching them to read but also keeping them home until the second grade to do it. Instead of going to kindergarten and first grade, her children learned to read and write and do the basics of math at a little school desk their mother set up in her office. (It was all legal, she explained, because children are not required to go to school until they are six, and her children did start at six, but instead of starting in first grade, as is normal, they were tested and passed with flying colors into second grade.)

Her reason for saddling herself instead of the schools with her brood was simple. She didn't like the way reading was and is being taught. By the time her children were ready for school, most schools had abandoned the tried-and-true phonics method for the "look-say" method, in which children are taught to memorize words by guessing at them from accompanying pictures. "The children are inflicted with endless pages of 'Look up,' 'Look down,' 'Quack-quack, said the duck' and similar nonsense. They end up unable to spell and with an artificially limited vocabulary," she explained.

Using an old standard textbook called *Reading with Phonics*, Schlafly spent two hours per day teaching. "I did it in twenty-minute segments. With one child you can do in two hours what they do all day in school. The rest of the day, they helped put dishes in the dishwasher or worked in their coloring books or rode their bikes. I mean, what else is kindergarten but a waste of time and a place to pick up germs?"[2]

"Every morning," Anne recalled, "Mother would ask if I wanted my lessons in the morning or in the afternoon. I'd usually pick the morning and then I'd be free for the rest of the day to read or go swimming or practice the piano.

"Mother wrote several of her books with me on her lap while she was typing," reported Anne. "One of my earlier rec-

---

[2] Delighted with her children's success, Schlafly became a proselytizer. "Parents teach their children to ride a bike, to swim, to cook, to sew, to drive a car," she wrote in *The Power of the Positive Woman*. "Why not teach your children to read—the most important skill of all?" Schlafly was unable to convince any of her friends to follow suit. They balked, claiming that either Phyllis or her children had special abilities. She did convince Willie Bea Reed, the family housekeeper for twenty-five years, to teach her daughter. Willie's success matched Phyllis'. Willie's daughter entered school in the second grade, reading two years above her grade level and became a straight-A student.

ollections of Phyllis," said her sister-in-law Eleanor, "is her remarkable ability to be surrounded by a lot of activity, little children playing and crying and yelling. You'd call Phyllis and while she was on the telephone talking to you, she'd be typing and there would be a gurgling, cooing sound from one baby on her lap, and the noises of two or three others close by playing games."

Critics repeated that Phyllis and family have carefully crafted this supermom myth. But back in 1965, long before ERA, when Schlafly would have been taken more seriously had she sold herself as a Harvard-educated political scientist, period, St. Louis *Globe-Democrat* staffer Jane Clark reported:

"With a boisterous brood of six to care for, how does Mrs. Schlafly find the time to write—especially on the serious subjects with which she deals? To her, it's no problem. . . . She feels no need for an ivory tower where she can retreat and shut off the household hubbub. She works in her library—'the most active room in the house.' There with her are several of the children and she keeps a small desk near her own so that the preschooler can keep busy alongside her. 'The only talent I really claim to have is the ability to work in the midst of bedlam.' She did admit that she does a great deal of her writing and research after 10 P.M. when the last of the children was bedded down."

"She's able to shut out everything else," said Betsy Birmingham. "Very few women are. If the kids are running around and spilling the jam and the cocoa, you feel that you have to go and see what is going on. She is totally able to let them go on with the jam and the cocoa and not get up." Betsy added that the Schlafly children seemed to be very well trained. They probably didn't spill much jam or cocoa.

On the cover of a scrapbook Phyllis kept as a high-school student is a drawing of a Girl Scout in her crisp green uniform and yellow bandanna, her cheeks naturally rosy, her red hair gleaming in the sun. Next to the drawing, Phyllis wrote, "My idea of a beautiful girl."

"If there's anything that has given me and my sister stamina at our age," said Phyllis' sister, Odile, "it's our good health. My mother scrimped and saved on many things but never, ever on food. Roast beef on Sundays. We ate off the same roast half the week, but we always ate well and on schedule. That's where our money went."

Phyllis brought that same concern with good food and good eating habits into her marriage. In 1950 Fred commented (in verse) on the "special" bread his wife baked and the bottled water she insisted on using at all times (before the fluoride controversy). In 1975, Fred told New York *Times* reporter Judy Klemesrud, "We particularly agree on national defense, anti-communism, opposition to détente, exercise, and good nutrition. We avoid many of the things that often hurt a marriage, such as alcohol and cigarettes, and we stick to foods that are not overrefined." Putting "good nutrition" in the same sentence as national defense, anti-communism, and opposition to détente shows just how important healthy food was in the Schlafly household.[3]

Back in 1950, when nursing a baby was unfashionable and even discouraged by obstetricians, Phyllis insisted on breast feeding. Back in 1950, when not loving Wonder Bread was considered downright un-American, Phyllis was already a health-food enthusiast.

Nephew Tom Schlafly, thirty-two years old, recalled out-

---

[3] "I never had a cup of coffee in my life until ERA came along," Phyllis said. "When ERA came into my life, I had to have something to keep awake so I could get through all the things I had to do." Caffeine is surely about as far as Schlafly goes in the stimulant department. Kathleen Teague, a friend and fellow STOP-ERAer, said that once in a while "when she's really relaxed, if you really push it, you can sometimes convince her to have a single glass of white wine."

ings to Aunt Phyllis' twenty years ago. "The thing that struck me most was she had sort of a strange diet for her children. Whenever I'd go there, there was always lots of wheat germ and none of the junk food that I was consuming. And she monitored mealtimes. She made sure we ate this food that I thought was fairly strange."

Betsy Birmingham's daughter Claire had a similar childhood memory: "I remember we used to have to eat that God-awful peanut butter. Phyllis was really into health foods. The only kind of sugar we could have was brown sugar. We used to have hamburgers or eggs for lunch—nothing else." The Birmingham children used to ask for peanut butter and jelly sandwiches, so Phyllis went to some health-food store she had found "God knows where" and bought organic peanut butter. "It was just awful. But whenever we went up there we had to eat just exactly what Phyllis said. She didn't allow any junk food or sweets. Phyllis would lay out the menus and she would execute them."

John vividly remembers what he called "Mother's health-food phase." "She would drive every Monday morning to a farm fory-five minutes away to get twelve gallons of raw, unpasteurized milk and twelve dozen fertile eggs. We weren't allowed to have anything in the house made from white flour or white sugar, except birthday cakes. [For his birthday one year, Roger got a loaf of home-baked bread with a candle on it.]

"We had hot Roman Meal for breakfast, with brown sugar, honey, wheat germ, and real cream. In the afternoons, when we came home from school, if we wanted a snack, we had scrambled eggs. But the thing I remember best was the peeled tomato in a little plastic cup that I had to take to school as part of my lunch every day. Everyone else had a salami sandwich on white bread."

For two years straight, Roger's sole lunch at school was

tuna fish. That was the only thing he liked that he could take in his lunch box that was on "Mother's approved list."

Far from ignoring her children, friends and relatives insisted that Phyllis kept an uncommonly tight rein on them. She is, said Claire Birmingham Hanlon, who worked for the Schlaflys as a governess one summer, a firm believer in the maxim, "The devil makes mischief for idle hands."

According to Claire, the children were all organized all the time. They had work or activities or projects or sight-seeing or music lessons—they all took music lessons. They were never allowed to just sit. They weren't allowed to watch television— "only certain programs and then they had to be special."

"She was always very organized," recalled Claire's mother, Betsy. "She had the children's day planned. They didn't just wander. There would be games for them to play and things for them to do. You didn't just visit."

Even parties were structured—for example, the Easter party that the Schlaflys held every year for 15 years. Each child was allowed to invite six classmates. The first hour was devoted to an Easter egg hunt. Next came the game of follow the string to a chocolate bunny. Then came competitions called "stunts" with prizes for relay races, jumping rope, basketball throws and chin ups. After refreshments (ice cream, cake and milk—never soda), came the scavenger hunt and later, as the boys grew up, a magic show put on by Roger and Andy.

Phyllis also monitored and sometimes vetoed her children's choice of friends. The regimen remained rigid in their teenage years. "There's not much beer drinking and stuff like that," said Betsy. "I ignore my children. I don't know what they do when they go upstairs. Phyllis always knew."

It is a very disciplined household, explained Claire—"old-fashioned, sort of like I imagine it was in Victorian England." Everybody must show up for dinner on time and dressed—no

T-shirts or bare feet allowed. Dinner was almost always buffet, and Phyllis and Fred were almost always there. It was the only time of the day or night that Phyllis did not answer her constantly ringing telephone. The children were expected to report on their day's activities. "There was always discussion at the dinner table," added Claire. "In a lot of families, I don't care if the mother stays home or not, the kids eat in front of the TV and the parents never talk to them." Fred and Phyllis kept the conversation focused on the children. They did not discuss SALT or the ERA or the B-1 bomber.

(With one exception, said Anne. During the time the Senate was debating the Panama Canal treaties, "There wasn't a dinner we had—for like three months straight—when my father didn't bring up the tragedy of giving up the Panama Canal.")

When it came time for the first child to go to college, Phyllis, according to Betsy, "decided she wanted to keep him close to home and that was that. There certainly wasn't any room for debate." John went to Washington University.

Five years later, when the second son, Bruce, reached college age, he decided he wanted to go farther away from Alton. His mother decided differently. "Phyllis and Fred wanted him to go to Washington University so he could come home on weekends and they could keep in touch with him," explained Betsy. "They wanted to know what he was thinking really." He went to Washington University.

When the next son, Roger, reached college age—relatives call Roger a "free spirit" and "a rebel"—he said, according to Betsy, "I'm going to Princeton," and they said, "Well, we're not quite sure about that."

"Well, that's where I'm going," said Roger, and off he went —setting a precedent for the next two in line. Liza and then Andy also went to Princeton. (After Princeton, Roger went to graduate school at the campus Phyllis and Fred considered the most revolutionary in the country—the University of California at Berkeley.)

All the Schlafly children started school at SS. Peter and Paul, a parochial school in Alton, connected with the Schlafly family parish. At the junior-high-school level, the boys all transferred to the Priory, a private Catholic boys' prep school in St. Louis County run by Benedictine monks.

In the seventh grade, Liza transferred to Mary Institute, a nondenominational girls' school in Ladue, where she graduated as valedictorian.

For several years the Schlafly children rode a bus each day that transported a score of Alton children to private schools in St. Louis; one year the Schlaflys and a French student living with them filled a car of their own. "We were spending like two hours in the car every day," said Anne, "and it got to be too much." The other years, the children lived four nights a week with their Aunt Eleanor, not far from their schools.

Each and every one of the Schlafly children has been a consummate student, graduating from high school with top honors and proceeding to college to do likewise. "It's probably a good thing," said one relative. "I'm not sure Phyllis could deal with having less than superstar children."

"Do you ever feel out of sync with the times?" Diane Weathers asked Schlafly in a recent *Family Circle* article. "No," Phyllis answered, "because I don't see that my opponents succeed in making themselves or the people around them happy. I don't see that they have fulfillment, happy marriages, or the wonderfully successful children that I have."

Gladys Levis, the Schlafly's next-door neighbor and one of Alton's most ardent ERA backers, is barely on speaking terms with Phyllis,[4] but called her children "delightful, won-

---

[4] The break came much before ERA. They started out being friends when Phyllis first moved to Alton. "As we got to know each other better," said Levis, "we agreed to disagree on almost everything." In

derful, smart. They're great kids." But she added, "I feel sorry for them. Their mother is so controversial and it's been tough for them in many ways."

It must be tough to have their mother perpetually in the ncws, belittled on editorial pages of newspapers all over the country. "If I were opposed to the ERA, its enemies would convert me," wrote syndicated columnist Garry Wills. "Phyllis Schlafly, for instance, talks more nonsense per appearance than anyone I have ever heard." And in a July 1980 column, Wills wrote, "The clearest light in which to see Phyllis Schlafly is that of a pampered child who does not want to grow up because that would entail surrendering her very expensive toys."

It must be tough to glance through the "letters" section of *Newsweek* and catch a letter from an Atlanta woman condemning the recently exposed Chicago Police Department practice of strip-searching women arrested for minor traffic violations: "Although it's a practice I ordinarily wouldn't wish on my worst enemy, imagine the divine justice if Illinois resident Phyllis Schlafly had been among the thousands of women strip-searched by the Chicago police."

It must be tough to be the child of a woman who has become a symbol, an institution. National Public Radio satirists Warren Leming and Jerry Sullivan recalled a recent routine they wrote for NPR's "All Things Considered." "When President Carter ordered that public buildings not be cooled below seventy-eight degrees last summer, Leming created a character named Uncle Willie, who, in a takeoff on public-service commercials, advised children that if the thermostats in their homes were set lower than seventy-eight degrees, they should

---

1964, Phyllis had a dinner party and polled the people around the table on who they favored for the Republican nomination that year. Everyone picked Goldwater except the Levises, who picked Rockefeller. That, said Levis, was the beginning of the end of their friendship.

look in their parents' wallets, write down their Social Security numbers, and report them by calling a toll-free number in Washington. "Your mom and dad are cheating Big Brother if they set their thermostat below seventy-eight degrees," Uncle Willie said.

A woman in Illinois didn't get it. She called the station and said she had written letters to the University of Illinois trustees, the Daughters of the American Revolution, the Republican National Committee, the Federal Communications Commission, and Phyllis Schlafly.

If Phyllis Schlafly is controversial nationally, she is three times as controversial locally. Alton is not exactly a big newsproducing town, and Phyllis is the biggest thing to come out of the little river town since the 1930s, when Alton produced the tallest man yet on record—a nearly nine-foot, five-hundred-pound giant named Robert Wadlow.[5]

When the St. Louis chapter of the National Conference of Christians and Jews selected Phyllis Schlafly in 1975 as recipient of its annual brotherhood award, her selection stirred up such bitter controversy that the next year the conference abolished the award.

When, three years later, the Madison County Bar Association selected Schlafly as recipient of its annual Liberty Bell Award, a few furious members of the association—which had earlier endorsed ERA—tried unsuccessfully to push through

---

[5] Alton's third claim to fame—right after Phyllis Schlafly and Robert Wadlow—is Elijah Lovejoy, an abolitionist editor murdered by an Alton mob in 1837. At the time of his death, Lovejoy had been in Alton for fifteen months, having fled St. Louis, sickened by the sight of slaves being sold on the block in the heart of downtown. Illinois, of course, was not a slave state, but Alton was thick with slave owners and sympathizers. After the Lovejoy murder, the town, according to a newspaper account of the time, was "loudly scorned and denounced. The progressive people who had given the city its good name moved away."

a "resolution of disclaimer" charging that the selection was "outrageous and an embarrassment to the bar."

Being Phyllis Schlafly's daughter during the ERA battle has got to rank as one of—if not the—toughest roles of the decade.

Phyllis Schlafly had three sons before her first daughter was born, in 1958, and christened Phyllis Dodge Schlafly. In 1975, when Phyl, as she was called, started college at the recently turned coed Princeton, the battle over ERA was at its height, and, on many campuses, her mother was Public Enemy No. 1.

So Phyllis Dodge Schlafly changed her name to Liza. "It's all right with me," her mother commented at the time. "She shouldn't have to fight my battles." With a surname like "Schlafly," though, Liza certainly did not conceal the link, and, once she got to Princeton, didn't seem to mind. "There were a lot of students with famous parents at Princeton," she explained. "It was no big deal."

Today, Liza Schlafly is a law student at the University of Virginia—a self-confident, tall, slim, pretty young woman determined to be accepted for her own accomplishments—and in the accomplishments department she could provide even her mother with some stiff competition.

Journalism is one of Liza's several strong interests. After graduating as high-school valedictorian and editor of the school paper, she won a coveted spot on Princeton's daily and then landed an internship with the pro-ERA, liberal Chicago *Sun-Times*. Liza calls another interest—in languages—"a hobby" (her college major was economics), but she speaks or reads French, Spanish, German, and Russian.

At first meeting she appeared shy, although she was not so much shy as she was a direct and deliberate speaker. If a question required a two-word response, two words it was—no small talk or chatter to fill the gaps. She was serious at twenty-one and was probably also serious at seven and at thirteen.

One summer, Liza worked in Washington for conservative columnist M. Stanton Evans and lived with Virginia STOP ERA leader Alyse O'Neill and her family. Liza befriended a college girl across the street who was dating a member of the New York Jets. "I remember [Liza] saying to me, 'Mrs. O'Neill, can you imagine dating a football player?' It just struck me so funny because everybody else was fawning all over that girl just because she was dating a football player."

Next-door neighbor Gladys Levis told a reporter recently that her children and the Schlaflys' took piano lessons from the same teacher and that at recitals Liza was always the only performer whose parents weren't in the audience. Without hesitation, Liza confirmed the report: "That's correct. They had better things to do. I didn't care. It hasn't blighted my life. To me there's nothing more boring than listening to a bunch of beginners. My parents are very busy people. I didn't resent it at the time."

When it really counted, Liza said, her mother gave full attention to her children. "She never believed in leaving education to the educators, and I'm grateful for that. Teaching me to read is one of the best things she ever did for me. Our education was supplemented with extra language instruction, math instruction, trips to interesting places, tutorials, camps. She tried to find our interests and stimulate them and that takes time."

Is she close with her mother? "I'd characterize my relationship with my mother as a teacher-student relationship. We don't see each other that much. We don't talk about every picky detail of our lives."

Does she agree with her mother? Claire Birmingham Hanlon recalled a comment her mother made after returning from Liza's coming-out tea. Liza, Betsy said, was developing a personality of her own and an identity separate from her mother's. "She was looking into having her own beliefs," Claire explained. "If those turned out to be those of her mother then I think it was an independent decision, not something that was forced down her throat."

The beliefs did turn out to be very similar to her mother's, although Liza has resisted her mother's suggestion that she speak out publicly against ERA. "I agree with my mother's basic premise," Liza explained. "You go out and do what you want to do. You don't sit around complaining and expecting the government to do it for you. That's what is basically wrong with the women's liberation movement. It did a lot of good, but also a lot of harm because it blames society instead of placing responsibility on the individual. The women I admire are those who have made a success in a traditionally man's world. I don't admire women who are really only successful in the women's movement and sit around whining."

Liza plans a career in journalism or law—perhaps a combination of the two. "I most certainly plan to have a career. That's a given. I plan to have a career and a family. I don't consider them mutually exclusive."

Twenty-nine-year-old John Schlafly, born in November 1950, a month after his parents' first anniversary, two years before Phyllis lost her first race for Congress, has been, perhaps, affected most by his mother's controversial career. Not one of the Schlafly sons likes to give interviews, but John is most adamantly opposed. "John just has a fit about reporters coming into the house," Phyllis explained. "He's supportive of everything I do, but he simply doesn't like having his home or life invaded with my causes."

Phyllis, according to Claire Hanlon, "just dotes" on John, whom she feared might be her only child. (There was a five-year gap between the birth of her first and her second child, and her doctor had assured her that John would be her one and only.) "I try to respect John's desire for privacy," Phyllis said, "and protect him from reporters as much as possible."

Asked if he thought his mother would run for office again, he answered, quickly, "I hope not." Although politics is obviously not one of their shared passions, mother and son do have several interests in common—including music. (Relatives say that John had the talent to become a concert pianist if he had wanted that career.)

A new shared interest is law. In January 1980, a year after his mother, John graduated from law school (University of Miami). He then returned to Alton, where, much to his parents' delight, he joined his father's firm. "He has found his career," said Phyllis happily. Before settling into law, John worked at several manual-labor jobs and for a St. Louis engineering consulting firm. (He is a graduate electrical engineer.)

Joe Schlafly, who went to school with John at Priory, described him as "shy, but extremely competent, talented and, once you get to know him, an exceptionally nice person. I asked him to play the organ at my wedding. He could have just sat down and played beautifully without a rehearsal. But he spent a lot of time preparing for it and did just a superb job. It was delightful—exactly the sort of thing John would do."

Thin—slight—with dark, curly hair, intense, bright eyes, and Phyllis' straight bearing, John said he doesn't think his mother's notoriety has hurt his social life. "Most of my law school friends would just rather not discuss ERA. And when it came up, I could see that the conversation was just not going to get anywhere and so I changed the subject."

John was the only one in his law-school class who was elected to both the academic honorary and service honorary societies. He was musical director and pianist for the annual law-school show spoofing professors, sharing his mother's talent for parody. And while going to law school full-time he also worked part-time for a Miami law firm. He obviously also shares his mother's energy.

Anne Schlafly described her brother Bruce, the Schlaflys' second son, a twenty-six-year-old intern, as "an all-American boy"—handsome, smart, athletic (a wrestler and a runner). His Great-uncle Carl Pfeifer described him as "probably the best-rounded and the smartest, basically, of all the Schlafly children—a real brain and handsome. Bruce impressed me particularly because when I was in the hospital, very sick, he came to see me. He stayed by my bedside and when the doctor made his rounds, Bruce questioned him very closely."

Bruce is "looser" than his siblings, said Betsy Birmingham, more easygoing and outgoing. When Phyllis refused to let him leave the area for college, he accepted the prohibition, went to Washington University, and graduated in electrical engineering as president of the engineering honor society. Four years later, he received his M.D. from Washington University Medical School.

(Every one of the four Schlafly boys, in fact, majored in electrical engineering, even though not one of them plans to practice it—a result, relatives said, of the strong influence Fred Schlafly has had on his sons. "I steered them toward it," Fred explained, "because there's no chance for confusion or errors in engineering. There's 100 percent truth. It's not like history or political science. I didn't want them wasting time on errors." Phyllis, of course, did not object, as her father was also an electrical engineer.)

Roger, the next son, who rejected the prohibition on out-of-town colleges, breezed through Princeton in three years—also in electrical engineering—*summa cum laude,* graduating at nineteen. Tom Schlafly described Roger as "almost the prototypical eccentric genius." Betsy Birmingham agreed: "I think he's marvelous. He's so brilliant and so strange." He has a mop of frantic curls—a cousin called it the Schlaflys' "one and only Jewish Afro"—and definitely a mind of his own.

"Roger," said Anne, "is kind of the genius of the family." By the time he was twenty, he had graduated from Princeton, gotten his master's from Berkeley, and passed his orals and all his course requirements for getting his Ph.D. (He got his Ph.D. in June 1980, age 23). All that remained was writing his thesis and passing two foreign-language tests. Roger was strictly a math and science person—never cared at all about languages. He passed his French exam the first time. He failed German because he hadn't ever taken a course in German. On the second try, all he knew were the indefinite pronouns and he passed it. He is so good at math that even though he didn't know any German, he could solve each problem and then figure out what the German word had to be.

"He liked to stay up late at night," recalled Claire Hanlon, "until, say, two in the morning and then get up at nine or ten —rather than go to bed on time and get up at seven. Phyllis likes everyone up at seven to start the day. She let it be known that Roger's late hours were not exactly her idea of right living. But that's the way he was and by the time he was fifteen or sixteen, you couldn't really tell him what to do. Roger is a free spirit in that, if he wants to do something, he'll do it."

"When he was at Priory," said Joe Schlafly, "he had no use at all for Latin—for certain subjects that were not scientific. He didn't have any interest in it. And he said, 'I'm not going to take them. This is irrelevant to what I want.' If he did take them, he didn't apply himself. I'm sure his mother said, 'Now, Roger, you ought to broaden yourself a little and not just do math and science. You ought to take a little French literature here and a little bit of this and that.' And Roger said, 'I'll have none of that.'"

"Fred told me," Carl Pfeifer recalled, "that it took quite a bit of talking to get Roger to do what was necessary to graduate from Priory on the subjects that he didn't think were worthwhile, such as English. They finally did persuade him. I don't think that Fred lays down the law very often. I think he really laid it down to Roger on that one." He must have, because Roger graduated sixth in his class. (He is now a member of the faculty of the University of Chicago, Mathematics Department.)

Andy, the youngest son, a senior at Princeton, is the Schlafly child who most resembles his father—tall, broad, square-jawed, and good-looking.[6]

Andy is a serious athlete, a serious student (he graduated first in his high-school class). Following in his sister's footsteps, he is also on the *Daily Prince* staff, although his specialty is sports writing. His major? Electrical engineering, of course.

The youngest Schlafly child, Anne, was born a few months after her mother turned forty. Her goal, Anne said with perfect poise and confidence, "is to be a success."

Anne, whom Phyllis calls "the light of my life," is an extrovert. "None of the others is an extrovert," said Phyllis. "And Anne is so refreshing." She sings in the choral group, acts in school plays, debates ERA in speech class, and, after semesters of avid letter-to-the-editor-writing, joined the staff of the school paper—the youngest reporter ever.

When Anne was twelve, she accompanied her mother to KMOX Radio (St. Louis), where Phyllis was being interviewed live. Twenty minutes into the interview, the newsman suddenly switched on the mike in front of Anne, and, with no warning whatsoever, said, "We have Phyllis' daughter with us in the studio. Anne, what do you think about ERA?" Anne answered, without a moment's hesitation, "Well, it's not just

[6] Not one of the six resembles each other. John and Andy don't look any more like brothers than willowy Liza and petite Anne look like sisters. And not one of them looks like their mother. "The standing joke of the family," said Phyllis, "is how many people have come up to me and said, 'Phyllis, you have the most beautiful children, and the funny thing is, not one of them looks like you.'"

because of my mother, but I'm against ERA. I sure don't want to be drafted."

Unlike her siblings, who think reporters range from being pests to being downright malicious, Anne loves to give interviews. "I tell all my siblings if reporters call them, just send them to me. I'll be glad to do it. I love it. I think it's so much fun.

"I grew up among all this politics stuff more than any other of the kids. I was born in 1964 and that was really a big year for Mother. [She worked avidly for Barry Goldwater.] In fact, the story goes, I was supposed to be born on Election Day, but I turned out to be a little bit late [November 16].

"I like to say I had a pretty normal childhood, but then, what is normal? It was slightly different, though; I mean, how many kids do you know who got to get out of school early to have their picture taken by *Newsweek?*" When her mother starred one week in Garry Trudeau's "Doonesbury," Anne was ecstatic. "That's really making it," she explained.

She is also her mother's most passionate defender. "Everybody in my family is proud of her. We all admire her and stuff. And well, I think she's really fantastic. Not only what she has done in politics, but I think she has been a really great mother. And she came to my piano recitals." Anne also raves about her mother's cooking, listing her specialties as meringues, soufflés—chocolate, cheese, spinach, and eggplant—Thanksgiving turkey with wild-rice dressing and, of course, buckwheat cakes.

How close are the children to their mother? As Liza said, she's not the sort of parent with whom you'd review every detail of your life. "Mother kind of has two sides to her," explained Anne. "You see the frosty side—the totally efficient politician. You've never seen the family side of her. She's a mother and she acts like a mother. And I feel that I can go to her and talk to her about a problem or whatever."

Do the children have to make an appointment to talk to her? "Of course not," said Anne, then adding that because her mother usually drives her to school on Monday morning and picks her up on Friday, "I'll save a lot of my problems to then to talk about. Also, I talk to my mother just about every night on the phone." The drive to school is also, according to Anne, the time when mother and daughter say the Rosary together. "Mother has said her Rosary every day since she first got into the ERA fight."

There is also what Liza called the "student/teacher" aspect of Phyllis' relationship with her children. Phyllis does not want her children to consider her as a peer or a pal. "Phyllis is like my mother," explained Claire Hanlon. "You're considered a child until you're about thirty."

Most of the time, on most issues, Phyllis claims that her children agree with her. Not one of them favors ERA, although Phyllis describes Bruce and Andy as apolitical and Roger as a tease. ("He likes to tell Mother he's all for ERA just to get her goat," explained Anne.) "ERA is not the biggest thing in my sons' lives," Phyllis said, "although if pinned down they'd be against. . . . The children are generally supportive. I won't say they agree with every idea I have, but in general they agree with what I am doing."

When she lectured at Princeton, Roger loyally brought most of the Math Department to hear her. Afterward, when she asked him how he liked it, he said, "You told me more about ERA than I ever cared to know."

Joe Schlafly said he wouldn't label his cousins conservatives so much as he would label them individualists—people who think for themselves. "They're not in any sense their mother's puppets. Like their father, they have tremendous talent of their own and they'll live by that. Obviously they've been affected by Phyllis' beliefs and have factored them into their viewpoints."

"We're all so completely different," Anne explained, "and

we have different interests, and most of us are going into different things."

"They're all highly competitive," said Phyllis. "Everybody in this family is competitive. They all have built separate lives and interests. They're every one of them, well, individualists. I guess it must be in the genes."

9

Sisters

Phyllis Schlafly's children may feel a certain compulsion to compete with their mother. But at least there is a full generation's gap to soften any pangs of inferiority they may, from time to time, feel. What about Phyllis' sister?—five years younger, but still, especially as she reached young womanhood, her sister's peer.

As Phyllis the academic wonder grew into Phyllis the public person, she became a special case. Phyllis Schlafly is, after all, as often loathed as loved; reviled as revered. Being the sister of a famous person can be tough. Being the sister of an infamous person can be even tougher.

Odile Stewart Mecker is forty-nine years old, the wife of a C.P.A., Robert Mecker, and mother of two daughters, ages twelve and fourteen. She lives in the St. Louis suburb of Ladue—as wealthy as it is Republican, just a curving, tree-lined mile from the home where Fred Schlafly grew up.

The physical resemblance between Phyllis and Odile is strong. Odile has even brighter blue eyes than her sister's. Odile is shorter, not quite as thin, with clipped, fine, fairish hair, and, although younger, has a more weather-beaten complexion than her sister's. Odile appears to spend more time outdoors, but, like Phyllis, she is delicate rather than rugged, with the same look of good breeding.

She dresses conservatively in a brown wool skirt and flowered blouse. She looks like she was born to drive blond children in a wood-sided station wagon. Her home is tastefully furnished; a blazing fire on a chilly February morning, good furniture, oriental rugs, a scattering of antiques, a grand piano, on the walls the old photos of St. Louis, with which her mother planned to illustrate her history of the city. Her voice is like her sister's, but more formal and notably precise—always "an advocate." She would, it seems, be as unlikely to drop a syllable during casual conversation as she would to drop a profanity.

Phyllis' sister-in-law Maie Schlafly described Odile as "literal, very literal. She's not the kind of person you'd joke around with." And, indeed, there's barely a trace of frivolity, silliness, even lightness about her. Missouri STOP ERA leader Ann McGraw called her "a neat person. She's a lot more down-to-earth than Phyllis. . . . Maybe she's just as bright."

She's serious, all right, but, on the other hand, she seems like the sort of person who would linger over lunch to chat with a friend about a new novel or a new neighbor. She is easier to talk to than her sister. In the course of a conversation with a stranger—a reporter she has never met—she revealed two or three quite personal facts and feelings. She seemed more concerned about the dynamics, the politics, of her family than about the dynamics and politics of the country.

She is not more personable than her sister, but she is more personal. "I haven't even asked you if you're married or have children," she apologized to the reporter before launching into a description of her pet project—no, not stopping ERA, but setting up day-care centers in neighborhood high schools that would, she explained, "serve a wonderful dual purpose." The high-school students—girls and boys—would staff the center by spending a few periods a week caring for the children and learning what it means to be a parent. ("I think child abuse is one of the most hideous problems facing us today.") No need for "Big Brother's" help or for expensive professionals, she explained, when every neighborhood has a building full of teen-agers to whom small children could more easily and joyously relate.

"If you're ever a parent, you'll find out that caring for a child, not to mention children, can be the most exhausting and exasperating job you'll ever have. They whine, they squabble, they can be utterly irrational. You may as well try to reason with the family dog."—not the sort of statement one would ever expect from sister Phyllis, who has never, ever hinted (on record, at least) that being a mother is anything but an unadulterated delight.

Odile followed in her sister's footsteps—literally, step by step. Phyllis went to City House, Odile followed; Phyllis went to Washington University and majored in political science; Odile followed; Phyllis went to Radcliffe and then to work in Washington; Odile followed.

Was Phyllis a tough act to follow? Yes, admitted Odile, but being Phyllis' sister "hasn't been a burden for me. I certainly admire her tremendously. I think she's a very great person. She has always been that way—always been just a model and a leader in a quiet way. Not in an obvious way. I've certainly never achieved what she has. . . . She is an extremely brilliant person."

Phyllis hasn't been a burden, Odile explained, because she "never tooted her own horn." And their parents were smart enough and kind enough "never to draw any comparisons between us. And there were plenty of occasions to do that. Phyllis was always a super student. Always got A's in everything. And I didn't. I would get A's in things I really worked hard at and was interested in, but most of the time I was pretty much of a B student. So I do feel that my parents probably could have drawn a lot more comparisons and made me feel less than I was if they wanted to, but they never did and I'm very grateful for that because I could really be devastated by all she has accomplished. I mean her depth and her world are so large. Everything just falls into place. She's just a most extraordinary person."[1]

Today, Odile is one of her sister's staunchest defenders. Shannon Schlafly—a niece through marriage—teaches film at Washington University and says that when criticism of Phyllis —no matter how trivial—appears in the Washington University newspaper, Odile "always" writes in to complain.

"Now that Phyllis has her law degree," Odile said, "I think she'd be well qualified for the Supreme Court," her voice betraying not a speck of facetiousness. "She's very thorough in her research. She's Republican, she's conservative, and she's Catholic. But just because she has had different views on various issues, like the Panama Canal and communism and ERA, I don't believe that detracts from the thoroughness of her research and her first-rate intellect."

She characterized the relationship as "close," with a qualifier: "Of course, we're 5½ years apart. Growing up we didn't have the same friends and we weren't doing the same things at the same time. So there was not much in com-

---

[1] Phyllis didn't remember that her younger sister was much impressed with her as they were growing up. "I think the biggest impression I made on Odile in those years," Phyllis said, "was when I used to get long-distance phone calls from an army lieutenant stationed on the West Coast during World War II. He would call from a pay phone, and the sound of five dollars' worth of quarters being dropped in the phone increased my status with Odile more than anything else that happened to me in high school or college. She didn't see how a phone call to me could possibly be worth five dollars."

mon. . . . But our family was close. We had nothing else but the family and we did everything that we did pretty much together with the family. . . . There's nothing closer than blood relations and we certainly have quite a bond." Odile, said Ann McGraw, is also very grateful for "how sweet Phyllis is to their mother" and for the time, energy, and money that caring for the eighty-four-year-old woman consumes.

There was a time when the sisters' bond cracked, almost broke; when Odile left the Catholic Church and married a divorced man. She's now a Presbyterian like her Scottish grandfather. "Phyllis and Fred could not understand why I did not choose to carry on with the faith, and it really caused a problem."

Has the rift healed? "Well, we don't talk about it. That's why I can't really sit down like I am with you and talk to Phyllis about any problems I might have with my children or the family or the home." Besides, Odile added, being close with Phyllis "is not the same as being close with anyone else." Phyllis, she explained, has always solved her own problems herself and she expects others to do likewise. While she'll offer advice happily, she's not one to sit down and listen to the gory details of other people's lives. "She has too much on her mind," said Odile. "In other words, I could not sit down with Phyllis like this for two hours and take that kind of time with her to discuss a problem."

Odile opposes ERA and has given some time and money to her sister's cause. "ERA sounds good on the surface, but it's a broad sentence and I believe it can become a field day for lawyers. That's why I think the legal profession is behind it and most of the local bar groups are behind it. They see a lot of business in it for themselves."

Like her sister, Odile feels that women can and always have been able to do anything they want to do if they want to do it badly enough. Her elaboration on the above is guaranteed to trigger apoplexy in even the least strident of feminists. "The

The morning after Phyllis Schlafly's 1952 primary victory over a heavily favored male lawyer, the St. Louis *Globe-Democrat* reported, "Mrs. Phyllis Schlafly cooks her husband's breakfast Wednesday morning after winning the nomination. ... She doesn't let political successes interfere with her wifely duties." (Credit: St. Louis *Globe-Democrat* photo)

In July 1960, Phyllis Schlafly, president of the Illinois Federation of Republican Women, hosted a Hawaiian Hukilau for Sen. Barry Goldwater (left) and Sen. Hiram Fong. Four years later, Schlafly's *A Choice Not an Echo* would propel Goldwater into the Republican nomination for President. (Wide World Photos)

Maureen Reagan, daughter of Ronald Reagan and Jane Wyman, steadies the chair from which Phyllis Schlafly addresses supporters in her 1967 race for the presidency of the National Federation of Republican Women—which proved to be the most bruising battle of Schlafly's career. Maureen, then an ardent "Phyllis fan" later vigorously lobbied for ERA. The two are no longer friends. (Credit: Wide World Photos)

Phyllis Schlafly works her farmers' booth, which traveled a fifteen-county-fair circuit during her 1970 campaign for Congress. She is flanked by "Schlafly girls" who helped pin on buttons, distribute literature, and sing campaign songs composed by the candidate. (Credit: Duffy Lowrance)

Phyllis Schlafly pounds in a point in testimony before an Illinois House committee in 1974. One lawyer/legislator upbraided her for testifying without benefit of a
law degree. A year later, she started law school and she is now a member of the
Illinois bar. (Credit: Dale Wittner)

Phyllis Schlafly rallies the troops in the rotunda of the Illinois Capitol in June 1978 —shortly before House members nixed ERA for the second time that month. Schlafly's rallies almost always include placards, banners, songs, skits, parodies, homemade pies, cookies, bread, and television coverage. "It's the best show in town," marveled one reporter. (Credit: UPI photo)

Phyllis Schlafly dispenses ammunition to the troops—equal parts apple pies and placards. (Credit: Dale Wittner)

April 12, 1978: Schlafly and Company singing "Here Comes Playboy Cottontail" (*Playboy* had been a generous financial backer of ERA) at the Illinois Capitol grab media attention from a League of Women Voters Legislative Day. "She turned a serious League event (at which ERA strategy was announced) into a three-ring circus," complained State Rep. Susan Catania, an ERA backer. (Credit: Wide World Photos)

only thing that holds women back in the business world is that they do not want all the extra responsibility; women want to get home and be with their families. You don't make fifty thousand dollars a year working forty hours a week and taking vacations. It would be a very rare job where you could make a top salary and not have to work your tail off. I think probably that's the reason why a lot of men don't promote women to the more time-consuming jobs. The women would like the money but they wouldn't like the overtime. Any business wants to make money and will promote the best person, male or female, who can get the job done."

This is a particularly astonishing analysis, considering that Odile herself suffered the sort of sexism that would turn most traditional women into raving feminists. But she wasn't converted to feminism by her misfortune any more than her father was converted into a New Deal Democrat by his.

She swerved from Phyllis' path for the first time at Radcliffe, where, instead of pursuing political science, Odile earned a master's in business. In Washington, she went to work for a brokerage firm.

"I was the first girl hired by this firm to do the actual filling of the orders that the salesmen would bring in. I was there two years and it was really a fascinating business. I decided I wanted to be a stockbroker"—a courageous, naïve decision for a "girl" to make at a time when the stock business was strictly male territory.

But she had that Stewart self-confidence and drive, so she headed back to St. Louis to start her career and build a clientele. She got a job as a secretary at Merrill Lynch, figuring it would be a matter of months before she could convince the partner there to send her to New York for the training program, a prerequisite to getting licensed as a stock salesman. She was there a year when she realized that her boss had no such intention. "He hired two young punks [male] just out of college—three years younger than I—and sent them right on up to New York for training. And that really bothered me. Although I can't say I was angry. I didn't really know how to feel anger at the time. I was just very disappointed and I tried to figure out how I could overcome this sexism. For weeks I put in a lot of overtime. I only took fifteen minutes for lunch. I would read the Dow Jones every day."

Her efforts were not appreciated. "One day while studying *The Wall Street Journal,* the boss noticed me, came over, and stood silently behind me until I could feel his presence—a great-big, good-looking, strong man—over my shoulder. 'Miss Stewart, just what do you find there so interesting to read?' And I said, 'Well, Mr. Bitting, I'm just trying to improve my knowledge so I can better understand what the men are saying in the letters they're writing to their clients and that I'm typing up.' And he said, 'Well, I suggest you return to your typewriter and just do the job you were hired to do.'"

She decided it was time to leave. A younger partner at a local firm was willing to take a chance on her. G. H. Walker and Company had just opened a branch in Clayton, a suburb adjacent to St. Louis, and needed people. Odile stayed with Walker for sixteen years, and when she left to devote full time to her children, she was still the only woman in St. Louis selling stocks. Today, there are many more.

"I was very successful—well, certainly for a girl." When she left she was making double the income of any man in her office.

In many ways, Odile led an even more liberated, unconventional life than her sister. She remained single until she was thirty-four, marrying in March 1964, eight months before Phyllis gave birth to her sixth child. Before that, she lived alone in her own apartment, "which was just unheard of in our social strata. You just might as well have been a woman of the streets." She met her husband, Bob Mecker, when, to impress Mr. Bitting, she took a course Mecker taught in analysis of financial statements. (Mr. Bitting still wasn't impressed; he advised her again to stick to typing.)

"Before we had our first child, Bob did tell me that he wanted me to stay home if we had children. Well, as most things with me, I just took that under advisement and let it pass because I thought, 'I'll handle this when the time comes.' When our first child was born, I was out of the office for about two months. We had an apartment right behind the office—we lived in Clayton—and my boss was very nice about putting in a telephone for me and an intercom so I could check back to the office to get quotes and place orders. I carried on my business at home while taking care of my baby. Eventually my boss wanted me to come back to the office. I'd walk home for lunch, see the baby and put her down for her nap. It worked out beautifully and Bob saw that and he didn't complain about it and of course the money was welcome. When the second child came, I was home a little longer. Funny thing, I didn't feel as comfortable about going back to work.

"I quit when the children were three and five and I don't know how I lasted as long as I did, doing two jobs. I finally realized that I just couldn't do both. It wasn't that I couldn't cope with the physical part of it, it was the mental part. You have two different lives. It got to the point where the children were so demanding. You can't come home and just relax and enjoy the home like husbands do. Children are very draining. And that's what I didn't need when I came home after being on the phone all day. Although I loved my work, I just felt that I couldn't handle both and keep my sanity. I just don't understand how my sister did what she did—did so much and had so many children and kept hers. It's amazing."

Now Odile invests the family income, reads *The Wall Street Journal* avidly, and contemplates with great satisfaction three standing job offers from brokerage firms.

"Odile Mecker is," said a former colleague (male), "one of the best brokers in the business, male or female. She did more to advance the cause of women as brokers—just by her example—than six busloads of feminists out to eradicate sexism could do in five years."

10

1952: "Powder-Puff Candidate for Congress"

In February 1949, a month before she met Fred Schlafly, Phyllis Stewart got a letter from Professor Arnold Lien, chairman of the Political Science Department at Washington University, urging her to return to the university as a doctoral student. When her former professor received a wedding announcement instead of an acceptance letter, he was soundly disappointed: "I regret . . . that we cannot add your name to our list of super-excellent Ph.D.s," but, he added, he was sure she would find some way of serving her community.

Some way? Phyllis hadn't been in Alton for a month before she was volunteering with a vengeance. She was a director of the Alton YWCA, a captain in the Community Chest drive, a discussion leader of a League of Women Voters group, a fund raiser for the St. Louis Symphony, president of the Radcliffe

Club of St. Louis, a director of the local chapter of the National Conference of Christians and Jews, and commentator on a weekly radio broadcast sponsored by the Conference. She was writing papers on housing problems for the Citizens' Housing Council and studies of voting behavior for the Social Planning Council, and giving speeches around town on everything from financial planning to Alger Hiss.

A fellow YWCA director recalled, "Phyllis then was exactly like Phyllis now. She didn't do just one thing like most of us. She did fourteen and she did them all well. With Phyllis, volunteering wasn't social, it was dead serious."

Between fund drives and board meetings and party rallies (she had also begun volunteering for the Republican Party), Schlafly gave birth in November 1950 to the first of her six children.

For two years Phyllis Schlafly played the role of the young matron about town. "One of Alton's most prominent civic leaders," a reporter from the Alton *Telegraph* called her. But then came 1952—the year of General Dwight Eisenhower's first run for the presidency.

"That was the year that everybody knew a Republican was going to be elected," Schlafly recalled. "It was the end of the Truman era, people were fed up, and we Republicans knew it was going to be our year." Schlafly had caught the campaign bug.

One night, early in 1952, Fred and Phyllis were at home with their young son when the Madison County Republican chairman and his delegation came calling—on Fred. Their mission was to persuade him to run for Congress. A Republican lawyer from St. Clair—the other county that comprised the then 24th District—had already filed, and Madison County Republicans thought Fred was the best man to challenge him in the primary, and then to take on the very popular Democratic incumbent, Melvin Price, in the general election. (Price was so popular that, some twenty-eight years later, he still represented that district [now the 23rd] in Congress.)

Fred barely pondered the request before saying "no"— firmly. "Fred didn't have the slightest interest in running," recalled his wife. "He was too busy with his law practice. Besides, his interest was always in issues—not elections." They sat in the Schlafly living room and talked and talked and the county chairman started looking upset and said he didn't have any other strong candidate and time was running out and what was he going to do?

Finally, in desperation, someone asked, "Well, Mrs. Schlafly, why don't you run?" "We kicked that around," Phyllis recalled. "We only had one child. One thing led to another and I agreed."

When she announced her intention to challenge the St. Clair Republican in the primary, Phyllis Schlafly became an instant "item." Why? Not because she was likely to win— everyone who followed local politics knew that one had to go back before the Civil War to find a Madison County resident who had made it to Washington. Representatives of the 24th District always came from the more populous St. Clair County.

She was a hot news story because she was the first woman —ever—from either county who was brash enough to seek a nomination from the blue-collar 24th District—and to seek it as a Republican in an overwhelmingly Democratic district. The Radcliffe-educated debutante was, in a word, a curiosity —as curious as if a black Republican that year were trying to become governor of Alabama.

So Phyllis Schlafly, who had worked her way through college firing rifles and machine guns in an ammunition plant, was taking on a man's job again; competing in a man's world; something she would do again and again in the coming years.

Whatever toughened the competition, stiffened the challenge, Schlafly had always welcomed. She may have had a shortage of funds and a shortage of chances to win in '52, but, as always, she had no shortage of confidence. "Interviewed with Thomas Sherman of the *Post-Dispatch* to get a job. Must have been an unlucky day. I didn't get it," she wrote shortly after high-school graduation, and in the intervening years, not a drop of that confidence dissipated—a good thing, because she was going to need all the confidence she could muster for this battle.

Her opponent in the primary was East St. Louis lawyer John T. R. Godlewski, who had the big advantages of hailing from St. Clair County, having the Republican organization solidly behind him, and being male and a lawyer.

If she made it past Stage I—which none of the "experts" thought possible—Stage II loomed even larger. Price was already serving his fourth consecutive term. He was a Democrat in a district that hadn't gone Republican since 1932. "Anybody who doesn't carry a union card couldn't possibly get elected in that district," wrote a *Telegraph* reporter at the time.

Schlafly stunned everybody, except perhaps herself and Fred, by clearing the first hurdle, winning the April primary in what was widely described as an "upset." Not only did she "upset" Godlewski, she also slaughtered him—carrying her own county by more than four to one and even racking up substantial leads in some areas of St. Clair County.

The morning after the April primary, the St. Louis *Globe-Democrat* reported that "a 'powder puff' candidate who conducted a slam-bang campaign came through with a resounding victory . . . mowing down a male opponent for the Republican nomination for Congress. . . . The attractive Alton housewife and 'political scientist deluxe' scored an impressive triumph." Running over the story was a photo of Phyllis Schlafly in a frilly apron, frying an egg: "Mrs. Phyllis Schlafly cooks her husband's breakfast Wednesday morning after winning the nomination. . . . She doesn't let political successes interfere with her wifely duties," the caption assured readers.[1]

Schlafly's present-day critics would be tickled to know that the woman who said she could not find a single redeeming value in the "women's lib" movement suffered all the ravages of sexism. Almost three decades later, reminiscing about that campaign, she betrayed just a hint of annoyance (mostly amusement) that no matter how shocking her attacks on her opponent or the Truman administration, reporters invariably referred to the source as "the good-looking blond candidate" or "the Alton housewife" or the "powder-puff candidate." And the puns were unrelenting. The *Globe-Democrat* headlined a story, "She's running for Congress and not just on face value" and then reported, "The East Side's 'powder puff' candidate making her debut in the real-life political arena has good looks, a cause, lots of get up and go."

A *Post-Dispatch* reporter covered a campaign speech first by quoting Schlafly: "Only a Republican victory this year will end the striped-pants diplomacy of the New Deal, including the vertical stripes worn by [Secretary of State] Dean Acheson and the horizontal stripes now worn in jail by his good friend, Alger Hiss." "Someday," the reporter sneered, "it would be nice to hear the speaker pursue this subject of stripes still further . . . and tell us all about the stripes worn by peppermint stick candy, seersucker suits, zebras, barber poles, skunks, rainbows, and the U.S. flag."

In her role as ERA spoiler, Schlafly became famous for grabbing every chance to let people know that she breast fed all six of her "babies" and possessed a multitude of motherly virtues. Back then, the candidate would undoubtedly have preferred to be questioned about the A-bomb than about her

[1] Even back then, reporters were skeptical of Schlafly's domesticity. The editor who cropped that photo back in '52 wrote in blue grease pencil across the bottom: "HA!"

apple cobbler—but apple cobbler it was. "She does all her own shopping, most of the housework, she enjoys cooking. Her culinary specialty is apple cobbler, but she seldom tries her hand at needlework," reported the women's editor at the *Post-Dispatch*—who was frequently assigned to cover "The Alton Housewife" while the political editor—male, of course —covered Price.

During the ERA battle, Alton reporters could barely hide their squeamishness in the presence of "anti-feminist" Phyllis Schlafly. Back then, they could barely hide their squeamishness at the prospect of sending a woman to Washington.

Alton, after all, is a hub of industry—located at the confluence of the Mississippi, Missouri, and Illinois rivers. Bottle plants, steel mills, lime plants, boxboard companies, cartridge plants, flour mills, brick plants, and breweries line the banks. It's a tough town, a river town, the sort of place that would have felt more comfortable with Mel Price—a former sportswriter—in Washington.

But if the "powder puff" candidate was not taken as seriously as she would have liked, it didn't seem to puncture her self-confidence. She had decided that she was going to become not just a good speaker, but also a great one, and so, in familiar Phyllis fashion, she worked at it—hard. Her reputation as a crowd rouser spread so quickly that the Republicans asked her to keynote their state convention in Springfield in June 1952—two months after her primary victory. Schlafly, who recalled "slaving" over the text, delivered a speech that one reporter called "smashing," noting that the audience of five thousand on a broiling hot, humid day applauded every paragraph.

So sure was Schlafly of her speaking skills that she challenged Congressman Price—who had experience, recognition, and a research staff on his side—to a debate. "It is a fine Illinois tradition for candidates for high public office to debate the issues of the day," Schlafly wrote him. [In 1858, Abraham

Lincoln and Stephen Douglas held the seventh and last of their famous debates in Alton.] "I therefore challenge you to debate throughout the district all the important issues of this congressional campaign."

Schlafly and Price debated Truman's handling, or "mishandling," as Schlafly charged, of the Korean War at a League of Women Voters forum in Alton City Hall. Price, the veteran congressman, spoke in generalities. "We have no other course but to continue to resist the advance of communism." Schlafly, the twenty-eight-year-old new mother, got right down to basics, leaving many in the audience aghast, and not a few offended by her audacity. The very idea of a woman—and such a young woman—talking tactics. We should blockade the coast of China, she advised. We should bomb the bridges on the Yalu River (used by Chinese Communist soldiers to come south and attack our troops, she explained). She then launched into a detailed comparison of Russian MIGs to American Sabers and a statistic-studded account of the U. S. Army and Air Force's decline from the world's best to second best.

Korea was a major issue in this campaign, as Vietnam would be when she ran for Congress again in 1970. The blackest spot on Truman's record—and, by extension, Price's —Schlafly charged, is the Korean War. "My husband's young cousin was killed recently by the Chinese Communists in that war," she said at a rally. "There was absolutely no reason for his death." Schlafly blasted Truman's conduct of the Korean War for the same reasons she would later blast Lyndon Johnson's conduct of the Vietnam War.

"We gave half of Korea to the Russians, and then didn't arm South Korea. Then when the Communists attacked, we weren't equipped." She believed, like she would twenty years later, that Russia was the only victor. Every day of fighting in Korea sapped the United States' defenses and morale and strengthened Russia's. The United States should have stayed out of Korea unless it was prepared to fight to win by arming the South Koreans and Americans to the teeth and then bombing vital targets.

"The American GI has been sent into battle against an enemy who greatly outnumbers him, who has a better tank than he has, and who has more and better planes than he has." She referred often to a mother in Colorado whose eighteen-year-old son was killed in Korea. She sent his Purple Heart back to the President with a letter, "Soldiers need help when they are fighting, not medals and scrolls after they are dead."

In lamenting the fact that volunteers for combat duty were in short supply, and that one third of those reporting to their draft boards pleaded a debilitating ailment, Schlafly said, "American boys feel their heroism is wasted in a war that the Truman-Acheson administration will not permit them to win." And then a quintessential Schlaflyism: "If the Truman administration had fought the Chinese Communists as hard as it is fighting the steel industry, the war in Korea would have been over long ago."[2]

On the domestic front, Schlafly charged Price with being an unquestioning champion of "big government and big spending." She advocated a balanced budget—at the time still within reach—as the best way to halt inflation. She dubbed Truman, "High-tax Harry," and pledged to work to reduce personal income taxes. "In the meantime," she suggested, "we should rename two months 'Taxember' and 'Spendember,' to reflect the fact that the average wage earner will hand over nearly two months of his wages to Uncle Sam. The American

---

[2] Ultimately Representative Price became chairman of the House Armed Services Committee and, in that role, finally—26 years after the campaign—won some words of praise from Phyllis Schlafly. In one of her syndicated columns she praised Price as a man who believes in a strong defense and who even criticized a President of his own party (Carter) for vetoing the nuclear aircraft carrier.

people are not too dumb to understand that the government should be the servant of the people, not their master."

Communist influence in the "highest levels of the U. S. Government" was one of the campaign's hottest issues, and Schlafly's charges flew. The New Dealers sent the "Reds" atom-bomb ingredients and a large drawing of the Oak Ridge atom-bomb plant. Federal bureaucrats were using a brainwashing technique developed by Chinese Communists to "cleanse" the brains of conquered people of their "longing for liberty and religion." In Washington, she said, "many government bureaus have developed extensive programs of brainwashing to push through socialized medicine and universal military training," which she denounced as "Prussian militarism." She hit Price specifically for voting against the investigation of Alger Hiss by the House Committee on Un-American Activities.[8]

The attacks, speeches, and news releases were unrelenting. In fact, Schlafly exhibited a passion for work during the '52 campaign that has been, perhaps, the secret of her success in the ERA battle. Maie Schlafly, Phyllis' elementary-school classmate and later her sister-in-law, recalled, "She started to work hard at a very young age when everyone else was playing Tarzan up in a tree, so when she ran for Congress like she was running for President of the United States, nobody in the family was surprised."

[8] Schlafly remained a vigorous supporter of congressional investigations. She believed that the House Committee on Un-American Activities (HUAC), whose demise she still mourns, had every right to investigate Communist Party members and agents. "I believe congressional investigations are one of the greatest features of our form of government," she said. "They are a great weapon for finding out the truth, and not only about communism. Watergate should have proved their value to those who did not understand it before." One of the few men Schlafly termed a "hero" was Congressman Martin Dies who, in 1938, created HUAC and became its first chairman.

A reporter for the *Globe-Democrat* described Schlafly as a campaigner of "untiring vigor" who gives the lie to that tired axiom about the "weaker sex." Schlafly's college feat of working a forty-eight-hour-a-week night shift at the ammunition plant, taking a full-course load at Washington University and graduating in three years, with a Phi Beta Kappa key and a scholarship to Radcliffe, was reported widely. "On the tender side of thirty, tireless and outspoken, she hit the hustings early in '52 with a vehemence that must have rocked Madison and St. Clair counties like a minor tremor," wrote one reporter.

Schlafly was then (as now) a firm believer in the maxim, "If you want it done right, do it yourself." As head of STOP ERA, she employed no fund raiser, public-relations agent, Washington lobbyist. Then, as now, she had a staff of one—herself. She was her own speechwriter, press secretary, researcher, scheduler, typist, messenger. "When I filed my financial report, it was about $2,000 for the whole year."

If elections were decided on the basis of energy expended, Schlafly would have won in a landslide. They're not, of course, and the landslide belonged to Price, who won by a margin of almost two to one, taking Madison County, not to mention his home county of St. Clair, and even Alton. A post-mortem editorial pointed out that Price was "one of the most popular representatives in Congress ever to run for office in the 24th District," but that Charlie McCarthy could have beat Mrs. Schlafly, assuming he ran as a Democrat. Although Ike's personality undoubtedly appealed to the average working man more than aloof, intellectual Adlai Stevenson's, Ike's party didn't. Eisenhower lost the district by the same margin as Schlafly.

The next morning not a reporter cared whether Phyllis fried Fred an egg or ordered him to toast his own English muffin.

Twenty-five years later, during a debate with Betty Friedan at the University of Illinois, Schlafly, who had by then lost two races for Congress, said, "The fact that there may be only

18 women out of 535 members of Congress does not prove discrimination at all. The small number of women in Congress proves only that most women do not want to do the things that must be done to win elections—drive all those thousands of miles, shake all those strangers' hands, eat all those third-rate chicken suppers. I've put a lot more into politics than most women would be willing to. To most women, it isn't worth the price. They like to devote their energy to other things—like having babies." Schlafly did not bat an eye.[4]

She made the statement in answer to a question from a woman who was convinced that discrimination, and discrimination alone, is the reason why such an infinitesimal number of women make it to Washington. Most of the audience obviously agreed with the questioner, if the groans that greeted Schlafly's analysis were any indication.

Another woman in the audience, who ran for the state legislature on an ERA platform and lost—badly—was furious. "That woman has no shame—to stand up there and say with a straight face that sexual jealousy and fear isn't at the bottom of it all. You know, she ran for Congress herself. I'd love to know what she said when she lost. Phyllis isn't one who likes to lose and I bet if she could have blamed it on her sex, she sure as hell did."

A couple of days after the 1952 election, a reporter asked Schlafly, "Did you lose because your name is Phyllis, not Phillip?" "No," she replied, "I lost because I ran in the 24th District and I'm a Republican, not a Democrat. It's as simple as that. My sex had nothing to do with it. Oh sure, there were

[4] Today, the biggest handicap women seeking elective office face, Schlafly frequently says, is "voter perception that they're just like all the other libbers—Bella Abzug and the rest." As evidence, she pointed to Jane Byrne's victory as mayor of Chicago and Margaret Thatcher's as Prime Minister of the United Kingdom, both of whom won without seeking feminist support. (In fact, women's groups worked against Margaret Thatcher and, to a lesser extent, Jane Byrne.)

people who voted against me solely because I'm a woman, but then there were people who voted for me for the same reason. It all evened out in the end." Schlafly had refused to make a special pitch for the woman's vote. "I'm running on the issues that affect us all," she said. "If these issues strongly affect women, so much the better for the cause of good government" —and that was as much mention as Schlafly ever made of her sex.

Congressman Price, now in his midseventies, frail, his hearing and memory fading—he didn't remember how he voted on the ERA extension, for example—did remember his race against Phyllis Schlafly more vividly than any of his eighteen others. "It was the most spirited of any," he recalled. "There was nothing dirty about it. I know she's always accused of distortions, but you can't prove that by me. I remember nothing of the sort. It was really a most intellectual campaign—a nationally oriented issues campaign.

"It was," Price said, "like she was running for national—or at least statewide—office. She was clearly knowledgeable about the national scene. Trouble was, the voters weren't." The voters were interested in what was happening on the Mississippi River in Madison and St. Clair counties, not on the Yalu River in North Korea.

Most of all, Price added, "They were interested in unions. She had no more chance of winning as a Republican running from this neck of the woods than"—he paused for what seemed a long time, his eyes half closed—"well, than Barry Goldwater had of winning the presidency in '64."

11

1964: "A Choice Not an Echo"

In 1964, Phyllis Schlafly wrote *A Choice Not an Echo,* a campaign book that changed the fortunes of the Republican Party in that election year and caused a rift among its members that has yet to heal.

The little seventy-five-cent self-published and self-distributed paperback packed such a powerful punch that—most analysts agreed—it pushed Barry Goldwater over the top in the June 1964 California primary, a victory that provided the momentum that helped Goldwater win the hotly contested Republican presidential nomination the next July.

Choice was the first of Phyllis Schlafly's nine books and by far the most successful. It sold three million copies, yet Schlafly did not place a single ad, or contact a single bookstore buyer. Advertising consisted solely of word of mouth— wives urging husbands to read it, and bosses telling secretaries. Mass distribution was accomplished via precinct captains, who ordered it in bulk and left it on their neighbors' doorsteps; ministers who passed it out at the end of the Sunday service; heads of organizations such as the Knights of Columbus, the Rotary, and the John Birch Society, who ordered it and sold it to members.

"I never tried to get a publisher for it," Schlafly explained. "In the first place, I didn't think any publisher would want it. In the second place, there was not time." She wrote it in January and February 1964, sent it to the printer in March, and had finished copies to ship at the end of April—three months before the nominating convention, six months before the election. "You can't get any publisher to move that fast. I had to get it out. The book would have been worthless if it hadn't been printed immediately. The election would have been over." So Schlafly, who was most comfortable doing things for herself anyway, started her own publishing company, called it Père Marquette Press (after the Jesuit missionary and explorer who discovered the Mississippi), and successfully self-published all but two of her nine books.

In the days before mass-market paperbacks, *Choice* represented a publishing milestone. Very few books—except dime-store Westerns and such—were published, originally, as paperbacks. It had to be a paperback, Schlafly figured, because it had to be cheap, small enough to carry in pocket or purse, and light enough for a precinct worker to cart a load around in a shopping bag. It was written to be read, to change minds —"not to sit on a shelf or win any literary awards."

It certainly did not win any awards, or even respectable reviews, but it did get read. In many ways, *Choice* resembled a pamphlet more than a book—its author a twentieth-century Tom Paine writing with all the urgency of Paine at his most populist. *A Choice Not an Echo* never made the New York *Times* best-seller list, but it was a best seller in every other sense of the word. Nothing like it had ever been published before; indeed, nothing quite like it has been published since.

It's chapters were short, shocking, and studded with sensational charges that sounded just believable enough to keep readers turning 121 pages. Schlafly aimed the book at people who felt ineffectual; who feared that some sort of conspiracy controlled everything from the size of their tax bill to the outcome of the last presidential race. There were a lot of people out there who felt vaguely emasculated. Three million bought it; probably ten times that number read it.

In September 1964, Alyse O'Neill, later chairman of Virginia STOP ERA, was en route to a National Federation of Republican Women (NFRW) Conference. A friend had given her "this funny-looking little paperback." O'Neill carried it around in her purse for weeks before she finally had a chance to read it on the plane. "I immediately ordered a hundred copies. I told everyone, 'Read this book. It has so many answers.' I sold the hundred to neighbors and members of my women's club and ordered another five hundred." When Phyllis came to Miami, where O'Neill was then living, Phyllis called her, obviously curious to meet this supersalesman. "I introduced Phyllis to people at teas and other places and her book sold like hotcakes."

"I can remember a Labor Day family picnic in 1964," said Martha Hume, a childhood neighbor of Schlafly's. "My father-in-law had a straw picnic basket full of Phyllis' book. Most years he'd be running around passing out beer. This year he was passing out *A Choice Not an Echo* and I can tell you, if you declined the offer, you wouldn't have gotten any beer. It was like he had just discovered the Bible and wanted to convert his loved ones."

At the time she wrote *A Choice Not an Echo,* Schlafly had become—for a woman—a respected voice in the Republican Party. In hotly contested races, she had been elected a delegate to the Republican National Convention in 1956 (pledged to Dwight Eisenhower) and an alternate delegate in 1960 (pledged to Richard Nixon). She was elected president of the twenty-seven-thousand-member Illinois Federation of

Republican Women in 1960 and re-elected in 1962. Strictly as a volunteer, she traveled some one hundred thousand miles through Illinois, speaking, organizing, and leaving people impressed. She was much in demand as a speaker for Lincoln Day dinners and Republican candidates' fund raisers because her speeches were hard-hitting, provocative, and many sparkled with political parodies poking fun at liberal Democrats.[1]

[1] Schlafly's Republican appearances during the 1956 presidential campaign, for example, often included such songs as these:

AVERELL HARRIMAN

(to the tune of "Davy Crockett")

I got elected with some votes to spare,
Ditched young Roosevelt to clear the air;
I'm a New Dealer with political flair,
Especially since I'm a millionaire!

Averell, Averell Harriman,
Tammany candidate.

I got the delegates 'cause I've got the dough,
Forget about Yalta, say I didn't go;
Tammany controls me, got me in tow,
I'll be nominated and not so slow.

Averell, Averell Harriman,
Tammany candidate.

ADLAI STEVENSON

(to the tune of "A Wand'ring Minstrel I"
from *The Mikado*)

A wand'ring jokester I—
A man of puns and smirking,
Of left-wing leanings lurking,
The same old trifling Adlai!

In September 1964 at a convention in Louisville, Kentucky, she was unanimously elected first vice president of the National Federation of Republican Women.

During the 1950s, Schlafly also made dozens of speeches across the state in her capacity as national-defense chairman and then as a state officer of the Daughters of the American Revolution. She filled many of those engagements accompanied by a nursing baby (Bruce in 1955, Roger in 1957, Liza in 1958, and Andy in 1961). "I could always find a woman who would be glad to watch my happy baby in a buggy rather than listening to speeches," Schlafly recalled.

Also in those years, Schlafly made two amateur attempts at self-publishing. Her bibliography called *A Reading List for Americans,* printed in 1954, was followed in 1959 by another called *Inside the Communist Conspiracy.* Both made use of her background as a librarian and were compiled to counter what Schlafly claimed was a more potent weapon than the hydrogen bomb: "World ignorance of Communist tactics, strategy, and objectives . . . American failure to grasp the fact that we are already engaged in total war with the Communists." The reading lists were widely reprinted and used in connection with seminars and schools on Communist techniques of the Cold War era, some of which Schlafly helped to arrange and some of which she addressed.

By 1960, Schlafly was doing research, writing, and speaking for the Cardinal Mindszenty Foundation—headed by her sister-in-law, Eleanor Schlafly. The Foundation was founded in 1958 by Eleanor and Father C. Stephen Dunker, C.M., a missionary who was imprisoned by the Chinese Communists,

---

The eggheads like my stuff,
The ADA is for me;
But voters still ignore me,
And Illinois has had enough,
And Illinois has had enough!

during which time he resolved to alert his fellow Americans to the threat of "atheistic communism." They named the Foundation in honor of Joseph Cardinal Mindszenty, a Hungarian cardinal who suffered twenty-three years of Communist torture and imprisonment for unflinchingly opposing totalitarianism and refusing to leave his homeland—becoming, in the process, a living martyr.[2]

In 1963, Schlafly devoted herself to fighting the Nuclear Test-ban Treaty, speaking to Rotary clubs and church groups and, finally, testifying before the Senate Foreign Relations Committee. Later that year, the St. Louis *Globe-Democrat* chose its hometown girl as its Woman of Achievement for 1963. "Phyllis Schlafly stands for everything that has made America great and for those things which will keep it that way," *Globe* publisher Richard Amberg said when he presented the award.

Also in 1963, the NFRW celebrated its twenty-fifth anniversary with a silver-anniversary banquet that drew Republican leaders from around the country to the ballroom of the Palmer House in Chicago. Schlafly, as president of the host federation, served as chairman and toastmistress. The choice of a speaker was hers. "I insisted on Barry Goldwater and I got him." Then she promoted the event with every bit of her boundless energy. So many Republicans showed up that the crowd overflowed from the ballroom into the Red Lacquer

---

[2] When Cardinal Mindszenty was forced to leave Hungary in 1971, he took up residence in Vienna, Austria. Eleanor and Phyllis rushed over to meet him and tell him what they had been doing with his name for the previous eleven years. "That was the most thrilling trip I ever made," Phyllis recalled. "Cardinal Mindszenty proved to be every bit as much of a hero as we believed him to be when we chose to use his name." As a result of her trip to Vienna to meet the cardinal, she befriended his longtime secretary, Father Joseph Vecsey, and they collaborated on a biography of the cardinal's early life titled *Mindszenty the Man*.

Room and she had to convince the senator to give his speech twice. "It was his first national Republican forum and it ranks as one of the most exciting days of my life," Schlafly said, as she gave a reporter a guided tour through a photograph-lined corridor outside her bedroom. At a central spot in this gallery of political highlights is a framed photo of a radiant Phyllis Schlafly with her guest of honor.

In early 1964, Schlafly was embroiled in an election fight for delegate to the Republican National Convention. She had been very impressed by Goldwater, and so, from the start, she pledged herself to him, a move that was considered controversial and even unpopular.

An editorial in the St. Louis *Post-Dispatch* urged voters to defeat her unless she repudiated a pamphlet being circulated throughout Illinois. The pamphlet smeared liberal Republican Charles Percy—then candidate for governor—by accusing him of being in cahoots with "Red Leaders," mentioning as evidence a meeting he had attended, without mentioning that also at the meeting were the Prime Minister of Canada, the chairman of General Mills, and the publisher of *The Journal of Commerce*. Schlafly claimed she had nothing to do with the pamphlet and, in fact, supported Percy. But she refused to repudiate it. Despite the *Post-Dispatch*'s displeasure, she won the election with the biggest vote total in a four-way contest.

The usually ignored delegate race got loads of publicity, and Schlafly found herself in the eye of the storm. Her zealous support of Barry Goldwater would keep her there for the rest of the decade.

In Schlafly's world—a world composed of heroes and villains, of patriots and "gravediggers"—Barry Goldwater was a hero, a "defender of the American way of life," whom she ranked with Washington, Jefferson, Madison, and Hamilton. "Barry Goldwater knows that the American military and nuclear power is the last best hope of the free world. . . ." Goldwater, she said, "combined the integrity of Robert Taft (whom she supported for the Republican presidential nomination in '52) with the glamor of Eisenhower." Besides, she added, she admired Goldwater for being a success at everything he tried, a general, a man of vast political experience, a successful businessman, author, a distinguished veteran of World War II and, best of all (in Schlafly's book), a man who still piloted jet fighter planes.

Schlafly's foes saw her as inflexible; her fans as highly principled—different ways of saying the same thing: She did not know how to compromise. And she recognized the same backbone, stubbornness in Goldwater. "The Republican Party must offer candidates who have strong moral and patriotic principles. If our leaders don't stand for something, they will fall for anything.

"Barry Goldwater is the one Republican who will win," Schlafly wrote, "because he will campaign on the issues of 1964. He is the one Republican who will not pull his punches to please the 'kingmakers.' . . . He is the only Republican who will truly offer the voters 'A Choice Not an Echo.'"

The above accolade was, of course, from *Choice*. Its author claimed, however, that her book was not a campaign puff piece (only one of the fifteen chapters was about Goldwater). She said proudly, though, that she had no doubt it helped Goldwater win the California primary and ultimately the Presidential nomination by knocking Nelson Rockefeller out of the running. She denied Goldwater asked her to write it.

Goldwater apparently did not see the manuscript before publication. He wrote Schlafly several weeks after publication, on May 11, 1964, that he had just seen it for the first time. He congratulated her on a "very well done" book and told her that he had an offer from a man who wanted to distribute *Choice* to every delegate at the convention the next July. That was ultimately done, again, with good results for Barry Goldwater. Most 1964 Republican delegates received many copies of *Choice* sent by constituents who wanted to persuade them to vote for Goldwater. "I remember one angry Pennsylvania delegate," Phyllis said, "who told me he had received seventy copies."

The red-and-white paperback, in fact, carried a cover portrait, not of Goldwater, but of a dark-haired Phyllis Schlafly smiling widely, exposing a set of gleaming teeth—a perfect match for her double strand of respectable Republican pearls. Except for the title and author, the only words on the front cover were "the inside story of how American Presidents are chosen." The back cover contained a three-paragraph expansion. Goldwater's name was nowhere to be found.

Schlafly insisted that the book was intended to be a history of Republican National Conventions (one of her longtime "hobbies") that would incidentally promote Goldwater's candidacy. It would do that by warning people—particularly delegates—of how the "kingmakers" had, in previous years, selected the presidential nominees of Republican National Conventions and defeated candidates whom they couldn't control—thereby "cheating" the "grassroots" out of their choice.

"Just as I have made myself the country's No. 1 expert on the ERA," Schlafly explained, "years ago I made myself the country's No. 1 expert on Republican National Conventions. I think they are a fascinating American institution. I have either been a delegate or intimately in attendance at all Republican National Conventions beginning in 1952, and I probably know more about their history, their functioning, their dynamics, and their results than anyone in the country. This part of my life has always been exciting, dramatic, and fun."

Like all of Schlafly's books, the core came from speeches. *Choice* was born of a speech delivered in December 1963, a month after the Kennedy assassination. "I didn't want to give an out-and-out political speech because I thought that was inappropriate and so I started developing this idea as a historical speech."

By studying Republican National Conventions, Schlafly attempted to prove that the eastern internationalist wing of the Republican Party—the J. P. Morgans and the Rockefellers—whom she labeled "kingmakers," had dictated the choice of every Republican nominee since 1936. Why? To preserve their "America last, pro-Communist foreign policy" in which, she claimed, they had a vested interest.

How so? Schlafly argued that during the Roosevelt administration, for example, the "kingmakers" were intent on protecting their heavy investments in England and Western Europe by keeping a President in power who would be sure to lead the United States into World War II.

Since the end of World War II, "the U.S. foreign giveaway programs have become immensely profitable for certain Americans. . . . There are large profits to be made in acting as depository or fiscal agent . . . for the recipients of these immense sums." (Between 1946 and 1963, "foreign giveaways," she claimed, totaled more than the total assessed valuation of America's fifty largest cities.) The kingmakers, she maintained, "are not opposed to the New Deal–New Frontier–Fast Deal Policy of deficit financing. . . . Since they dominate the consortium which fixes the interest rate the government has to pay on its obligations, they have no incentive to see deficit financing stop."

When necessary, she charged, the kingmakers would even deliberately choose losers—wishy-washy washouts who would not campaign on the issues and consequently would lose. And that, she asserted, was just dandy in the kingmakers' opinion because, in many cases, the Democrat would be friendlier to their far-flung financial interests anyway. In action, Schlafly's theory went as follows:

The kingmakers chose Wendell Willkie in 1940 because they knew that this former Democrat would not campaign on the chief issue of that year, which was "Roosevelt's policy of consenting to Stalin's invasions of Poland, Romania, Finland, Latvia, Lithuania and Estonia—while committing American boys to fight Hitler." In 1944, Thomas Dewey never mentioned the Republicans' best issue—how the Roosevelt administration "manipulated and invited disaster at Pearl Harbor."

In 1948, Tom Dewey again did not campaign on the major issue which, according to Schlafly, was Communist infiltration of the government. The Republicans finally won in 1952, because Eisenhower, after consulting with conservative Robert Taft (from whom the kingmakers had stolen the nomination), agreed to run a hard-hitting campaign on "corruption, communism, and Korea."

In 1960, the kingmakers decided that Nixon was too conservative and so set their sights on one of their own, Nelson Rockefeller—in Schlafly's book, definitely on the "villain" side of the ledger. When the kingmakers realized they couldn't beat Nixon, they tried to compromise him—succeeding when Nixon made a pilgrimage to Rockefeller's Fifth Avenue co-op, where Nixon accepted Rockefeller's platform changes and the kingmakers' vice-presidential candidate, Henry Cabot Lodge—"one of the darlings of the internationalist clique, one of the discredited hatchet men of the smear-Taft maneuver in 1952, and also of the get-McCarthy[3] cabal in 1954." (Schlafly also accused Lodge of, in her eyes, an unforgivable sin: laziness. She quoted *Newsweek,* "He canceled five of seven [campaign] appearances in Kansas City in order to watch television.")

[3] Schlafly's next-door neighbor, Gladys Levis, frequently told reporters that during Joseph McCarthy's heyday, "Phyllis fed him information." Schlafly called the charge "preposterous. I never had any contact with McCarthy or with his office or with anyone acting in his behalf. I never wrote McCarthy a letter and I never got one from him." She did, however, strongly support congressional investigations of Communists and, from her writings, it appeared that she believed McCarthy had been smeared. When Schlafly compiled her reading list *Inside the Communist Conspiracy,* she included two books by McCarthy (out of 115), which, several reporters implied, proved some sort of collusion between the two.

Nixon pulled his punches, "pulling a steady retreat from the conservative and anti-Communist principles which alone could bring victory for Republicans—and blew the election." (Rockefeller, Schlafly noted with undisguised glee, failed even to carry his own state for Nixon.) Schlafly even saw the kingmakers' long arm in the fact that when Nixon abandoned California after his gubernatorial defeat in 1962, he moved into the cooperative building in Manhattan owned and occupied by Nelson Rockefeller.[4]

The press soundly ridiculed *Choice*, ignored it, or linked it to other "ultra right-wing" books and then denounced the group. William Randolph Hearst, Jr., condemned *Choice* as a "book of fantastic political indictments and a monotonous reiteration of purported conspiracies." An editorial writer for the Minneapolis *Tribune* charged *Choice* was "full of false statements" and "guilty of phony documentation," concluding, ". . . it does seem that Mrs. Schlafly has a special call on our sympathy. Anyone who sees so much duplicity in her fellow men, so much evil in the hearts of national leaders, so many plots and conspiracies, must be a sorely troubled, unhappy person." Syndicated columnist Drew Pearson damned

[4] Although Schlafly supported Nixon at two Republican National Conventions (1960 and 1968), in early 1970 she began criticizing him openly for failing to carry out his 1968 campaign pledge to restore clear-cut U.S. military superiority. By 1971, with Nixon's planned visit to Red China in the headlines, Schlafly was talking publicly about "taking a vacation" when it was time to work for his re-election. She even claimed that a poll she conducted indicated that "Nixon is certain to lose the next election," and she pushed Ronald Reagan instead. When Reagan declined to run, she threw her support to Congressman John Ashbrook. "President Nixon promised," she said in a 1973 CBS Radio "Spectrum" broadcast, "that we must never allow America to become the second strongest nation in the world." After a detailed comparison of American and Soviet missile strength, she concluded, "The fact is we are already only the second strongest nation, and it happened under Richard Nixon."

Choice by including it in his list of favorite reading of the "radical right." Jim Kulp of the Alton *Telegraph* blasted *Choice* in an article headlined "Facts Take a Beating in Rightist Books," sparking the long-term acrimony between the *Telegraph* and its most famous reader. When Kulp got to Schlafly's book, though, the only inaccuracy he cited was that she called the Bilderberger Society the DeBilderberger Society and claimed that the Society's meetings were secret when, according to Kulp, they were not.

(Ironically, corroboration of *Choice*'s central charge came from a most unlikely source—Tom Wicker, then a Washington correspondent for the New York *Times,* a newspaper that Schlafly called "the chief propaganda organ of the secret kingmakers." "The most bitter resistance to Senator Goldwater centers in the eastern internationalist power structure that for two decades has dictated Republican nominations," Wicker wrote in the August 11, 1963, *Times* magazine. "The members of that elite will not lightly relinquish their party to Barry Goldwater.")

Jim Kulp was one of many journalists who linked *Choice* to the John Birch Society and then declared its author guilty by association. "The main premise of Mrs. Schlafly's book that a group of eastern 'kingmakers' has selected Republican presidential nominees in recent campaigns is an echo of a similar point made years ago by Robert Welch, founder of the John Birch Society." Kulp claimed that the Society was "among the first organizations to buy, distribute, and promote the book," citing as evidence the fact that it was sold in the Alton American Opinion bookstore, a known Birch Society outlet. (He failed to mention that *Choice* was also carried by Marshall Field's, Kroch's & Brentano's, and most bookstores and newsstands.)

The "grass roots" apparently didn't care what the book critics said (or didn't say) or whether the John Birch Society or Attila the Hun endorsed *Choice,* distributed it, or even financed it.[5] People read it—many of them people who hadn't read a book since the sixth grade, if then—and they passed it on to their friends. A man came up to Schlafly after a speech in Peoria, Illinois. "Your book is the first book I ever read," he said. "I couldn't even get through *Tom Sawyer*."

In some parts of the country, Republican state committees tried to suppress *Choice* by refusing to handle it in the official headquarters, but *Choice* fans would sell the book under the counter. In California, the state chairman of the Goldwater Campaign Committee, former U. S. Senator William F. Knowland, implied during a press interview that *Choice* was not acceptable campaign literature. At the same time he was publicly criticizing it, he plagiarized several pages and used them under his own byline in the Goldwater for President campaign newspaper.

Schlafly predicted in *Choice* that after Nelson Rockefeller stumbled and dropped out of the race, the kingmakers' choice to replace him as the man to beat Goldwater would be Governor William Scranton of Pennsylvania, a name almost unknown to rank-and-file Republicans. When readers saw the Scranton scenario unfold before their eyes—after *Choice* was already in their hands—many became positively fanatic about getting others to read it.

It was the distribution of a million copies of *Choice* in California that truly turned the tide to Goldwater—from Rockefeller, who had been the leading candidate, supported by nearly all the major newspapers, networks, pundits, and pollsters.

In an election postmortem, Stephen Shadegg, a top Goldwater aide, said that Schlafly's book contributed heavily to Goldwater's victory in the crucial California primary. Gar-

---

[5] Schlafly denied getting money from any person or organization. "Putting up my own three thousand dollars to pay the printer was the biggest risk I'd ever taken," she said. "It paid off. It sold and sold. I didn't need any money from anyone."

diner Johnson, Republican National Committeeman for California, agreed, calling it "a major factor in bringing victory to Barry Goldwater against the terrific assault of the press, the pollsters, and the paid political workers of the opposition." (Goldwater was accused of wanting to abolish Social Security, win the war in Vietnam by "nuking" the North Vietnamese, and—by a leading newsman on CBS-TV—launch his campaign in Munich, where the *Führer* launched his.)

"The guy who distributed *Choice* in California was a man who ran a door business," Schlafly recalled, "so he had a loading dock. We shipped the books out there and he stood out on his dock and would give these boxes of books to people. We were selling them at cost, which was ten dollars a box (of one hundred books). Goldwater workers would come and count out ten dollars of their own money in dollar bills and silver. Those people worked their precincts and knew where every vote was. They would take my book and pass it out and, lo and behold, they would have another hundred Goldwater votes that they didn't have before."

In an interview with a St. Louis *Globe-Democrat* reporter in April 1964, Schlafly described Lyndon Johnson as extremely weak and handily beatable. Famous last words: LBJ ended up carrying forty-four states and the District of Columbia, making Goldwater the biggest loser since Alf Landon in 1936, who carried only two states.[6]

---

[6] Schlafly later blamed the Goldwater debacle on Republican liberals who refused to accept the "grass-roots" choice. "Like spoiled children," she said, "they took their marbles and went home." However, months before the election, Schlafly implied that Goldwater didn't stand a chance. In *Choice* she quoted from *Time* magazine: "A lot of the kingmakers think that President Johnson, all things being relative, has done a good job." Then she quoted Walter Lippmann: "The old established ruling powers in the Republican Party—the banking, industrial, and publishing magnates . . . are either in favor of the election of President Johnson or at least are not strongly opposed to it."

Three years later, in 1967, when Schlafly braved a bitter battle for the presidency of the National Federation of Republican Women, Goldwater remained neutral—although the strongest opposition to her candidacy stemmed from her gung-ho support of his presidential bid. (The powers in the party feared that Schlafly, who enjoyed zealous support among precinct workers—doorbell ringers, envelope lickers —would steer the party to a replay of 1964 with another unyielding, unelectable conservative.) In a letter written shortly before the '67 election, Goldwater praised Schlafly, calling her "a friend of long standing. . . ." But he also praised her opponent.

In late 1979, Goldwater published his political memoirs, *With No Apologies* (written with Stephen Shadegg). Goldwater devoted a number of pages to the California primary, a chapter to the '64 convention and the campaign. Not once did he mention Schlafly, her potent little paperback, or even its title, which became his campaign slogan and one of the most memorable in campaign history. Schlafly's name was not even in the index.

In a room off the living room of her Alton home, atop a video machine—on which Schlafly watches tapes of herself during televised debates and interviews—is a bust of Barry Goldwater. Across the room is a portrait of Cardinal Mindszenty. "Both men," Schlafly said, "are heroes in my life."

12

1967: "The Queenmakers"

When Phyllis Schlafly wrote *A Choice Not an Echo* in 1964, she surely never suspected that she herself could be the next victim of the "kingmakers," that she was composing a scenario for her race in 1967 for the presidency of the National Federation of Republican Women (NFRW).

Of all the controversies of Phyllis Schlafly's controversial career, none has been quite so tumultuous as the battle for this unpaid, not particularly prestigious or powerful "women's" position.

By the time the election was held in May 1967, there had been so many bitter charges and countercharges, so much maligning and vilifying, that at a debate between the two candidates a few days before the election, they refused to shake hands, even for photographers, and would not speak to each other except publicly into the microphone.

As unanimously elected NFRW first vice president, Schlafly was unquestionably in line for the presidency. But the male leadership of the Republican National Committee (RNC)—still reeling from the Goldwater disaster three years earlier—decided that Schlafly was too conservative to lead its official "ladies'" auxiliary. It was the ladies, after all, who were out in the precincts, ringing doorbells, licking envelopes, serving the lemonade at rallies—in other words, getting the men elected. Under the leadership of a Goldwater conservative like Schlafly, the ladies might prefer to man the mimeograph for Ronald Reagan than for George Romney or Nelson Rockefeller.

When the NFRW nominating committee members met to choose their candidate—an endorsement tantamount to election—they passed over Schlafly and tapped Southern Californian Gladys O'Donnell, hardly a screaming liberal, even in Schlafly's terms. O'Donnell had worked for Robert Taft in 1952, for William Knowland, for Nixon when he ran for governor of California in 1962, for George Murphy, and for Ronald Reagan.

But the adjective used most frequently to describe O'Donnell was "mild"—a word that by no stretch of anyone's imagination could be applied to Phyllis Schlafly. Reporters frequently described O'Donnell as "accommodating," the sort of woman who would support such liberals as Governor Rockefeller of New York or Governor Romney of Michigan or Governor Scranton of Pennsylvania, all new members of the Republican National Committee. Schlafly put it a bit differently: "The men in the Republican National Committee (the "kingmakers" of this battle) know they can control Gladys O'Donnell and they know that they can't control me."

Rockefeller, Romney, and Scranton had all been Goldwater rivals for the nomination in '64. Their presidential ambitions were by no means stilled and they were not about to take the chance of letting Schlafly still them again. Who knew? She might write *A Choice Not an Echo, 1968,* which would endorse Ronald Reagan, and order her legions of ladies to distribute the book door to door. "Already some of the Republican governors . . . are starting a quiet campaign to prevent the automatic accession of Mrs. Phyllis Schlafly . . ." columnists Evans and Novak reported in 1965.

At a September 1965 NFRW board meeting, it was, reportedly, the men "in the perfume-filled rooms," led by moderate RNC chairman Ray Bliss, who engineered the ingenious bylaws change designed to prevent Schlafly's ascension to the presidency. They changed the biennial convention, at which officers are elected, from even to odd years. The ostensible reason was so women could be back home working the precincts in even years—election years—instead of off at a NFRW convention.

Tom Littlewood of the Des Moines *Register* reported what he considered the real reason: "To give the moderates until 1967 (instead of 1966, when the convention normally would have been held) to devise a way of heading off Mrs. Schlafly . . ." Richard Dudman of the St. Louis *Post-Dispatch* agreed: "If the election had been held as scheduled in 1966, Republican leaders foresaw a strong possibility that Mrs. Schlafly would win on a nomination from the floor because conservatives control many of the forty-two hundred individual woman's clubs."

Dudman also reported that "a group of party leaders planned the maneuver in several secret strategy sessions . . ." lending credence to Schlafly's *Choice* charges of "smoke-filled rooms" in which kingmakers, or in this case, "queenmakers," called the shots, flouting the will of the "grass roots."

Gladys O'Donnell, to Schlafly's amazement, mailed as part of her campaign literature a news article from her hometown paper that stated, "National GOP Chairman Ray C. Bliss is generally credited with manipulating Mrs. Schlafly out of the NFRW presidency last year. . . . The device used was deferral of the scheduled 1966 election to this year."

But if Schlafly could have gotten nominated from the floor and elected in 1966, what was to keep her from doing likewise in 1967?

For the convenience of members, NFRW meetings alternated between cities east and west of the Mississippi. It was time to go west to Los Angeles. But in the meantime, Schlafly had been speaking in Southern California, particularly conservative Orange County, and drawing big crowds. It was clear that even though O'Donnell, the "official" federation nominee, was from Orange County, California would be strongly pro-Schlafly. The Federation Board voted to move the meeting from Schlafly country to Washington, D.C., where, Schlafly later charged, the RNC was headquartered and its leader, Ray Bliss, could keep a tighter rein on the ladies. Also, delegates from the more liberal northeastern states were more likely to attend a convention in Washington, D.C., than one in Los Angeles.

In January 1967, the Federation's Board met in New Orleans to select a nominating committee that would, in turn, select the Federation's official choice for president. Paul Hope of the Washington *Star* covered the meeting: Federation leaders "planned to see that a nominating committee was named tomorrow who will select Gladys O'Donnell."

Schlafly complained at the time that the "men don't have enough respect for the women of the Federation to let them choose their own leaders." Van Wolverton, an editorial writer for the Lindsay Schaub News Service, reported, "Ray Bliss, a man possessed with the idea of party unity since the shattering GOP defeat in 1964, apparently had one too many nightmares about an ultraconservative as NFRW president. Through his influence he got the nominating committee to bypass Mrs. Schlafly and propose a California woman . . . for the top job." Governors Romney and Rockefeller both were reported to have had staff members in New Orleans jockeying to influence the committee's selection.

In March 1967, two months before the May election, Schlafly was screaming "purge"—another attempt by the "New York liberals to purge from office those who whole-heartedly supported Senator Goldwater in 1964."

At that point, Schlafly was better known nationally than any other woman in the Federation. She had been traveling all over the country making speeches at the rate of three a week. The typical NFRW woman—a conservative—loved her. She was popular and she knew it. Under Federation by-laws, she could be nominated from the floor at the convention and challenge the "official" nominee, and that was, precisely, what she planned.

In the spring of 1967, during the weeks before the election, Schlafly's charges flew fast and furious, many, apparently, perfectly justified. The outgoing president of the Federation, Dorothy Elston, a self-proclaimed O'Donnell backer, had received a letter from Barry Goldwater in which he disputed claims by Schlafly's opponents that her election would split the Federation wide open and render it impotent in electing Republicans. "You and I both know that the election of either of these fine ladies will not be a slur on any member of the Republican Party and will not have a divisive effect, and further, that under the leadership of either, the Federation will unite to carry out its true function, which is the election of Republicans all across the land."

He proceeded to praise O'Donnell, describing her as a "longtime worker in conservative causes" and thus denying Schlafly's claim that the election was a "purge" of Goldwater's supporters. And then he went on to praise Schlafly, whom he called a "friend of long standing. . . . Anyone familiar with politics at all must be familiar with the fantastic work done by this fine lady."

Elston released the letter to the press and to presidents of clubs around the country, most of whom would be voting delegates. But the letter she released was minus Goldwater's praise of Schlafly and minus his assertion that her election would not divide the Republican Party.

Apparently Elston did not know that Goldwater had sent Phyllis Schlafly a copy of his letter. When reporters called Schlafly for comment, she released the remainder of the letter. Reporters then hurried back to President Elston, who admitted she had cut the missing paragraphs. She explained that she deleted the parts helpful to Schlafly because "I do not agree with it."

Her position as president demanded it, and Dorothy Elston proclaimed her neutrality loudly and frequently. More loudly and more frequently, Schlafly proclaimed Elston "the real campaign manager" for Mrs. O'Donnell. In any case, Elston refused to answer Schlafly's charges.

"The charges," Elston said, "only prove her political immaturity, which is one reason the nominating committee feels she is not the person to fill that sensitive position." Being painted as a divisive force more interested in polemics than practical politics infuriated Schlafly. She stressed that in her three terms as president of the Illinois Federation "We had a period of harmony unmatched by any other state." Federation membership in Illinois rose by 45 percent.

She trotted out her record of service to all Republican candidates, liberal and conservative, focusing on the latest victory: 1966, when Illinois Republicans enjoyed a rare triumph, winning not only a Senate seat for liberal Charles Percy, but also a House seat, forty seats in the Illinois legislature, and the Cook County Board presidency. The Illinois Federation adopted a "Statement of Sentiment" "heartily" supporting its former president and calling her a "loyal and indefatigable Republican."

Ironically, Schlafly encountered the most vehement opposition practically in her own backyard, from her next-door neighbor, Gladys Levis. The Alton District Women's Republican Club and the Godfrey (a town adjoining Alton)

Women's Republican Club came out solidly for Schlafly. In the meantime, Levis and some friends seceded from the Alton District Club and started their own, the Alton League of Republican Women.

As its president, Levis signed a letter explaining why she wouldn't support Schlafly: "Mrs. O'Donnell has a constructive philosophy while her opponent is an exponent of extreme right-wing philosophy . . . a propagandist who deals in emotion and personalities where it is not necessary to establish facts or to prove charges. . . . It is necessary only to make them in a style so sweeping that it triggers the adrenalin and blanks the need to think. The membership of the NFRW wants a Choice, not an Echo of a disaster they would like to forget."

At that time, the men in control of things expected ladies to be ladies; to be seen and not heard. Federation leaders were respecting those wishes. Phyllis Schlafly had other ideas of women's proper place in the party, and she obviously didn't care what the men thought of those ideas. She wasn't going to go quietly.

Two months before the election, Schlafly staged a one-woman invasion of Republican National Headquarters. She walked into Dorothy Elston's office, located down the corridor from Ray Bliss's, demanding to see a list of delegates who were certified to vote at the Federation convention. Mrs. Elston was at a luncheon on Capitol Hill and her staff refused to let Schlafly see the lists without their boss's approval. The refusal sparked a 2½-hour verbal battle between Schlafly and Liz Fielding, the Federation's public-relations director.

Fielding first pleaded with Schlafly to withdraw as a presidential candidate on the grounds that she was "tearing the party apart." When this failed, Fielding began quizzing Schlafly on her beliefs, specifically on whether she or her husband Fred were then or ever had been members of the John

Birch Society. (Phyllis and Fred Schlafly have always denied ever having been JBS members. The Birch Society membership rolls are secret.)

Schlafly finally realized her mission was impossible and left, with Mrs. Fielding at her heels, still pleading with her to withdraw, saying, in effect, that the men know what's best for the party. En route to the elevator, they encountered Ray Bliss. Fielding told him what she was trying to do, adding, "Men in the party think we women are stupid enough as it is without this." "You said that, I didn't," Bliss responded, ducking into his office.

Fielding made a final, fruitless stab at changing Schlafly's mind. "We've all been working twelve to fourteen hours a day and eating at our desks dealing with the fuss that you have stirred up around the country, and now we're infested with cockroaches." The exterminators, Fielding said, were due that very afternoon. "Well wouldn't the press like to know that?" Fielding asked. "Five minutes after Phyllis Schlafly came to Republican headquarters the exterminators arrived!"

"I won't tell them if you don't," Schlafly responded, as she ducked into the elevator.

One of the more intriguing ironies of the Federation battle was that if there was a feminist on the front—a strong-willed woman who was not going to tolerate any dictation from the boys in the bureaucracy—that was Phyllis Schlafly. The Federation fight rates a whole chapter in Schlafly's fourth book, Safe—Not Sorry, published in December 1967, seven months after the election. In "The Purge" she sounds suspiciously liberated.

"The Republican Party is carried on the shoulders of the women who do the work in the precincts, ringing doorbells, distributing literature, and doing all the tiresome, repetitive campaign tasks. Many men in the party frankly want to keep the women doing the menial work, while the selection of candidates and the policy decisions are taken care of by the men in the smoke-filled rooms," she wrote, and then, continuing in her style of referring to herself in the third person, "In Phyllis, they recognize one who could not be neutralized or silenced, and who would fight for women to express their ideas in matters of policies and candidates commensurate with the work the women do for the party."

Schlafly pledged to wrest political decision making from the "kingmakers" and told Marie Smith of the Washington *Post*, "The more we let their [women's] voices be heard in politics, the better off we are. . . . Women should have a role beyond stuffing envelopes and stirring coffee."

Gladys O'Donnell was as different from Phyllis Schlafly as Pat Nixon is from Bella Abzug. A widow and a grandmother who flew her own plane and ran the family's oil business, O'Donnell gushed to reporters, "This is the first elective office I've ever run for in my life. I never dreamed that I would run for anything." (She had never held an office in the NFRW.)

O'Donnell proclaimed herself a "simple garden-variety of uncomplicated Republicanism." Watching a Schlafly/O'Donnell luncheon debate before the Woman's National Press Club a few days before the election prodded Edward O'Brien, the St. Louis *Globe-Democrat*'s Washington Bureau chief, to observe: "Mrs. O'Donnell's self-portrait in the confrontation was of a mild, well-meaning lady who . . . will rock no boats if elected."

Obviously, Schlafly did not see herself as a pretty centerpiece for the head table. She planned on being as much of an activist nationally as she had been in Illinois. "My objective in seeking the presidency," she said, "was not to sit at head tables and listen to twenty speeches about Republican unity. My principal objective was to elect the right kind of President in 1968."

The irony of ironies in the Federation race was that Schlafly's now famous six children were used against her. "The candidacy of Mrs. Phyllis Schlafly . . . may be affected more by the fact that she has a large family than by her ultraconservative tendencies," wrote the Alton *Telegraph*'s Jim Kulp several months before the election.

The outgoing president, Dorothy Elston, an elderly woman with neither husband nor children, told reporters that she did "not think it's right that a woman with responsibilities to husband and children should be running for the Federation presidency." Many members, she added, are concerned that Mrs. Schlafly—whose children then ranged from two to sixteen—would even want the job. "She must end up neglecting one or the other to do it right. How can she do it (handle the presidency) and spend time with her family, I don't understand. This is a woman's organization. You cannot duck the six kids."

Suddenly a new "rule" materialized—namely, that the Federation president had to be willing to live in the Federation apartment in Washington, D.C.—as it happened, a one-bedroom apartment that Elston, who lived alone, rented and that would be perfect for O'Donnell, who also lived alone.

Schlafly protested. "The fact is there never was any such rule binding on the Federation, and the Federation does not even have an apartment in Washington. The Federation merely pays the rent on an apartment that Mrs. Elston selected and lives in. The immediate purpose was to give the false impression that this 'rule' barred me from the presidency because everyone knew I could not put my six children in a one-bedroom apartment."

She pointed out that there were only two Republican women's clubs in Washington, D.C.—and so it was ridiculous to require the president to live there and run the Federation's Washington office. "I expect to be a leader and keep in contact with the clubs—not be an office manager," Schlafly said.

Elections are won, she added, "by working in the precincts. The Republican Party's best workers are mothers of young children. They are not looking for favors. They work selflessly. The party needs the image of youth. It's high time the Federation had a president who is the mother of young children."

The race had suddenly become a battle of the generations —a contest between youth and age—as was clear to anyone who saw the debate between the two at the Women's National Press Club. Schlafly, forty-three, was hatless and wore a bright dress, referring several times to her six children, her family duties, and her work in the precincts with her children by her side. O'Donnell, in contrast, wore a conservative blue suit and large white hat. She looked like the stereotype of a Federation president. "Some of the correspondents were impressed by Mrs. Schlafly," wrote a reporter for the Medill News Service. "Little was said about Mrs. O'Donnell."

Schlafly commented that Federation leaders "got what they deserved" when Californians for Schlafly distributed campaign literature with photographs in which Schlafly, according to O'Donnell, "is made to look like a beautiful glowing thing about twenty" while a photo of the sixty-three-year-old O'Donnell "had been retouched to make me look like I just dragged myself out of an irrigation ditch."

And so the Federation was about to experience the first contested election in its history. Normally decorous, collected, white-gloved Republican matrons were stirred to a fevered pitch. Typically, fifteen hundred delegates—one from each club able to finance the trip—showed up. This time five thousand delegates and alternates, plus a packed gallery of spectators, choked the sweltering Sheraton Park Hotel ballroom.

Mary McGrory wrote in the Washington *Star* of "riotous scenes of booing, weeping, and teeth gnashing." Staid Republican ladies hissed and catcalled, bickered and brawled at formal sessions. Several women collapsed from the excitement. Schlafly charged that at a credentials committee hearing, "one of my supporters fainted and was thrown out while she was unconscious."

That corridor, outside the credentials committee hearing room, was undoubtedly the hottest spot in the hotel. The credentials committee members decided who could and who could not vote and, Schlafly charged, they heavily favored Gladys O'Donnell. "My supporters are being harassed mercilessly," she complained. "They're being disqualified as voting delegates for utterly inane reasons." Isabel Shelton reported in the Washington *Star*, ". . . it was obvious to those standing in the corridor watching the proceedings that most of the contested cases involved delegates who favored Mrs. Schlafly rather than Mrs. Gladys O'Donnell."

Schlafly delegates waited in line for as much as twelve hours in the unair-conditioned corridor while the credentials committee, whose chairman was O'Donnell's Virginia campaign manager, met in closed session. Mrs. Gladys Mitchell traveled all the way from Laguna Beach, California, to vote for Schlafly. "This is impossible," she snapped as she stomped toward the elevator. Her case had still not been heard after ten hours, she said, and she was going home. "I didn't come here to sit in a hallway. They treat you like animals waiting for slaughter."

Delegates from eleven pro-Schlafly Missouri clubs, including Eleanor Schlafly, the rebel candidate's sister-in-law, were ousted on what Ann McGraw (later a leader in the Missouri STOP ERA movement) called "unjustified technicalities." (Their state treasurer was one day late in forwarding dues to Washington. Schlafly charged that pro-O'Donnell delegates from hundreds of clubs that had paid only half their dues were allowed to vote.)

Even busing was an issue in this election. On voting day, several busloads of women arrived from New York, Pennsylvania, New Jersey, and Michigan. They were taken, Schlafly charged, immediately to their state headquarters, given badges, instructed how to vote, herded to the voting area, and then put back on buses and driven home without ever going to the convention floor or participating in the convention. There were four hundred of them, she claimed, or, as the election turned out, almost enough to make a difference in the results.

President Dorothy Elston, Schlafly contended, had illegally denied the convention the right to accept or reject the credentials report. "We don't know how many delegates were present and entitled to vote," she complained. "What is Mrs. Elston hiding?" Schlafly asked. "The names of the women who were bused in to vote?"

On election eve, Dorothy Elston hosted a lavish reception —for delegates, congressmen, and other VIPs. She invited Gladys O'Donnell to stand in the receiving line but pointedly excluded Phyllis Schlafly. "Out where I come from, that is sort of like eating peas with your knife at a formal dinner," Schlafly commented. Then she announced that while Californian O'Donnell stood in the official receiving line, Californians for Schlafly would be hosting their own reception.

Reporters pronounced the rump reception the livelier of the two. Refreshments included pink punch, petits fours, and a foot-long eagle, which Schlafly adopted as her campaign symbol from Barry Goldwater, whose campaign workers wore gold-eagle pins in their lapels.

Maureen Reagan Sills, daughter of Ronald Reagan and Jane Wyman, and president of a strong pro-Schlafly club in Orange County, California, provided the entertainment. She stood atop the piano in her stocking feet leading a sing-along.[1]

---

[1] Today, the once cozy relationship between Schlafly and Maureen Reagan has cooled considerably. Maureen (now divorced) endorsed ERA and has even gone on speaking tours—one with presidential daughter-in-law Judy Carter. When Maureen Reagan wrote an article for *Redbook* claiming that "the ERA ensures only that if a woman chooses to work outside her home . . . her pay will be equal to that of a man holding a similar job," Schlafly blasted her for being wrong (ERA does not apply to the private sector and so does not insure

Schlafly, a particularly powerful speaker when she's angry, was also denied the opportunity to address the convention. And so were her supporters, she complained. The abortive attempts by Schlafly backers to make themselves heard resulted in one of the convention's more ludicrous scenes.

In the final session, Schlafly's supporters shouted, stood on chairs, and waved their arms to force Elston's recognition of their last-minute protests of the conduct of the election. Mrs. Whitworth Taylor of Cincinnati tried in vain to raise a point of parliamentary procedure, finally leaping onto the press table, where she stood eye to eye with Dorothy Elston, still screaming, "Madam Chairman, Madam Chairman."

President Elston, frail, elderly, pale, and exhausted from the sound and fury of it all, was in the midst of announcing an award to the woman who had brought in the most new members. Mistaking Mrs. Taylor for the super recruiter, Mrs. Elston presented the astonished Mrs. Taylor with an engraved medal. The unexpected honor left her speechless, mouth hanging open. Public-relations director Liz Fielding, realizing the mistake, leaped to the press table, stood on tiptoes, and snatched the medal out of Mrs. Taylor's hands, nearly knocking the Cincinnati housewife into the lap of syndicated columnist Mary McGrory.

Minutes later, before the vote count was announced, Schlafly's supporters filed a formal election protest that fo-

---

equal pay for equal work), and added, "Much can be learned about ERA by the type of woman *Redbook* chose to write those articles. The first was written by Maureen Reagan, a young woman who had divorced two husbands by the time she was twenty-five, and now tells reporters: 'I'm looking for the person I'd most like to divorce.'" (Schlafly explained that the reason she chose the eagle as her symbol was because "the eagle is almost the only creature that keeps one mate for a lifetime.") In spring 1980, Reagan, once as staunch a Republican as Schlafly, announced that she was considering running for the California Senate as a Democrat.

cused on the alleged voting machine irregularities. The crux of the complicated complaint was that ballot security men whom Schlafly had hired were "not allowed to check out the counters—in other words to cast a test vote and make sure machines recorded votes accurately." (The convention referred the challenge to the Federation's Board of Directors, which eventually voted 58 to 2 that the election was "legal in all its aspects.")

Five years later, at a Republican reception in Washington, a man came up to a prominent Federation officer long active in Republican politics. "I just had to tell you," the man confessed. "It's been on my conscience all these years. I was the one who fixed the voting machines used by the Ohio delegates (Schlafly's biggest voting bloc) in order to switch votes away from Mrs. Schlafly and to the other candidate at that women's convention in 1967." Then he disappeared in the crowd. The woman, who remained neutral in the election, said that she was "shocked" to learn that the Ohio machines had been "fixed" so that the vote was reversed. The vast majority of Ohio delegates cast votes for Schlafly, which were recorded as votes for O'Donnell. "That information I confirmed later. Phyllis was not being paranoid as everyone had thought. And I learned of even more dirty dealing, including the busing. There is absolutely no doubt that but for the tampering Schlafly would have won that election."

Gladys O'Donnell had predicted that she'd win by a 2–1 margin. She won by just over 400 votes—1,910 to 1,494.

When the results were announced, Schlafly, willowy in a pink linen dress, "P.S. I love you" streamers fastened to her chest with a gold eagle pin, shook O'Donnell's hand, smiled, turned, and headed for the door. As if on cue, an estimated 3,000 women, some sobbing, a few shaking their fists, followed their leader to a rump session in the hotel's basement.

In the corridor, a supporter called Schlafly "the women's leader in America." The crowd cheered. Incensed over the alleged "busloads of women" and "fixed voting machines" that had snatched their victory, others screamed for revenge.

Schlafly then headed for a press conference, her troops in tow, where she charged that the election had been "stolen." "This controlled and rigged election has constituted an election fraud that has robbed a half million federated Republican women of their representation."

Rebellion was in the air. Schlafly raised the possibility of forming a "grass-roots organization made up of just plain American women and mothers who believe in the cause of constitutional government and freedom." The crowd cheered.

A supporter from Illinois offered a charter for a new organization to be known as the American Federation of Republican Women. The crowd cheered some more. "I think we should do it," one woman wrapped in a "Phyllis Power" banner shouted. "After all, you have two baseball leagues, National and American."

Just when it looked like the Republican Party was headed for American and National leagues of Republican women, Maureen Reagan came to Ray Bliss's rescue. She said she was "fighting mad" but "this is not the time to make a decision like this. . . . If we put one fourth of the energy into this organization that we would have put into a new one, we won't need two ball clubs."

"Go home and think about it," Schlafly told her fans. "Pray about it. And then write me what you want to do. I am not going to lead you into anything you don't want to do." When she got back to Alton, she wrote the three thousand women who had traveled to Washington on her behalf and urged them to work through the Federation to elect the "right kind of [U.S.] President in 1968."

She didn't practice what she preached. She worked—was a delegate, in fact—for Nixon, but she severed ties to the Federation. She didn't start a competing organization until 1975, when Eagle Forum was incorporated. By then, she claimed the NFRW had lost at least 100,000 members. A past president of the Federation puts the number at 180,000, at least. By 1980, the once nearly half-million-strong organization had only 280,000 members left. The reason, the official explained, was O'Donnell's "very weak presidency." The women working the precincts were hungry for meaty programs—campaign technique workshops, lobbying instruction, etc.—and "literally all Gladys did was establish something called Queen Isabella Day, the day the Queen gave her jewels to Columbus, I think." (O'Donnell's other accomplishment was helping push ERA through the U. S. Congress. She died in 1973 at just about the time Schlafly turned the tide against ERA.)

What Schlafly did that summer of 1967 was far more potent and effective over the long run than starting a competing women's organization. She launched *The Phyllis Schlafly Report*, a monthly newsletter through which she could communicate current news and opinion to her growing number of followers. Vol. 1, No. 1 was mailed in August 1967 to the 3,000 women who supported her at the NFRW convention the previous May. By 1980 the number of subscribers had grown to 35,000. In addition, Schlafly established the Eagle Trust Fund to receive donations in support of causes espoused in the newsletter; funds that subscribers might previously have donated to Republican clubs or organizations.

So, when Schlafly launched the STOP ERA movement in 1972, solely to prevent ratification of ERA, she had a ready-made core of female political leaders—her loyal supporters from the NFRW convention. In Schlafly's words, "They had received a postgraduate course in politics at the NFRW convention in 1967." She also had a ready-made means of communicating with them—*The Phyllis Schlafly Report*, in which, since 1972, Schlafly relentlessly attacked ERA. And she had a modest cushion of funds in the Eagle Trust Fund to finance the anti-ERA activities of those first years.

In August 1967, three months after the election, when Dorothy Elston got word of the *Report*'s imminent publication, she called a press conference and charged Schlafly with "subversion . . . because her activities seek to undermine the effectiveness of the National Federation." What she didn't realize, apparently, was that Phyllis Schlafly didn't care if the Republican establishment thought her subversive.

Two new bylaws were also proposed—both obviously aimed at Phyllis Schlafly. One required "the removal of Federation officers for speaking to the detriment of the organization, its policies, objectives, or ideals. Another required local clubs "to conform to the objectives and bylaws of the National Federation." (Schlafly charged that the changes would transform the Federation into a Soviet-style dictatorship and called it a "bold attempt by Federation officials to move power from local women's Republican clubs around the country and centralize it in Washington.")

And so Schlafly had, in a sense, been forced to become a free agent, a role that suited her to perfection. When her supporters tried to draft her for another try at the NFRW presidency, Schlafly declined, firmly, without a minute's hesitation.

She remained an elected Republican precinct committeeman, but slowly her base of support switched from the Republican Party to what she called the "grass roots"— Republicans and Democrats, urban Catholics and southern fundamentalists, Mormons and Orthodox Jews, blue-collar ethnics and white-collar suburbanites—an unlikely but potent coalition that would battle ERA with such astonishing success.

But before the ERA battle started in late 1971, Schlafly, in 1970, tried once again to get elected to Congress. The experience, coming three years after the NFRW race, left her thoroughly convinced that her base of support had turned national and bipartisan and that the anti-Washington theme that permeated the 1967 battle (and the ERA battle) was more convincingly used by someone who was attacking the government than by someone who was seeking to become a part of it.

13

1970: A Woman's Place Is in the "House"

Phyllis Schlafly has a great—almost a naïve—faith in the political process. After losing the race for President of the National Federation of Republican Women in 1967 and charging it had been "stolen" from her, she told her dispirited supporters that the ballot box was their only redress. The ballot box—what she considers a fundamental difference between the United States and the Soviet Union.

"America can be saved," she wrote later that year, "if citizens elect congressmen who are for keeping America strong." In 1970, Schlafly decided to do her part to "save America" by accepting a plea from Republican county chairmen to run for Congress. (She had impressed party leaders in 1968 by winning a hotly contested race for delegate to the Republican National Convention.)

Since her unsuccessful 1952 race for Congress, she had been redistricted out of the 24th District, where Representative Melvin Price still held sway. This time she would run from the 23rd, a predominantly rural and small-town district, sprawling across the width of the state, stretching from the Mississippi above St. Louis to the Wabash River on the Indiana line.

Her Democratic opponent, then six-term Congressman George E. Shipley, was considered vulnerable. Republican state candidates regularly carried the 23rd, by some 15,000 to 20,000 votes. Before Shipley's election to his first term in 1958, the district had been represented in Congress by the same Republican for 16 years, and in '58 Shipley scored an upset with only 187 votes to spare. In his 1968 race, Shipley had won re-election by a relatively small margin over a political neophyte.

Political analysts and editors called the race "a tossup." The National Republican Congressional Committee gave it a "top priority" rating. The 23rd was the only one of Illinois' 24 congressional districts considered likely to change hands. That, coupled with Schlafly's national reputation for strong opinions, brought newsmen swarming into the district.

Shipley, obviously, could have done very nicely without all the attention. "He was used to just breezing along," explained a campaign aide. "Now, all of a sudden he had these New York *Times* reporters snooping around, analyzing his record."

"Why are all these reporters from New York and Chicago interested in our district?" Shipley asked a group of supporters. "I'll tell you why. It's because of Mrs. Schlafly and her controversial record. It's because of all those books she has written." Shipley quickly labeled Schlafly "with all her degrees and breeding and books" an "egghead." He played up this "intellectual" angle for all it was worth, and it turned out to be worth quite a bit.

It would be hard to imagine two candidates with styles as different as the then forty-eight-year-old "good ol' boy" Shipley and his forty-six-year-old aggressive, articulate, aristocratic opponent. Shipley was an ex-Marine from the oil town of Olney, former sheriff (like his father before him) of Richland County, who, in his spare time, hung out at the restaurant he owned in town. Shipley had joined the Marines out of high school and he was downright proud of his modest education.

Schlafly, on the other hand, was the "intellectual," the author of five books, the Radcliffe graduate with perfect posture and poise and manners—who knew how to serve tea and with which fork to eat her salad. She had worked her way through college as a gunner in an ammunition plant and she never let her campaign audiences forget that, but the oil riggers and farmers must have found it hard to imagine her ever getting sweat or dirt on her prim Republican dresses.

In campaign styles, they were also a study in contrasts. Shipley was a back-slapper, a hand-shaker, a man of the people whose wife had insisted on staying in Olney while her husband commuted back and forth to Washington, spending as little time in the latter and as much in the former as possible. "My family doesn't like Washington any more than I do," Shipley said frequently. "This is our country," he'd say at county fairs, his arms outstretched as if to embrace the rich farmland.

Shipley campaigned by mingling in small meetings of veterans and laborers. Schlafly, on the other hand, conducted a whirlwind campaign complete with saturation mailings, television appearances, and "big name" endorsements. Switch on the radio to catch the farm report and out boomed John Wayne: "The reason I like Phyllis is that she talks straight. She is the kind of person we can count on to do something about the big-spending politicians who are wasting our hard-earned tax dollars." Switch on the TV for a football game and Gerald Ford was saying about Phyllis Schlafly: "America is worth fighting for and Phyllis is the kind of stand-up person we all need in Washington to get the job done. I know Phyllis stands for everything that makes America great."

Voters opened their mailboxes to find a letter from Barry Goldwater soliciting votes and funds—and she needed a lot of the latter. Her campaign cost nearly six times as much as her opponent's. She had such prominent contributors as W. Clement Stone, multimillionaire head of Combined Insurance, who kicked in $33,492, just about the total tab for Shipley's whole operation. This is not to say that Schlafly didn't get checks for $5.00 and quarters taped on the inside of envelopes. But those donations came as frequently from Nashville as from Alton, from Tempe as from Olney. Shipley was a local boy of whom few outside the district had ever heard. Schlafly was a Republican celebrity, a conservative prophet with a faithful, fervent, and national following.

The 23rd District was composed of farms, small towns with dwindling populations, played-out coal mines, depleted oil fields. Alton, with forty thousand residents, was the closest thing to a city in the district. The district's concerns were more basic than the megatonnage gap between Russia and the United States and the perils of disarmament.

"George Shipley's the best thing to happen to this district since electric power," said one farmer. Shipley was better known for his letters of congratulations and sympathy to the folks back home than for any concrete achievements. But because his interests were purely local, he could prime the pork barrel with the best of them. As a member of the House Appropriations Committee, he regularly tacked on local projects to bills—a new reservoir, a new dam, a new federal building for Alton, the latter to counter Schlafly's charges that he had ignored the west side of his district.

If a constituent got tangled up in federal red tape or if he found himself tangling with a bureaucrat, Shipley would graciously and efficiently untangle him. On weekends, Shipley the ombudsman invariably hung around the county courthouses talking to voters about their problems or, as one put it, "just chewing the fat."

Schlafly, on the other hand, was a national figure with a national constituency who had an undisguised fascination with national issues. She blasted Shipley for voting for "welfare giveaways . . . while only a few crumbs of our tax dollars come back for the needs of the 23rd District. It is not fair to tax the hard-working people in our small cities and rural areas to put large subsidies into fancy transportation systems and into the pockets of freeloaders who won't work."

And so Schlafly was off and preaching on a national issue —on the evils and even the "immorality" of the welfare system. Her audience undoubtedly agreed, but also undoubtedly would have preferred to hear about the new dam that might affect their jobs or their crops. "We've been shortchanged too long," Schlafly said about George Shipley, ultimately turning that into her campaign slogan. Not too many voters agreed.

Shipley didn't even bother responding to Schlafly's attacks. She challenged him to a debate. Shipley refused, pleading too heavy a schedule. "There is a need for a new voice in Washington to speak up for our kind of district," Schlafly persisted. "Congressmen from a district like ours are only in a minority and unless they speak up we aren't going to have representation. I don't think he can do it. If he won't debate here, he probably won't do it in Washington." Probably not, but as long as he made it to the county courthouses every Saturday morning, it didn't really matter that his grasp of national and international issues was a bit shaky.

Schlafly stuck to her issue-packed campaign to the bitter end but never could get Shipley to join her. Shipley stuck to his road-tested "You know me, I'm one of you" style. While Schlafly attacked Shipley for not showing leadership on the Soviet-adventurism-in-Africa issue, Shipley, at a Labor Day picnic, attacked Schlafly for "writing a letter to one of our neighbors over in Breese and misspelling the name of the town. And not only that," Shipley said, his sweat-soaked shirt open at the neck, "the second time she used the name she also stuck a "z" in there."

Despite a rather rocky relationship with the Alton *Telegraph*—sparked by a staffer's pan of her first book—Schlafly won the paper's endorsement. The editors found her national and intellectual perspective refreshing and also relished the prospect of having a congresswoman sure to make national headlines and waves.

"Few people on the political scene can match Mrs. Schlafly's skill and intelligence. She is exceptionally able and articulate. We recommend that voters give her the opportunity to put her excellent qualifications to work. . . . She has the potential to become one of the nation's foremost legislators."

The *Telegraph* found her intellect impressive. The locals didn't. Her brains and her sex became hot issues.

A couple of weeks before the election, Shipley complained that Schlafly's degrees, her Phi Beta Kappa key, all the books she has written are "irritating my people"; people whose doubts about women mixing in men's work "go double for brainy women. . . . She gives the impression she's an expert on military affairs and foreign affairs," Shipley said. "I say I'm not an expert on any of these things and I need the guidance of the people in the district." Schlafly issued detailed position papers on defense and other foreign and domestic topics. Stumping in a fire-and-brimstone style, Shipley would pull off his coat and tie, shove up his sleeves, and shout, "You know me and I know you. You are my kind of people. The greatest in America."

Associated Press reporter John Beckler asked one man on the campaign trail what he thought of a woman running for Congress: "She's got six kids, hasn't she? You'd think that would give her enough to do."

"Who here thinks my Harvard-educated opponent ought to

quit attacking my foreign-aid votes and stay home with her husband and six kids?" Shipley thundered. "We do," came the reply from families at an Indian-summer barbecue. "I don't tell her how to take care of her family. And she shouldn't tell me how to take care of my constituents."

The scoldings obviously worried Schlafly because she studiously avoided mentioning her children in her campaign literature. In light of her later crusade against women's liberation, Schlafly's response to these—by today's standards, outrageously sexist attacks—was intriguing.

"My opponent says a woman's place is in the home," she told a luncheon audience in the basement of the Christian Church in Shelbyville. "But my husband replies that a woman's place is in the House—the U. S. House of Representatives." (The same year, running for Congress in New York, another woman, Bella Abzug, used the same clever rejoinder—and that was the one and only time the two ever had anything in common.)

If anyone worried about Schlafly being a member of the weaker sex, they didn't worry for long. Maintaining a pace that only those who have tangled with her over ERA could comprehend, Schlafly drove some 40,000 miles and flew thousands more. It took 3½ hours to drive from one end of the district to the other.

She met voters at hog competitions, at tractor pulls, and at demolition derbies. She stood at factory gates to talk to workers as they changed shifts and to cast off the country-club cloak in which Shipley had wrapped her. (It didn't help when the St. Louis *Post-Dispatch* belittled her fund-raising appeal by noting that it "appears right next to a picture of Mrs. Schlafly in a good-looking fur coat." The fur, Schlafly protested, was shirred raccoon and six years old.)

Schlafly's inexhaustible energy fueled the frenzied pace, but so did her corps of faithful—indeed, fervent—mostly female volunteers. This was more than a campaign to them. It was a mission. "They worked for me as they had worked for no candidate before," Schlafly boasted. In most campaigns, women stuff the envelopes and stir the coffee while men make the strategy decisions. In the Schlafly campaign, in nearly every one of the fifteen counties comprising the 23rd District, a woman called the shots.

Schlafly's campaign organization was a harbinger of STOP ERA, whose stunning success depended largely on decentralization. Local people mapped local strategy, but Schlafly —not an aide or a campaign manager—was the final, the chief strategist. She relied on her workers' judgment, but kept tight control over everyone and everything—absolutely everything.

Uncharacteristically, early in 1970, she hired a Chicago advertising firm with a successful sideline of handling political campaigns. The firm had mapped out every detail of the campaign and was ready to flick the "on" switch in the crucial two months before the election. Suddenly the ad agency withdrew, citing a "difference of opinion over the approach." The problem, it seemed, was that Schlafly insisted on keeping control of the campaign's every last particular, down to the most arcane detail. Campaign strategy, set designs for TV spots, typeface for brochures all came under her personal scrutiny.

Schlafly never got Shipley to discuss, much less debate the issues, but that didn't stop her from writing, talking, and moralizing about them.

Inflation—then still single-digit—was a big one. Shipley, as a member of the Appropriations Committee, had done nothing, she charged, to cut federal spending and help halt the shrinking value of the dollar. She advocated balancing the budget and radically slashing taxes when, unfortunately for her, the country had not yet been struck by Proposition 13 fever. She talked about slashing the federal bureaucracy in terms that would not be repeated until Jimmy Carter jumped into the White House off an anti-Washington platform.

While campaigning, she said, she met a man who "put it to me bluntly. When I asked him to vote for me . . . he looked at me sternly and said, 'Are you in office now?' I replied, 'No, I'm not.' 'Then I'll vote for you.' This man's remark expresses how people are fed up with how the present Congress has been living it up with our money, lining their own pockets and turning their backs on the taxpayers, who are paying the bills."

The congressional battle was waged at a time when the phrase "long, hot summer" struck terror, not only in the hearts of city storekeepers, but also small-town folk who feared brigades of bayonet-brandishing welfare cheaters swarming down Main Street looting, raping, and trampling on cherished values and traditions. Schlafly's militantly law-and-order campaign was antiriot—ghetto or college—with a vengeance.

"Do you like the way the campus rioters and police killers, bomb throwers, arsonists, and other terrorists seem to get away with their revolutionary acts?" she asked in a fund-raising letter. "Are you fed up with the politicians who do nothing about the criminals who stalk our streets but harass the law-abiding with 'gun control' . . . ? Something is happening to our great country and I'm not willing to sit by and let it happen."

Schlafly argued that the massive federal welfare program had created a permanent class of impoverished—morally, financially, and physically—people whom federal spending had sapped of any innate incentive to pull themselves up by their bootstraps, as did the Jews or the Italians or the Irish. A hot campaign issue was ghetto riots, and Schlafly preached that poverty didn't cause them and that spending money to eliminate poverty wouldn't stop them—and, in fact, might stimulate them. "To believe that race riots are not caused by people, but by conditions such as rats and poor housing, is as silly as to believe that illegitimate babies are not caused by people but by conditions."

The idea of trying to stop riots and crime via huge doses of federal aid was, Schlafly argued, based on two false assumptions: (1) that poverty causes riots and crime and (2) that a large percentage of Americans are hopelessly trapped in poverty. "Contrary to general belief, many rioters are not economically deprived slum dwellers but have jobs with medium incomes." Liberals, she added, are committed "to the absurd proposition that men do have the 'right' to be criminals—if they lack an automobile, or a color TV, or if their garbage has attracted rats."

If poverty was not the cause of crime and rioting, what— did Schlafly tell voters—was? Riots, she said, are nourished by federal spending and sometimes ignited by Communists.

"Riots and crime cannot be stopped by spending vast sums of money to wipe out slums and poverty, however worthy those objectives are.[1] If living conditions in 'ghettos' were improved 1,000 percent tomorrow, the agitators and Communists would only say, 'See, we told you that riots would get you better housing, more automobiles, and color TV sets: Get your gun and your Molotov cocktail, and we will take over the country!'

"Riots don't just happen—they are organized by outside agitators and armed guerrillas, by various civil-rights and New Left groups saturated by Communists . . . and by federally financed poverty workers . . . who think the only way to solve the problems of the 'ghetto' is to burn it down."

---

[1] Schlafly, at least, was consistent. If she opposed spending money to conquer poverty, she also opposed spending money to conquer space. "We should forget about flying to the moon and build our nuclear capability until it is so overwhelming it would be ridiculous for any nation to attack us. Space flight is a luxury we cannot afford."

During appearances at county bake-offs and PTA crafts fairs, she raised the specter of black militant H. Rap Brown: "Get you some guns. . . . Violence is necessary. . . . If Washington don't turn around, you should burn Washington down. . . . Blacks stopped moaning 'We shall overcome' and started swinging to 'Burn, baby, burn.' That was our Declaration of Independence and we signed it with Molotov cocktails and rifles." She quoted Stokely Carmichael's definition of "Black Power": "When you talk of Black Power, you talk of building a movement that will smash everything Western civilization has created."

College rioters enraged Schlafly even more than ghetto rioters. In 1970 it seemed that students were shutting down colleges at the rate of one per week to show their displeasure over the war in Vietnam in general and the Cambodian invasion in particular, and—Schlafly added—upcoming final exams.

She told campaign crowds that colleges should immediately expel any student who destroyed property or disrupted classes. Financial aid should be revoked from students who participated in riots, and professors who backed student rioters should be denied tenure. Invariably, she would recall her own college career during World War II when she toiled forty-eight hours a week to pay for her education.

Only the eldest of the Schlafly children was in college at this point, but his mother kept close tabs on him—so his mind wouldn't be "polluted" by radicals, but also because she simply did not believe that going off to college transformed a teen-ager into an adult. It is a major responsibility of college administrators to serve *in loco parentis*, she said.

"I reject the idea that our colleges and universities are the private domain of the faculty and students. Taxpayers have prior rights . . . and parents have prior rights. . . . After parents have scrimped and saved to send our children off to college we have a right to expect that they be taught truth, a reverence for our moral codes, respect for the U. S. Constitution and flag. . . . We have a right to a guarantee that they will not be taught revolution, criminal acts, drug use, or immorality. . . ." Schlafly was particularly proud of a note that came attached to a campaign contribution. "This donation for a most worthy cause is made from the small salary of just a plain worker. It will possibly be needed to help in sending my child to college but if things continue in the direction they are headed, there will be no colleges as we knew them twenty years ago."

The gut-wrenching issue of 1970 was Vietnam, a hideously unpopular war that seemed as if it would never end and certainly never end in victory for the United States. The war was a particularly emotional subject in the 23rd District because it was, after all, the farm and small-town boys who were disproportionately represented among the crippled and killed.

Most people are surprised to learn that, from the start, Schlafly opposed sending troops into Vietnam—and not because she had a dovish bone in her body. In 1964 in *A Choice Not an Echo* she wrote, "The Johnson administration is sending American boys nine thousand miles away to fight and die against the Communists in Vietnam—the Johnson administration won't do anything at all about the Communists only ninety miles away in Cuba." LBJ, she said a year later, was "advancing communism while getting American boys killed under the guise of fighting it."

Shipley, a onetime hawk, was for admitting defeat and retreating. "Retreating" and "admitting defeat" were words not in Schlafly's vocabulary. Now that the United States was in Vietnam, she said, it should fight to win.

The United States could win with little loss of American and South Vietnamese lives if it would do what it had always done—until the Korean War: Fight to win. She quoted the commander-in-chief of the U. S. Pacific Fleet as saying that our Seventh Fleet could "do the job in a day or two if only the Administration would give the Navy orders to put a naval quarantine on Haiphong Harbor (Soviet ships were freely trading with the North Vietnamese and thus being supplied with weapons used to "kill American boys," she charged). She praised Admiral Ulysses S. G. Sharp, who testified in the Senate that all military targets in Vietnam should be bombed (with non-nuclear bombs).

The Vietnam War, she said, lasted much longer than World War II, when the United States defeated two very powerful enemies on two distant fronts. Her explanation of why the United States let itself lose lives, dollars, and prestige in Vietnam was—like most of Schlafly's explanations of complex issues—simple, and parallel to her explanation of why the United States got and stayed mired in Korea. LBJ vetoed the solutions advocated by his military advisers, even though his own re-election hung in the balance, because he was afraid that if we won in Vietnam, the "Soviets would launch a nuclear attack on the United States. The Soviets would have little to fear because we have lost the overwhelming nuclear superiority we had before the days of Johnson and his Secretary of Defense, Robert McNamara. We have no antimissile defense to shoot down Soviet missiles."

She called the war in Vietnam a "gigantic trap designed by the Soviet Union to drain away our resources" and keep us from building up our defenses. "We spent $130 billion, which was shot up or used by the enemy, while the Soviets spent the same amount on weapons they can ultimately use on us." The Soviet Union was the only beneficiary. "The Soviet Union," she charged, "is now blackmailing us into offering up thousands of American boys as hostages and sacrifices in Vietnam in a war we are not permitted to win. If the Soviets can blackmail us into this betrayal of the flower of our youth, they can blackmail us into anything, including the surrender of the United States."[2]

If the Communists, according to Schlafly, reaped rewards from Vietnam, they also profited from foreign aid—or "foreign giveaways," her preferred phrase. One morning, 23rd District residents found leaflets hanging off doorknobs. They were left compliments of the Schlafly for Congress Committee and featured a rather startling charge: "Our present congressman is responsible for Communist Yugoslavia getting $40 million of our tax money for new roads and for giving $480 million in interest-free loans to foreign countries even though the roads in our district are in a deplorable condition. I am 100 percent against such aid. Roads should be built in our district, first."

Schlafly had gone too far this time. Shipley, obviously, was not single-handedly responsible for Communist Yugoslavia getting new roads. (Shipley had supported the triennial authorization bill for the International Development Association, an affiliate of the World Bank, which does make low-interest loans for foreign road-building projects.)

Shipley watched a group of supporters dismantle a huge circus tent that had covered some four thousand Democrats at a rally the day before, while he told Warren Weaver of the New York *Times,* "I voted against foreign aid thirty-nine times since I came to Congress, against every authorization bill and every appropriation. I believe in voting my district. These people know better than to believe that sort of thing.

"She says George Shipley's responsible for high interest rates, the war and campus unrest, and unemployment. I

[2] Schlafly offered a second solution to the Vietnam War, along with bombing Haiphong Harbor: "The main Soviet objective was to divert U.S. defense spending away from nuclear weapons and into conventional weapons. If the United States went ahead with strong antiballistic-missile systems, the Communists would lose their reason for continuing the war and a settlement could be reached."

thought that was President Nixon's responsibility, not George Shipley's."

The leaflet, Shipley claimed, brought him an unexpected windfall of small contributions from people "who were turned off by the rhetoric. One man wrote me and said he wasn't planning to vote because he wasn't crazy about either of us until Schlafly's campaign literature convinced him that I was the better man, so to speak."

When Schlafly lost again (by a margin of 53 to 47 percent), reporters speculated that her sex was the reason. "Most political observers believe Mrs. Schlafly's sex is a handicap in a district far removed from any influence of the women's liberation movement . . ." wrote AP reporter John Beckler. Schlafly disagreed. She refused, as she had in 1952, to blame her loss on sexism. She said during the campaign: "I don't think it's an issue. If it is, I think it will even out." She said afterward: "I think you'll find there are some bigoted people who voted against me because I was a woman. I think that that was probably balanced off by people who might have voted for me because I was a woman. In the overall picture, I don't think that hurt."

The reason she cited for losing in the 23rd in 1970 was essentially the same reason she cited for losing in the 24th in 1952: "If that hadn't been a dreadful year for Republicans I probably would have won. You have to go back to 1934 to find such a bad year for Republicans." 1970 *was* a bad year, and an awful year for Illinois. Republicans lost the U. S. Senate seat long held by Everett M. Dirksen, and even the majority on the state Supreme Court.

Schlafly had the misfortune of being on the ballot in the first election after Republican Governor Richard Ogilvie pushed through the state's first income tax. She also had the misfortune of sharing the ticket with the late Ralph Smith, a former state senator running for the U. S. Senate who was out of his depth debating national issues. Schlafly and Smith were closely linked in voters' minds, not only because they were both from Alton, but also because, under pressure from Republican leaders, Schlafly agreed to a joint campaign.

But there was another reason too, one that Schlafly didn't mention; a problem that plagued her in all three of her runs for major offices—against Mel Price in 1952, against Gladys O'Donnell (for the presidency of the National Federation of Republican Women) in 1967, and against George Shipley in 1970.

Her opponents were never nearly as liberal as Schlafly accused them of being, thus depriving her of a proper foil, of someone to make her pithy campaign slogan—"A Choice Not an Echo"—truly applicable.

Schlafly consistently painted Shipley as a monochromatic liberal. "I am out to defeat the liberal Mr. Shipley this November." She harped on the fact that the AFL-CIO's Committee on Political Education (COPE) had given Shipley a 93 percent rating—as she called it, his "Walter Reuther/COPE rating." One campaign brochure stated, "Phyllis' campaign has already made such an impact that the Democratic opponent she faces in November is trying to pass himself off to the voters as a 'conservative.' But there is no way [he] can hide his longtime record of voting for nearly every extravagant giveaway spending bill that comes before the Congress."

Although George Shipley voted the liberal side on most money bills, he voted the conservative side on most social issues. "I probably have the most conservative Democratic voting record of the Illinois congressional delegation," he bragged. He had a high COPE rating, he explained, because he voted the way he thought his constituents wanted him to. (The district was heavy with small industrial cities and union members.) The conservative American Security Council rated him 89 out of 100 for selected security issues. The liberal Americans for Democratic Action condemned him for voting against ADA positions on civil rights and civil liberties (abortion, amnesty, busing, affirmative action, gay rights) four out of five times. He kept getting re-elected until he finally retired in 1978 after ten terms.

So Shipley—a known if bland commodity—garnered the liberal vote and too much of the conservative vote. In one campaign speech he startled reporters with this astonishing admission: "I guess I consider George Shipley the lesser of two evils."

To lose to the "lesser of two evils" was, understandably, hard to take, and Schlafly vowed it would be her last loss. "I've run for office and I wouldn't wish it on Betty Friedan," she liked to say.

A year later, she entered another fight, which would result in a political upset unrivaled in the annals of twentieth-century politics. At last she had found the ideal foil—the "women's libbers" who were trying desperately to get ERA ratified as the 27th Amendment to the Constitution.

But in the meantime, Schlafly had plenty to keep her busy. She would not be warning her countrymen about the "Soviet threat" from the floor of Congress as she had hoped. Instead, she immersed herself in getting her message out the best way she knew how—between the covers of her books, five of which had already been published, to bad reviews and big sales. Four were still to come.

14

"Saint Joan of the Space Age"

In August 1964, four months after *A Choice Not an Echo* was published, Phyllis Schlafly got a call from Rear Admiral Chester Ward, then living in Hawaii.

"Your book is every place I go in Honolulu," the admiral said. "Everybody's reading it and talking about it. The newsstands can't keep it in stock." He then asked her to collaborate on a book on what he called "the most important issue of our time"—the "survival" of America in the face of the "growing Soviet military arsenal."

"That was quite a shock," Schlafly recalled. She had met Ward briefly the year before when she and Fred heard him lecture on military strategy. She had been much impressed. But she did not want to write another book just then. She was president of the Illinois Federation of Republican Women, trying to carry Illinois for Barry Goldwater. She was spending hours each day filling rush orders for *Choice*, packing and carting them to the post office or airport. Besides, she had five children and was six months pregnant. She told the admiral she would think it over.

Then she told Fred about the call. Not only was he enthusiastic, he also insisted that she accept the offer. He liked Ward's approach to national defense, and he saw a great opportunity to put what he considered Ward's brilliant analyses into language the average American could understand via Phyllis' straightforward style. *Choice* was a best seller. Sticking to the same format and distribution promised, for the first time, a mass audience for a very specialized, technical subject.

One more phone call between Honolulu and Alton cemented a fruitful collaboration that lasted through five books and fourteen years (until Ward died in 1978).

Once they decided to write the book—a paperback campaign book of the same size and style as *Choice*—Ward started writing furiously in Honolulu, and Schlafly did the same in Alton. For the last week, Ward came to Alton, where they put the sections together, with Fred critiquing and proofreading. By this time, Phyllis knew how to move a book from manuscript to bound copies in an incredible three weeks, and by early September, boxes of *The Gravediggers* were flooding the mails. The same people who bought *Choice* bought the new paperback with, at Ward's insistence, the same picture of Phyllis Schlafly on the cover. Paraphrasing the famous line about Helen of Troy, Ward called that picture "the face that launched a million books." Two million copies of *The Gravediggers* were sold in two months of 1964.

The "gravediggers" is the label Schlafly and Ward coined to describe, in Schlafly's words, "the elite group of men, principally in the government, who are working for the unilateral disarmament of the United States despite the growing Soviet weapons threat." As used in the books, "gravediggers" was not a blunderbuss term applied to Communists, liberals, or anyone supporting cuts in the defense budget. It was a precise term to describe identifiable men who, Schlafly claimed, were responsible for the decisions to reduce the military power of the United States, thereby forfeiting the United States' once tremendous nuclear superiority to the Soviet Union.

Schlafly got visibly ruffled when an interviewer made the term "gravedigger" synonymous with "Communist." "They are not interchangeable," she insisted. "Gravediggers are not Communists. The book made that crystal clear. There is not the slightest innuendo that they were or are Soviet agents or spies or Communists."

The top "gravediggers," according to Schlafly and Ward in that book and later books, were Defense Secretary Robert McNamara (from 1961 to 1968) and, from 1968 to 1976, Henry Kissinger, first as President Nixon's national-security adviser and then as Secretary of State. Other leading "grave-diggers" included Harold Brown and Cyrus Vance, who held top defense posts in the Kennedy/Johnson administrations and then came back to pursue the same policies in the Carter administration.

Presuming to criticize such important people caused a lot of rumbling in high places. Admiral Ward, who had retired as judge advocate general of the U. S. Navy, still had many friends in the Pentagon. They told him that Secretary McNamara was so incensed over *The Gravediggers* that he assigned a team of men to work for two months, combing the book line by line, to see if they could make a case for court-martialing Ward. They finally abandoned the idea.

The next year, 1965, Ward stopped off in Alton after a trip to Washington, and another book—*Strike from Space*—was born. How did the two collaborate when they lived four thousand miles apart? Schlafly wrote half the book and sent it to Ward for reworking; he wrote the other half and did likewise. Every day's mail brought packages of reworked manuscript, back and forth, until both were satisfied with the result.

Ninety-seven percent of the collaboration depended on the mail. There was one personal visit per book, usually in Alton, and always a flurry of expensive phone calls as self-imposed deadlines approached.

Schlafly insisted that *Strike from Space* was "prophetic." She told a story of meeting an engineer she hadn't seen in ten years. "When I read *Strike from Space* in 1965," he told her, "I thought you were nuts. Now I give briefings for military personnel, and I tell them it was the most prophetic book ever written. It has all come true, just like you and the admiral predicted."

"It did make many predictions that were simply incredible to most people in 1965," Schlafly maintained. The collaborators predicted military strategy and diplomatic tactics, plus specifics on nuclear weapons and the Vietnam War, for both the Soviet Union and the United States. Their predictions were completely at odds with the prevailing ideology of the mid-1960s, with official Pentagon statements, and with practically everything the American people heard through the media. "Yet," Schlafly repeated, "our predictions have all come true."

What were some of the predictions? The principal predictions were (1) that the Soviets had made the policy decision to build strategic weapons as fast as they could until they achieved decisive nuclear superiority over the United States and (2) that, unbeknownst to the American people, an elite group of government officials (the "gravediggers") had made the policy decision to opt out of the nuclear arms race, cancel all the weapons they could get by with canceling, and allow nuclear superiority to pass to the Soviets.

Certainly it was difficult to believe such predictions in the mid-1960s. Those were the years when Defense Secretary Robert McNamara was repeating his assurance that "we can now and in the foreseeable future meet any military challenge with incontestable superiority in power." Those were the years when the prevailing ideology was that the only reason the Soviets were building intercontinental ballistic missiles was that they wanted to "catch up" with the United States, to achieve "parity," and that they would stop building when parity was reached. Those were the years when liberals assured the nation that all difficulties with the Soviets could be solved by treaties and negotiations.

Interestingly, the Schlafly-Ward thesis wasn't any more acceptable to the leaders of the conservative and anti-communist movement in the 1960s than it was to Pentagon officials. The prevailing dogma of the conservative leaders was that the communist threat was internal, not external; and they looked with suspicion on anyone who espoused the notion that the principal threat to the United States came from military weapons.

The John Birch Society journal *American Opinion* published a seven-page review of *Strike from Space* calling it "a shocking book," and "disputing its outstanding contention." The reviewer, Medford Evans, urged that the book be read by "adult conservatives only," and deplored "its possible influence on the politically immature and emotionally suggestible." He accused Schlafly and Ward of "propagating the Myth of Soviet Might," assuring Birch members that "that monster in the sky is pretty hard to locate."

"I believe," wrote Evans, "that it [the Soviet capability in nuclear technology] is parasitic, laggard, minor, perhaps to the point of imbecility. . . . And, I hardly mention the authors' gratuitous declaration, 'The gravediggers are not Communists.' . . . It is strange that so many Americans refuse obstinately to believe that there is Communist influence in our Government, while they readily believe, without significant evidence, that backward Russia has produced scientific miracles."

"I spent many days after that answering letters from conservatives who had been convinced that Soviet ICBMs were a figment of my imagination," Schlafly recalled. "Then, when they discovered that Chester Ward was a member of the internationalist Council on Foreign Relations, they thought for sure that I had been infiltrated. However, I knew that our analyses were accurate and that events would, unfortunately, ultimately prove us right."

Anyway, by this time, Schlafly had developed such a loyal following that thousands of readers would have believed her no matter what anyone said.

Strike from Space, which sold a half-million copies, did seem "way out" at the time. It was, for example, published in the years when no one else had the temerity to criticize the Kennedy decision to make America first with a man on the moon. Americans were convinced that the Soviets were racing them to the moon and that national honor depended on winning that race. When Wernher Von Braun was asked what Americans would find when they got to the moon, he answered, "Russians."

Schlafly and Ward called the race to put a man on the moon a "moondoggle" and charged that the Soviets "are *not* racing to the moon [because they] know there is no military value in that trip." Four years later, the New York *Times* reported (on October 26, 1969) that the Soviet Union "abandoned" its plan to put men on the moon, that some observers now believed that the Russians never had such a plan, and others believed that, if they did, it was scrapped in 1964. (Schlafly and Ward did not oppose space exploration. It was the "outrageous cost" of putting a *man* on the moon that they believed was not justified. Nearly all the benefits of space exploration, they argued, could have been achieved at a fraction of the cost without sending a man, whose life the United States was bound to spend every dollar to try to protect.)

As the election of 1968 approached, Schlafly and Ward collaborated on another paperback called *The Betrayers.* It restated and updated the indictment against the McNamara stewardship of U.S. defenses and called for the election of Richard Nixon because of his campaign promise, "We shall restore the strength of America."

"Chester never forgave me for insisting that our 1968 book endorse Nixon," Schlafly said. "He knew Nixon was a liar then; I still had hopes, and didn't break with Nixon until June 1971" (long before Watergate).

Chester Ward had an unusual career as a law-school professor, an architect, and as rear admiral in the United States Navy, ending his last tour of duty in 1960 after four years as judge advocate general. He retired early for the specific purpose of devoting the rest of his life to nuclear strategy without being beholden to any administration, university, foundation, or defense contractor. He moved with his wife to Hawaii, where he could pursue his studies without interruption. He held the Legion of Merit with a citation from President Eisenhower commending him for his contributions to the effective use of U.S. seapower and his "realistic" opposition to "the Communist conspiracy."

In Schlafly's office hangs a picture of Ward inscribed "To our Saint Joan of the Space Age." The admiration was mutual. "Chester was the greatest patriot I have ever known," Schlafly said. "He was clearly the pre-eminent American nuclear strategist, and I consider it a rare privilege to have worked with him. His understanding of nuclear strategy and of the personalities of the men who made that strategy (for both the United States and the Soviet Union) enabled him to predict the consequences of their actions ten years into the future. He was a marvelous combination of an original thinker and a consummate scholar who paid meticulous attention to detail. I never had to recheck any fact or conclusion he wrote me; he was always correct. It was a job, though, to translate what he wrote from the language of the strategist to that of the average American." The biggest job was yet to come.

In 1972, Chester Ward again stopped off in Alton on a trip between Washington and Honolulu, and *Kissinger on the Couch* was planned. They agreed at the outset that this would not be a campaign book or a paperback, but would be their major work, without the previous limitations of time or space —a full-fledged critique of the Kissinger strategy and a complete dissection of his *tour de force,* the SALT I agreements of 1972.

They worked three years on that book. Schlafly devoted as many hours to *Kissinger on the Couch* as she did to her entire three years of law school from the first day through the bar exam. Five thousand pages of manuscript were exchanged between them by mail, studied and sweated over until they were finally reduced to the 832 pages of the final book.

The book's title is a bit misleading, because it was Kissinger's *policies* that were "on the couch" rather than Kissinger himself. The book was, essentially, a strategic, political, economic, and psychological analysis of Kissinger's strategy and policies, which, the authors maintained, were the same as those of McNamara, who preceded him.

"I think *Kissinger on the Couch* is one of the most influential books ever written," Schlafly said, displaying not a twinge of doubt. But the fact remained, as the first of her books not available in paperback and not self-published—it was published by conservative Arlington House—it had a relatively small sale. Released in 1975, in the midst of her fight against ERA, Schlafly claimed the book was blacklisted in libraries, and it *is* hard to find.

"But U.S. policymakers must have read it," she insisted, "because I see the results. The knowledgeable people who agree with our conclusions make use of some of the original material in the book without giving credit. The knowledgeable people on the gravediggers' side have modified their positions so as to protect themselves in the future from the kind of criticism we dished out. Before *Kissinger on the Couch* was published, hardly anyone of importance would attack Kissinger's policies or SALT I. After the book was published, hardly anyone of importance would defend them. You notice how even Kissinger himself has done a turnaround."[1]

She had a point. Only three senators out of one hundred voted against SALT I in 1972 (James Buckley, James Allen, and Barry Goldwater). SALT II was not called for a vote in 1979 because at least thirty-four senators threatened to vote no, and the treaty could not have been ratified if they did. (And this was before the December Soviet invasion of Afghanistan made SALT II, for the time being, at least, a moot issue.)

Yet, Schlafly argued, "there were far better reasons to oppose SALT I. The difference in the vote count in the Senate is because of the powerful indictment of SALT I Admiral Ward and I presented in *Kissinger on the Couch*, which no one has ever been able to refute. We showed how SALT I had fourteen loopholes, carefully crafted to advantage the Soviets and disadvantage us, and how it leaves our cities naked and defenseless against incoming missiles." (If any senator used *Kissinger on the Couch* as a resource, he has yet to admit it.)

Many readers of Schlafly's other books found themselves terribly frustrated by *Kissinger on the Couch*. Those who liked their reading short and concise found the thick book, full of technical terms, simply overwhelming. Most of her Eagles, even those who bought the $12.95 book out of loyalty, probably didn't read it. Some of those who were deter-

---

[1] Shortly after *Kissinger on the Couch* was published, Schlafly told a reporter for the Chicago *Sun-Times*, "My book got the silent treatment from the press. But since it came out I notice that people don't defend Kissinger anymore. I think I could get that man knocked out of power."

mined to plow through it got angry at her for writing such a long book. One syndicated columnist told her that twice during the reading of the book, he threw it at the wall.

(Schlafly defended the length and immense detail of the book. "It is a textbook on U.S. and Soviet nuclear strategy— the only one available to the general public. Anyone who wants to understand SALT I and II, and the relationship between the United States and the Soviet Union, must be familiar with the history and the theories in the book. No other book puts it all together for the serious student.")

On the other hand, some of her fans among the more staid professional, military, and academic types cringed at the book's title, at some of its authors' rhetoric, and at their emphasis on the personal role of Henry Kissinger. Those critics believed that such a monumental contribution to strategic thinking was marred by the authors' focus on personalities.

A writer for the conservative *National Review* praised the book for its ". . . technical data . . . meticulously marshaled and lucidly analyzed. . . . Any layman with sufficient time and patience can come away from it with a basic understanding of the complex world of nuclear weaponry and defense strategy." But the reviewer panned it for its "polemical overkill. Kissinger, the villain of the piece, is variously depicted as a loon, a coward, a Svengali, a liar, and a traitor."

Schlafly, not surprisingly, disagreed. She considered the focus on and even the vilification of certain personalities perfectly proper. "U.S. policies don't make themselves. They are not made by anonymous, faceless zombies who cannot be identified. When men are given positions of great responsibility, we have a right to hold them accountable for their actions, especially when our lives are at stake, as well as the survival of our country. I think it is a cheat on the reader—and on the voters—to criticize national policies, while hiding the names of those who made the policies by saying only that 'they' did it, or worse still, that 'we' did it."

Invariably, that defense is followed by Schlafly's "roll call" of strategic weapons that have been scrapped over the past 16 years: "The B-70 and then the B-1 bombers, hundreds of B-47s and B-58s, the 550 Minuteman Is and IIs, which were destroyed when the Minuteman IIIs were put in the same holes, the second thousand Minuteman missiles, which were canceled before they were built, every plan for building mobile missiles, the Atlas and Titan I missiles, the Skybolt, the scrapping of 31 Polaris submarines by the ruse of 'retrofitting' them as Poseidon submarines instead of allowing them to become additional submarines, and every antimissile system ever proposed, including the scrapping of one only 24 hours after it was built. Those weapons were not canceled by 'we' or by 'they,'" Schlafly said without pausing for breath. "They were scrapped by identifiable men whose names should be known. The American people should hold McNamara accountable for the eight years he was in charge, and Kissinger accountable for the eight years he was in charge. The blame is about equally divided between them for the horrendous result that the eight-to-one nuclear superiority which America had over the Soviet Union in 1962 is gone, and the day is fast approaching when the Soviets will have the same margin over us.

"If the American people and the press were entitled to know every last detail of Watergate—the interplay of personalities, the motivation, and the confidential records and conversations—surely we are entitled to the same when it comes to the overriding issue of our national survival in the face of the Soviet missile threat. That is why *Kissinger on the Couch* not only dissects SALT I and the strategic theories behind it, its relationship to the oil crisis of 1973, to the other Middle East and Cuba crises, and to the Vietnam War and the *Pentagon Papers,* but also examines the personalities of Kissinger and of his associates making the SALT I decisions."

All the intellectuals were not turned off by Schlafly's style.

When she went to Princeton University in June 1976 for her son Roger's graduation, Nobel Prize winner Dr. Eugene P. Wigner, a Hungarian-born physicist, was receiving an honorary degree. When Schlafly met him at a reception afterward, he immediately recognized her name, gave her a long, searching look, and said, "But how can you know so much when you are only an American?"

The last book Schlafly and Ward wrote together was *Ambush at Vladivostok,* a paperback published in 1976, which Schlafly called "the poor man's update of *Kissinger on the Couch.*" It analyzed the preliminary SALT II agreement signed by Gerald Ford in Vladivostok in the Soviet Union.

The number of years Schlafly spent fighting ERA pales beside the number of years she spent fighting the "gravediggers." Ward's death in 1978 and the heating up of the ERA battle did not stop or even stem Schlafly's defense analyses, testimony, and writing.[2] And her reception got a lot warmer in 1979 and 1980 as the United States' relationship with the Russians got cooler.

Senator Richard Stone (D., Fla.), presiding at a hearing of the Senate Foreign Relations Committee on September 7, 1979, addressed the witness: "Mrs. Schlafly, early in your testimony, you provided quite a remarkable summary which is, I

[2] The simultaneous campaigns did, however, leave her rather disconcerted at times. When she gave a speech on nuclear strategy at the Executives' Club in Chicago in January 1975, the ERA battle was raging in Illinois. During the question period, which was supposed to be on the subject matter of the speech, one woman asked her, "Mrs. Schlafly, will you comment on the refusal of the Union League Club to admit women to two of its floors?" On the other hand, the editor of the specialized *Journal of Civil Defense* was enthusiastic about Schlafly's writings on defense, but obviously didn't understand her work against ERA. He identified her as a "feminist-lawyer-political analyst . . . avid campaigner for basic American moral values, controversial, and a hazard to proponents of pantywaist American foreign policy."

think, probably the most lucid that I have heard, of the difference between Soviet numbers [of nuclear weapons] and the American numbers as limited by SALT II. . . . In about two minutes, you summarized the strategic numerical difference in this [SALT II] treaty. Would you repeat that?"

Senator Jesse Helms (R., N.C.) took his turn at complimenting the witness. "Mrs. Schlafly, we appreciate your coming before the Committee today. You are a distinguished American and I congratulate our colleague from Illinois for having such a constituent as Mrs. Schlafly."

Liberal Senator Charles Percy (R., Ill.) responded: "We haven't always seen eye to eye, but I have always admired her many qualities of tenacity, perseverance, and her power of expression is unbelievable. It is one of the best testimonies I have heard. . . ."[3]

Senator Helms continued, "The chairman [Stone] and I were just remarking that there are very few witnesses who, while delivering testimony, could get up and walk over to a map, describe it, come back, and sit down without missing a syllable." He was referring to the fact that, in presenting her case against SALT II, Schlafly talked from a large world map showing U.S. dependence on oil imported from the Middle East and Africa. She showed how, in her opinion, SALT II would give the Soviets the power to cut off the flow of oil.

[3] Coming from Percy, that was quite a compliment. The two had been on a collision course since the midsixties. Percy was not only an ardent supporter of détente and the Panama Canal treaties, he also supported several measures that Schlafly totally opposed. He cosponsored a bill to "curb the population explosion" by allowing personal-income-tax exemptions for only two children in one family, supported public financing of abortions, the $5 million appropriation for the International Women's Year Conference, and the extension of time for ERA. By 1978, Schlafly urged her supporters not to vote for him for re-election. Percy, who anticipated no trouble getting re-elected, ended up in an exhausting, humiliating race against an unknown Democrat, a conservative on foreign policy issues, who nearly toppled him.

(That the Soviets would ever somehow block U.S. oil supplies seemed fairly farfetched at the time. But this testimony predated by three months the Soviet invasion of Afghanistan, which most observers agreed could give Soviet jet fighters the capability of striking Persian Gulf oil routes from Afghan bases, and so cut the oil lifeline on which the United States, Japan, and Western Europe depend.)

As usual, taking a complex issue and bringing it right home to the gut, she told the senators, "If you liked being in gasoline lines in June, you will love SALT II. . . . How in the world could we give the Soviet Union the power to cut off that oil and cause all the economic dislocations that would result?"

Schlafly, speaking without notes, gave Stone his requested two-minute summary of the SALT II Treaty. "SALT II allows the Soviets to have 308 heavy missiles. It does not allow us to have a single one. SALT II allows the Soviets to have about 1,500 ICBMs, but it allows us to have only 1,054. It allows them to have almost four times as many MIRVs on their land-based ICBMs as we have, and it allows those Soviet MIRVs to be 26 times more powerful than our land-based MIRVs.

"It allows the Soviets to have their submarines prowling our coasts with weapons that can reach all our major cities. But we are prohibited from building a cruise missile that will reach Soviet territory. It allows them to build all the Backfire bombers they want, but we are strictly limited on our bombers. . . .

"Nobody knows how many mobile missiles they have. Of course, mobiles were the big loophole in SALT I. . . . We don't know how many they have built and hidden. But under SALT II, we would be prohibited from deploying a mobile missile until 1982.

"The disparities are so tremendous that the whole thing is humiliating to us. In addition to the actual differences in power and number and throw weight and megatonnage,

SALT II gives the Soviets the perception of power. I don't see how they could respect us for signing such an unequal agreement."

Schlafly was confident that she knew what she was talking about on the complex subject of SALT II. She was not awed by being questioned by a lineup of senators in the imposing room in the Russell Senate Office Building, where the Watergate hearings had been held. After all, it was sixteen years and five books on nuclear strategy ago that she first appeared before the same Committee, in 1963, when Senator Sparkman (D., Ala.) was presiding. She gained even more confidence from the fact that she believed the years had proven her right.

Rereading her 1963 testimony against the Moscow Testban Treaty, Schlafly said, "I still stand behind every word of it. The criticisms I made then are just as applicable to the SALT II Treaty now being debated." Back then she testified, "Even State Department sources have conceded that some of the language in the Moscow Nuclear Test-ban Treaty is 'disturbingly imprecise.' This is a diplomatic way of saying that the treaty is shot through with legal loopholes that imperil the security of the United States. Senate ratification will give valid American promises, which will bind us, in return for worthless Soviet promises, which will not bind them.

"I wonder how many witnesses who testified in favor of the Moscow Test-ban Treaty in 1963 are willing to stand behind their words today?" Schlafly asked rhetorically, brandishing a copy of the yellowing hearing transcript and quoting Secretary of Defense Harold Brown, then the Defense Department's director of Defense, Research, and Engineering: "I do not believe that the Soviets can impair to an important degree our strategic superiority."

"Even Brown would have to admit that 'our strategic superiority' is long since gone," Schlafly said, explaining that in the modern space world, in which the lead time required to develop and build weapons can be ten to fifteen years, Pentagon officials must be held accountable for weapons-policy planning fifteen years into the future.

Then she switched to another transcript, this one from "Meet the Press" on October 28, 1979, when Secretary of Defense Brown was asked, "Mr. Secretary, Henry Kissinger has warned that, unless the United States takes dramatic steps to change the military balance, that the United States will face a massive crisis in the 1980s. Do you agree?" Brown replied, "It took us fifteen years to get in the situation where the momentum is against us."

"That's right. It did take fifteen years," Schlafly said, her tone smug but also angry. "And who was making the decisions fifteen years ago that headed us downhill in nuclear weapons, while the Soviets were building at a crash wartime rate? Harold Brown, when he was in the Defense Department and then when he was Secretary of the Air Force."[4] And then she lists a long line of other "gravediggers."

"That was the same crowd whose unilateral-disarmament decisions and deceptions I exposed in my three books on nuclear strategy in the 1960s. I identified the men when they were at the peak of their power, and I exposed their tragic decisions at a time when they could have been changed and thereby prevented our country's decline in world power and prestige, for which we are now paying a bitter price in Iran," Schlafly concluded—a week before President Carter called Soviet President Leonid Brezhnev a "liar" and the invasion of Afghanistan a violation of an agreement between former President Richard Nixon and Brezhnev.

Phyllis Schlafly waited many years for history to corrobo-

[4] In a speech to the Naval War College on August 20, 1980, Defense Secretary Harold Brown said that the Soviets now have thousands of highly accurate warheads and may already be able to wipe out our Minuteman missile force.

rate some of her early statements—for example, "The only agreement the Soviets have ever kept is the one they made with Hitler in August 1939, which started World War II"— and she is certainly not bashful about boasting, pointing to testimony by Henry Kissinger in 1979, before that same Senate Committee:

"We have placed ourselves at a significant disadvantage voluntarily. This is not the result of SALT. It is the consequence of unilateral decisions extending over a decade and a half, of a strategic doctrine adopted in the sixties, and of the choices of the present Administration. All these actions were unilateral and avoidable. Rarely in history has a nation so passively accepted such a radical change in the military balance."

Phyllis Schlafly couldn't have said it better. In one of the more startling ironies of her life, she found herself agreeing with Henry Kissinger or—as she would have it—found Henry Kissinger agreeing with her.

15

Declaring War on ERA

More than anything else—more than her crusade against communism, more than her crusade to get Barry Goldwater elected President, Phyllis Schlafly is famous for her crusade against the Equal Rights Amendment.

Given Schlafly's conservative background, an instant aversion to the amendment was what one would have expected. For as liberated as Schlafly herself was, she was never a fan of the women's liberation movement—with which ERA was closely identified. In her 1970 campaign for Congress, she had blasted the movement as "destructive of family living" and feminists as "selfish and misguided."

She had, after all, grown up in a very traditional family. Her mother worked and brought home the paycheck, but there was never a doubt that her father was the head of the house, the boss. Phyllis passed on that tradition to her children, raising her four boys and two girls with very clearly defined sex roles. She raised all six to be achievers, but she taught her boys that careers should be No. 1 in their lives, and her girls that careers should be No. 2, after family.

One would have thought that a constitutional amendment that was bound to spark unpredictable change and give more power to the federal government would have sparked serious misgivings not only in Schlafly but in most conservatives. However, in 1972, when ERA had passed both houses of Congress and was on its way to the states for ratification, it seemed, to most people, conservatives included, far from radical. ERA was nothing new—not by a long shot. It has been introduced annually in Congress since 1923. Although it might have sounded radical in 1920 when women, against fierce opposition, won the right to vote, a half century later, a constitutional guarantee of equality seemed long overdue. Even most conservative congressmen and state legislators found little wrong with ERA.

Times had changed. It was no longer socially or legally acceptable to discriminate against blacks and other minorities, and women began demanding that it be every bit as socially and legally unacceptable to discriminate against women. So they started agitating to push ERA out of committee onto the floor of Congress. Anyone who believed in simple equality, they argued, had to believe in ERA. It was so downright simple and just. All it said was:

1. Equality of rights under the law shall not be denied or abridged by the United States or by any State on account of sex.
2. The Congress shall have the power to enforce, by appropriate legislation, the provisions of this article.
3. This amendment shall take effect two years after the date of ratification.

Substitute the word "race" for the word "sex" at the end of the first section, women's leaders pointed out, and no politician in his right mind would have dared to stand up publicly and oppose ERA.

So it surprised no one that on October 12, 1971, the U. S. House passed ERA by 354 to 23; or that on March 22, 1972, the Senate approved ERA by 84 to 8. ERA opponents were hard to find. Support came from Democrats and Republicans, the left and the right. Birch Bayh was for it, but so was George Wallace. Ted Kennedy supported it, but so did Strom Thurmond. Bella Abzug promoted ERA as the Great American Panacea, but Spiro Agnew also had nice things to say about it.

Likewise, it surprised no one that, when Congress sent ERA to the states for ratification, it sent the states—conservative and liberal—into a mad scramble to be the first to ratify.

Hawaii could hardly wait. Within hours after word reached Honolulu of the U. S. Senate's approval, the legislature voted to ratify, without a word of opposition or debate. Nebraska, scurrying to be No. 2, passed it the next day, without a single dissenting vote. (Nebraska was in such a hurry, in fact, that it neglected to pass Section II of the three-section Amendment and had to pass it all over again six days later. Alaska passed Section I, but forgot Sections II and III.) The Delaware Senate passed ERA at 3:00 P.M. on March 22, an hour and forty minutes before the U. S. Senate passed it and submitted it to the states for ratification, a fact that brought a court challenge to Delaware's ratification.

Within that first week, New Hampshire, Iowa, Kansas, and Idaho ratified. Kansas, which devoted ten minutes to debate, was typical.

ERA passed by 205 to 7 in Massachusetts, but it also passed by 31 to 0 in West Virginia. Colorado passed it by 61 to 0. In no state was the vote even close.

Within a month, fourteen states ratified. The bandwagon

whizzed along and, within three months, twenty states ratified. Within a year, thirty states ratified. Only eight more were needed to make ERA a part of the Constitution. (The Constitution requires that three fourths of the states ratify [thirty-eight states]. Since 1919, Congress has required that states ratify within seven years. ERA's seven years expired on March 22, 1979.)

In March 1973—with nearly six years to spare before ERA's time limit expired—women's leaders predicted that within two months the eight states required to bring the total up to thirty-eight would ratify. "ERA will be part of the Constitution long before the year's out," said Martha Griffiths, then congresswoman from Michigan.

The congresswoman, who had shepherded ERA through Congress the year before, failed to take into account one factor—one person—Phyllis Schlafly.

As a religious, traditional woman, Schlafly found ERA distasteful. As a conservative, she found it appalling. A staunch believer that, when it comes to government, "less is better," Schlafly considered the second section of ERA, which gives enforcement power to the U. S. Congress, even worse than the first, which decrees a strict equality of rights under the law. The first section would require states to make vast changes in the laws in such private areas as marriage, divorce, child custody, and adoption. And the second section would effectively give Washington the power to rewrite those laws if they did not meet a national standard. "ERA would virtually reduce the states of this union to meaningless zeros on the nation's map," said Senator Sam J. Ervin—one of the very few critics of the Amendment—during Senate debate in 1972.

Schlafly, whose favorite target in speeches had always been "Big Brother" turning a once-diverse, vigorous, and independent country into a standardized, homogenized, helpless blob, agreed. And considering that Section II threatened to transfer some 70 percent of a state legislature's already rapidly dwindling power to the federal government, it was not hard to get a majority of state legislators to agree—especially when Schlafly presented specifics. Under ERA, she warned, the traditional family would become an endangered species.

When ERA was introduced into Congress in 1970, its sponsors omitted the Hayden modification, which had been part of the pending amendment for twenty years and stated: "Nothing in the amendment will be construed to deprive persons of the female sex of any of the rights, benefits, and exemptions now conferred by law on persons of the female sex." (for example, the "right" of a wife to be supported by her husband).

When ERA was on the floor of the Senate, Senator Ervin proposed nine separate amendments to ERA—all of which were defeated. The amendments would have retained preferential laws for wives, mothers, and widows and would have exempted women from the draft and combat duty.

Schlafly was disturbed by the fact that the ERA that was sent to the states compelled absolute equality—no amendments, no exceptions. (She said she would have supported ERA had Congress left in the Hayden modification or the Ervin amendments.)

Once ERA was ratified, the states would be forced to treat men and women equally under all circumstances, meaning that most laws requiring a husband to support his wife would become unconstitutional. Those laws obviously discriminated on the basis of sex because they did not impose the equal obligation on the wife to support her husband. The state of New York, for example, would have to change its law, which read simply, "Husband liable for support of his wife," to require mutual or reciprocal support.

Schlafly saw these changes, which experts on both sides of the issue agreed ERA would demand, as eventually weakening the traditional family. With the divorce rate soaring, young women would be less likely to leave the work force to devote themselves to husband and children. Becoming financially dependent on a male would be too big a gamble for many women to risk, especially because every year of not working would lessen their value in the job market.

The women who had already taken the gamble—the middle-aged, full-time homemakers with no job skills—would be, Schlafly decided, hurt most by ERA. (Not surprisingly, it was from this group that Schlafly drew most of her STOP ERA support.) Those women had gone into marriage in another era when it was assumed that it was the wife's duty to bear and raise children and the husband's duty to provide the support.[1] "ERA does not even include a 'grandmother clause,'" Schlafly was fond of saying.

The fact that ERA allowed no reasonable differences in treatment of the sexes would affect, Schlafly claimed, an enormous number of institutions. Women's colleges that received federal aid (about 99 percent of them) would not be able to continue admitting women only, because by so doing they discriminated "on account of sex." Protective labor laws for blue-collar women—such as those exempting women from compulsory overtime, allowing women extra rest periods and better restrooms, and putting a limit on weights they could be required to lift—would also be unconstitutional.

But to Schlafly these were minor ramifications in comparison with another law that would become unconstitutional if ERA were ratified—the federal law that exempted women from the draft and excluded them from military combat. While there was hot dispute over some of Schlafly's ERA-spawned horrors, there was no dispute over the draft issue. The House Judiciary Committee reported that, under ERA, "not only would women, including mothers, be subject to the

---

[1] It is true that many states, without ERA to compel them, have begun to sex-neutralize their family laws. However, Schlafly sees these new laws as fashionable but dangerous trends. Laws can be changed. A constitutional amendment can't be changed—except by another constitutional amendment.

draft, but the military would be compelled to place them in combat units alongside of men." That same year, Professor Thomas Emerson, writing in the *Yale Law Journal,* concurred: "The amendment permits no exceptions for the military. Neither the right to privacy nor any unique physical characteristic justifies different treatment of the sexes. . . ."

While others found the prospect of equality of sexes in the military heartening, Schlafly found it horrifying. Aside from the moral implications of men and women sharing foxholes, a coed military to Schlafly meant a weakened defense—according to Pentagon studies women have, on the average, 60 percent of the physical strength of men. The Soviet Army, she said ominously, is less than 1 percent female and its combat troops are exclusively male.

Schlafly saw several other by-products of ERA over which there was wide disagreement. The amendment's backers denounced these as "scare tactics," arguments that, they said, were about as sound as the flat-earth theory. Schlafly saw ERA as giving homosexuals the right to a marriage license and so the rights of married couples, such as the right to adopt infants. "ERA bans discrimination on account of sex, and it is precisely on account of sex that a state now denies a marriage license to a man and a man." She was not the first person to make this argument. In testifying before the Senate Judiciary Committee, Harvard Professor Paul Freund said, "If the law must be as undiscriminating concerning sex as it is toward race, it would follow that laws outlawing wedlock between members of the same sex would be as invalid as laws forbidding miscegenation." (Yale Professor Thomas Emerson disagreed: "ERA says you can't discriminate because of gender. It doesn't say you can't discriminate because of sexual preference.")

Schlafly also saw a link between ERA and abortion that has been, perhaps, the most controversial of her anti-ERA arguments. ERA, she said, would give women the constitutional right to an abortion because not to do so is discrimination—denying them their equal right with men not to be pregnant. When on January 22, 1973, the U. S. Supreme Court invalidated state anti-abortion laws, finding a right to abortion in the 14th Amendment (ratified in 1868 to give full citizenship rights to blacks), Schlafly pronounced the link strengthened: "No one else had ever seen abortion there for a hundred years, and abortion was clearly *not* intended by those who ratified the 14th Amendment. How much easier it will be to find an absolute, government-financed right to abortion in ERA!"

When Schlafly finished listing what ERA would do, she proceeded to what ERA would *not* do—guarantee equal pay for equal work; a point on which, again, both friends and foes of the amendment agreed. Like most provisions of the Constitution, ERA is directed to government, not individual, behavior. How a private employer treated his employee was not the business of ERA, and, in any case, a federal law—the Equal Employment Opportunity Act of 1972—already made it illegal for an employer to discriminate against women.

So she quickly labeled ERA the "Men's Liberation Amendment," arguing that it would transfer substantial old rights from women to men without giving women any substantial new rights in return.

For most people, first exposure to Phyllis Schlafly came in the mid-1970s, when she was already in the thick of the ERA battle. So they assume that the statements that opened this chapter—that Schlafly was a natural foe of ERA, born and bred to battle the amendment—are accurate. Even her closest associates tend to remember Phyllis Schlafly as opposed to ERA from the very start.

Thus it comes as a surprise to almost everyone that, back in 1971, Phyllis Schlafly, at home in Alton writing about ICBMs and megatonnage and warheads, was apathetic about

ERA. In fact, if pressed, she might have supported it. "I figured ERA was something between innocuous and mildly helpful," Schlafly recalled.

That year, Shirley Spellerberg, Schlafly's fellow conservative, was struggling to stop ERA from sailing through Congress and she tried to recruit her friend Phyllis, who declined. "Phyllis and I could have stopped ERA while it was still in Congress," sighed Spellerberg who, in the coming years as head of Florida STOP ERA, would spend hundreds of hours lobbying against the amendment. "I just couldn't get her to move."

Later in 1971, in December, a friend of Schlafly's asked her to come to Connecticut to debate a feminist on ERA. "ERA?" Schlafly replied incredulously. "I'm not interested in ERA. How about a debate on national defense?" Nothing doing. The friend insisted on ERA.

"I don't even know which side I'm on," Schlafly finally said in exasperation. She had other things on her mind, like the SALT I agreements, which would be signed in Moscow that next May and which Schlafly felt marked the beginning of the end of the United States as the premier nuclear power. With the presidential election less than a year away, she also had Richard Nixon on her mind. She could not support him in 1972. His policy of détente, not to mention his national-security adviser, Henry Kissinger, had made Nixon completely unacceptable, and she wanted to find a candidate who would be tougher in his dealings with the Russians.

"Look," the friend from Connecticut finally said, "I'll send you some background information on ERA. Just promise to read it. I know which side you'll be on after you do." She was right. Schlafly read the material and did some research of her own. ERA suddenly turned from innocuous to dangerous.

She was determined to stop it. It was too late to block approval in Congress—it had already passed the House, and the tide for passage in the Senate was too strong to turn. So Schlafly focused on the states—three quarters of which had to ratify ERA before it became the 27th Amendment to the Constitution.

The odds were certainly against Phyllis Schlafly. Still, she felt confident that if state legislators "knew what ERA really meant," they would vote not to ratify. At the time, even Phyllis' most fervent fans would have considered her a trifle presumptuous. But in retrospect, she had good reason for confidence. Until then, after all, nobody had mounted a national mass movement against the amendment. The very few individuals criticizing ERA were speaking locally, softly, and irregularly.

Phyllis Schlafly vowed to change all that. "I knew from the start," she said, "that I had found enough seriously wrong with ERA to stop it, or at least stall it, for an awfully long time, if only I could get the message out."

She realized that if she was going to get the message out she had to jump in the battle immediately, marshal the disorganized opposition, and march into the states. To the everlasting despair of ERA's confident backers, she did.

16

The Slaughter

In October 1972 Schlafly founded and appointed herself national chairman of STOP ERA. By February 1973, it seemed that just about every ERA news article contained the name Phyllis Schlafly in its lead. "Phyllis Schlafly led a group of opponents into Florida to carry off an unexpected defeat in the state Senate," reported one newsman. "The unexpected defeat in Illinois is seen as a result of intense political pressure led by Mrs. Schlafly," reported another. She seemed omnipotent, omnipresent.

It was a rare STOP ERA rally that Schlafly, armed with bullhorn and whistle and toy wagon full of leaflets and buttons, did not personally stage and direct. Her sense of public relations was shrewd. Photo- and evening-newsworthy activities abounded—a casket in the middle of a state capitol rotunda, a "Bury ERA" banner draped dramatically across—skits, costumes, special effects, refreshments, and smiling ladies.

In Illinois in April 1976, ERA was not scheduled for a vote, but Schlafly called a rally anyway, just to protest a Bella

Abzug-led march, planned for May, of several thousand ERA backers bused in from across the country. With the TV cameras whirring, Schlafly led her "girls" in her own composition of "Bella's Bunch Is Coming to Town" (sung to the tune of "Santa Claus Is Coming to Town").

> The buses are rolling all over the East.
> They start in New York till Springfield they reach.
> Bella's bunch is comin' to town.
> They couldn't get our local girls to vote for ERA.
> They had to advertise and bus,
> To try to get their way [etc.].

Two years later, in April 1978, Schlafly reduced an Illinois League of Women Voters Legislative Day to a circus—literally—by scheduling her own rally on the same day.

Ruth Clusen, president of the national organization, had flown to Springfield to announce that the League would contribute $150,000 to the Illinois ratification fight. Clusen was in the midst of her speech when the Reverend John Peck of Rockford began prancing around in a gorilla suit as a prelude to presenting a banana to Phyllis; the banana sporting a sign, "Don't monkey with the Constitution."

Soon after the Reverend Peck stole the show, it was Phyllis' turn. She announced to her troops that *Playboy* had contributed five thousand dollars to the pro-ERA cause and then led them in another original composition titled "Here Comes *Playboy* Cottontail":

> Here comes *Playboy* cottontail,
> Hopping down the bunny trail,
> Trying to buy the votes for ERA.
> Telling every girl and boy,
> You can only have your joy,
> By becoming gender-free or gay.

Given the choice between a dull speech and a gorilla-suited reverend, it's not hard to imagine where the television cameras lingered.

A month later, recalled Illinois senator and ERA activist Susan Catania, "We were sure we had the votes. Our people had worked for these legislators with the understanding they'd back ERA. Then Phyllis showed up marching bunches of women in frilly long dresses who told legislators that if they voted for ERA, they'd be in trouble come the next election. My colleagues came back to the chamber appalled, 'I didn't know all these women in my district are against ERA.'"

When Schlafly called a rally, women came—in crowds. Her organization became the envy of politicians, who watched her spirited, jam-packed gatherings and wondered, "My God, how does she do it?" For openers, organization—precise organization and a strict hierarchy of workers.

In Illinois, for example, she could rally a thousand women for a routine demonstration by notifying her top lieutenants—fifty-nine chairmen, one for each of the state's fifty-nine legislative districts. And that was nothing because, all told, she had twenty thousand people working for her in the state, some monitoring only their block or bowling team. She communicated frequently with all of them—from the lowliest to the most powerful—via chain calls and notices in her *Eagle Forum Newsletter*. Once she triggered the system, mobilizing twelve thousand people for a rally at the Illinois Capitol was simple—and foolproof.

But still, Phyllis Schlafly was fighting ridiculously tough odds. Everyone from Jimmy Carter to George Meany to Erma Bombeck was lobbying for ERA. That, however, just seemed to make Schlafly more determined. She was, after all, the same Phyllis Schlafly who had, fourteen years earlier, written about her hero Barry Goldwater:

"Any political leader can score a win if he has the votes in his pocket, just as any general can win if he has more men and more weapons. The true test of leadership is the ability to carry your side to victory when the odds are against you."

In a spectacularly shrewd political move, Schlafly turned the support of some of the country's most influential people and organizations from ERA's asset to its liability. She cast and relentlessly promoted herself as the underdog. She was David battling Goliath. She was the courageous, crusading individual battling the big, bad Washington bureaucracy—*even* the President of the United States.

Concentrating her attack on the White House, she performed brilliantly, blasting Jimmy Carter and Rosalynn Carter, charging that the First Family had a vested, even a sinister, interest in pushing through ERA. At the very least, she claimed, the man who was elected to uphold the Constitution was violating it by interfering in the ratification process, which the Constitution vests in the Congress and state legislatures.

"The only way they got ERA through Indiana," Schlafly bellowed through a bullhorn to a group rallied in Springfield, "was by telephone calls from Rosalynn Carter, who turned on her southern charm and told Senator Wayne Townsend, 'I'll campaign for you if you vote for ERA.'"

A month later, Phyllis and her Eagles picketed the White House. "Please Mrs. Carter, let us stay home and be mothers too," read one placard. "Article V of the Constitution gives ratification power exclusively to Congress and state legislatures," Schlafly told an ABC news reporter covering the rally. "Rosalynn Carter is part of the Executive branch. She wakes up every morning on an Executive branch bed. She made calls to a number of state legislators on an Executive branch telephone.[1]

---

[1] Schlafly was bipartisan in her criticism of the President and his wife. Two years earlier, she had led a demonstration in front of the White House to protest Betty Ford's lobbying of state legislators.

"Just the week before," Schlafly added, "members of the Virginia legislature telegraphed Mrs. Carter and asked her to keep out of their affairs." She pulled out a copy of the telegram: "Let us fairly debate the merits of ERA free from Executive branch pressure that violates our Constitution."

Just how active had the President been? Very, but, due to Schlafly's genius for public relations and just plain politicking, not very successful. The President said women need ERA. Schlafly said Washington politicians need ERA. The President whispered a promise in a legislator's ear; Schlafly whispered a threat in the other. For every one Washington lobbyist dispatched to the provinces by Jimmy Carter, Phyllis Schlafly dispatched a hundred STOP-ERAers—housewives from the legislator's own district who could make or break him in the next election.

Shortly after Election Day 1976, Rosalynn Carter hosted a luncheon for state legislators in Georgia and appealed to them to "give ERA to Jimmy as an Inauguration present." Schlafly took to television and radio denouncing Washington interference, and Georgia gave Jimmy and ERA another defeat.

In 1978, the President promised that he would take the Democratic National Convention to Miami if the Florida legislature would ratify ERA. Schlafly urged legislators to hold their ground, not to yield to "blackmail." The state forfeited fifty million dollars of business when Florida refused again to ratify.

The next year, the Florida Senate rejected ERA for the fourth time, despite intense lobbying by Governor Bob Graham and a group of Carter aides. According to a report from the Associated Press, "The governor tried to entice key senators off the floor so he and White House aides . . . could try to persuade them to change their votes." Following a huddle with Phyllis Schlafly, Democratic Senator Dempsey Barron complained to the press, "Senators are being pulled out of the

Senate and being threatened by the White House and other places." The STOP ERA ladies sent a bottle of Elmer's Glue-All in to each anti-ERA Senator with a note, "Please stay glued to your seat." The Senators stuck, and ERA failed again.

During his campaign in 1975, Jimmy Carter addressed the Oklahoma Senate: "I favor the ERA, but I don't think it would be appropriate for the President to try to involve himself directly in the deliberations of the Oklahoma state legislature or any other." Schlafly didn't let anyone forget that statement when, in February 1979, the Carters invited Oklahoma Governor George Nigh, his wife, and five key Democratic members of the Oklahoma legislature to lunch at the White House—to set strategy for pushing through ERA in Oklahoma. Phyllis called her Eagles out, in droves, and, later that month, Oklahoma ERA proponents failed even to get ERA to the floor for a vote.

Pounding away, Schlafly convinced legislators that ERA meant Washington breathing down their necks. So when President Carter asked Governor Nigh what he could do to help, the governor, a staunch ERA backer, pleaded with him to keep himself, his aides, his family, or anyone who smacked of Washington, out of the state.

A frustrated President ignored that advice and continued using traditional political pressure tactics to push ERA. North Carolina Congressman Lamar Gudger cast a key vote for the ERA time extension and got $1.6 million for the Asheville Airport. Gudger got his airport, but Schlafly got hundreds of women to the Capitol in a "prayer chain," and the Administration got another defeat for ERA in North Carolina.

On October 23, 1979, Carter held an "ERA Summit" at the White House for eight hundred ERA leaders and officials from unratified states. As reported in the New York *Times,* "Carter pledged the full support of his Administration, including such specific actions as . . . pointedly reminding un-ratified states of the need for the Equal Rights Amendment every time federal grants or loans are made."

To a press conference packed with reporters and network news cameras, Schlafly blasted the President for "blatant blackmail," adding for good measure, "During the week Iran was going down the tube, President Carter was sitting in the Oval Office telephoning North Carolina senators begging them to vote for ERA. That just proves what we've been saying all along. The real beneficiaries of ERA are the federal politi-cians and payrollers because they see it as an enormous transfer of power from the states to the federal government. People won't stand for that anymore. The whole momentum of the country is moving away from that."

In no state did Jimmy Carter lobby as avidly as in Illinois —the first state to ratify the women's suffrage amendment; the only northern industrial state that hadn't ratified ERA; the state that ERA strategists designated *the* key state—once Illi-nois ratifies, others will fall in line—and, of course, Phyllis Schlafly's home. Schlafly met him, and, so far, has beat him, every step of the way.

In December 1976, when the President was at the height of his popularity—a month after the election and a month be-fore the Inauguration—Carter, Vice President Walter Mon-dale, and the late AFL-CIO head, George Meany, all per-sonally telephoned wavering Illinois legislators. (Carter's daughter-in-law Judy made personal appearances.) On De-cember 16, 1976, ERA was defeated again. And things didn't get any better.

Phyllis and her Eagles lobbied legislators relentlessly, armed with loaves of homemade bread ("from the bread-makers to the breadwinners"), with jars of homemade jam festooned with red ribbons ("preserve us from a congressional jam; vote against the ERA sham"), and with homemade apple pies ("I'm for Mom and apple pie").

In May 1978 Carter traveled to Springfield to address a joint session of the Illinois General Assembly. "The eyes of the nation now are focused on the men and women in this chamber. What you do here in this chamber in the next few weeks might very well determine whether women do have those equal rights guaranteed in the U. S. Constitution or whether they do not."

Schlafly immediately called a press conference to charge that "someone high in the Chicago administration" had told her that President Carter threatened to cut off federal funds unless [then Chicago] Mayor Michael Bilandic pressured more Chicago legislators to vote for ERA. She charged that Carter sent Vice President Mondale to Chicago "to reinforce the threat that the Carter administration would make Bilandic's life miserable unless he used his power to force Chicago-area legislators against their will to vote yes on ERA."[2] When ERA came up for a vote a couple of weeks later, several legislators said they voted no because "we couldn't tolerate blackmail."

Illinois Republican Governor James Thompson was also working overtime for ERA that month, not to help President Carter, but to help himself—a politician with an acknowledged ambition for national office. Also, like many of the political leaders of the state that calls itself "the Land of Lin-

---

[2] Less than a year later, Bilandic was out of office, replaced by Chicago's first woman mayor, Jane Byrne, who promised "We will call people nicely and ask them to think it [voting for ERA] over and then pull the levers if necessary." In a candid interview with Byrne's assistant press secretary, Bob Saigh, Paul Zemitzsch of the St. Louis *Globe-Democrat* reported Saigh saying, "The federal government would be most appreciative and gratified if ERA passes in Illinois. That message has been brought by many different people in Washington to Chicago." The Byrne administration, he added, would receive "unspelled benefits from an appreciative Washington. There are no promises. . . . But it's nice to have them remember you."

coln," he was embarrassed that Illinois had attached itself to the cluster of ten southern anti-ERA states.[3]

One newsman reported that Thompson offered "jobs, roads, and bridges" in exchange for votes. Minutes before the vote on ERA, the governor telephoned legislators on the House floor. "Do you understand what's at stake here?" he asked Republican William A. Margalus. "It's the end of me as the leader of the party."

Thompson was working hard, but Schlafly was working harder. (In the course of Thompson's term, six Republican votes switched from the governor's side to Schlafly's.) Schlafly didn't limit her lobbying to legislators. "The Spoiler," as one columnist dubbed her, had a meeting with Thompson's lieutenant governor, Dave O'Neal, and convinced him, as O'Neal later put it, "These people are being ganged up on by the President, the Vice President, the governor, the mayor, even former President Ford and his wife." O'Neal called the same legislators his boss had called, but instead of pleading with them to support ERA, he urged them to "stick to your guns and vote against ERA." They did.

Jimmy Carter was not the only "celebrity" to visit Illinois. Also making personal appearances in Illinois during the days before the June 1978 vote were the real thing—Alan Alda, Marlo Thomas, Jean Stapleton, and Carol Burnett.[4]

[3] Also four western states—Oklahoma, Arizona, Utah, and Nevada. The southern states are Missouri, Arkansas, Louisiana, Mississippi, Alabama, Florida, Georgia, South Carolina, North Carolina, and Virginia. States that have rescinded their ratification fall into the same southern/western split: Kentucky, Tennessee, Nebraska, South Dakota, and Idaho.

[4] They came at the suggestion of ERA-Illinois lobbyists hired with $150,000 contributed by the League of Women Voters. (Patricia de Luna of Knight-Ridder reported that the California ERA Campaign Fund had spent $250,000 to send celebrities and dollars into unratified states.)

Phyllis Schlafly stuck to the tried and true—her ladies in long dresses, the homemade bread and apple pies, the catchy ditties, the telegrams, the threats of retaliation at election time. On June 22, 1978, after Carol Burnett beseeched legislators to vote yes on ERA—"I have three daughters. Unless they're protected by the Constitution, what's going to happen to them?"—ERA went down to defeat in the Illinois House, for the seventh year.

"They have the movie-star money and we have the voters," Schlafly boasted. "They buy lobbyists and we turn out the vote. They glorify ERA and we smash it." And that was no idle boast.

Two springs later, in 1980, ERA came to a vote again in Illinois. NOW president Ellie Smeal called that year's campaign "the most extensive in ERA's history." A Chicago rally the day before Mother's Day drew an estimated 50,000 people from 50 states, and a host of movie and television stars. Labor leaders, in their strongest show of support for ERA, contributed thousands of marchers and dollars and workers. It appeared that this year *was* different; that ERA *would* finally pass. Everyone from the President to the mayor of Chicago predicted victory. (So did Phyllis Schlafly, but her perennial claim that the pro-ERAers just didn't have the votes sounded, this time, like wishful thinking.)

Jimmy Carter invited leaders of the Illinois legislature to Washington and promised to "do anything that would be helpful." He kept his promise. Two black legislators, for example, threatened to withhold their yes vote to protest a new state human rights agency (a consolidation of three agencies). The President telephoned both men, invited them to the White House, and promised to set up meetings in their districts with federal housing and job officials. (They voted yes in exchange, Schlafly charged, for Carter's promise of a housing project in their districts.)

Mayor Jane Byrne also made an all-out effort. The House Majority Leader credited her with rounding up five new votes for ERA. Schlafly—joined by five female members of the House—immediately charged that Chicago ward committeemen were forcing Chicago legislators to switch from no to yes or lose hundreds of city patronage jobs in their districts. The charges drew little attention. Governor Thompson went to work full-time for ERA and was credited with picking up two new votes.

The vote was announced for Wednesday May 14. Hundreds of green-clad supporters and red-clad opponents waited in the House gallery from dawn to dusk, only to learn the vote wouldn't be called. A head count showed ERA two votes short.

While Schlafly, surrounded by reporters, claimed victory, Rep. John Matijevich, a Democrat and ERA's sponsor, speaking from the House floor, blasted Gov. Thompson. "I am certain that the governor has provided virtually nothing." House Minority Leader George Ryan, a Republican and ERA advocate, sprang to his feet, "The difference," he shouted, "is that we are not led by the mayor of Chicago because we've got two jobs. . . . We speak for ourselves." Thirty house Republicans petitioned the governor to stop lobbying for ERA and let legislators vote their consciences. Thompson suggested that the pro-ERA people wait to call another vote until January 1981 when tempers had cooled and the new legislature had been seated. (Several pro-ERA candidates won in the primaries and many observers believe that ERA really does have a good chance of passing in 1981.)

Wednesday was a bad day for the pro-ERA side. Thursday was worse. An anti-ERA legislator charged that television producer Norman Lear had set up a $200,000 slush fund to push through the Amendment. (Days earlier, Lear had donated $500,000 to establish a pro-ERA "Edith Bunker Memorial Fund.") Two legislators claimed a colleague had told them he'd been offered $10,000 to support ERA. The charges were never substantiated. But another charge that surfaced that day was substantiated. On June 5, a Sangamon County Grand Jury indicted a NOW field organizer on charges of bribery and solicitation, both felonies. The NOW volunteer was alleged to have offered a legislator a $1,000 campaign contribution (she wrote the offer on the back of her business card and signed her name) to vote yes on ERA.[5] Thompson pleaded again with pro-ERAers to postpone a vote until early 1981, or, at least, until after the election in November 1980, during the lame duck session, when legislators from anti-ERA districts could, perhaps, be convinced to vote yes.

NOW leaders ignored him. ERA came up for a vote again on June 18, preceded, again, by predictions from everyone, including Thompson, that this time they had the votes. Schlafly, passing out bread and posing with babies, told reporters, "They always say they have the votes. I don't think they do." When the vote was finally called at 6:00 P.M., after hours of counting heads and lobbying, ERA fell a whopping five votes short—three fewer than the last vote in 1978.

Within a year after Phyllis Schlafly entered the battle, the ERA bandwagon started losing steam. In 1974, only three states ratified. In 1975, only one state ratified, but sixteen states rejected. In 1977, one state—Indiana—passed ERA (by only one vote after fierce lobbying by Rosalynn Carter), but nine states defeated or tabled it. In 1978, ERA proponents failed to win a single ratification, while STOP ERA

[5] On August 23, 1980, an eight-woman, four-man jury found Wanda Brandstetter guilty of bribery but innocent of solicitation. Her attorneys immediately filed an appeal.

defeated the amendment in six states. In Illinois that year, the House turned down what one reporter dubbed "the star-crossed amendment" for the seventh year straight. 1980 marked the ninth year that the Illinois legislature had grappled with ERA and rejected it.

So in the first twelve months of its life, the year before Phyllis Schlafly got her troops mobilized, ERA amassed thirty ratifications. In the next eight years, it accumulated a measly five. To add insult to injury, five of the thirty-five ratified states, convinced that their yes votes on ERA had been hasty and wrong, voted to rescind their ratification—the first state to do so being Nebraska (the very state that had rushed to be No. 2), after a legislative breakfast meeting with Phyllis Schlafly.

If rescissions are held to be legal, and this is a big "if"—an "if" that may ultimately be decided by the U. S. Supreme Court—then the ERAers' net score for seven years of back- and budget-breaking work was zero. In March of 1973 they had thirty ratifications; in March of 1980 they still had thirty.

In 1979, ERA made constitutional history by becoming the first amendment ever to reach its seven-year limit still unratified. The year before, Congress, under enormous pressure from the pro-ERA side, took the unprecedented step of extending the time for ratification from the original seven years (March 22, 1979) to ten years, three months (June 30, 1982). The year 1981 marks nine years since Congress sent ERA to the states for ratification—an extraordinarily long time considering that since 1917, when Congress began setting seven-year limits, no amendment had ever required more than three years, eleven months for ratification. The average time for ratification is sixteen months, and the most recent amendment—the 26th Amendment, lowering the voting age to eighteen—required less than four months. The controversial 19th Amendment (women's suffrage) was ratified in fourteen months, twenty-two days.[6]

Convincing Congress to pass the extension was a life-and-death victory for the pro-ERA forces, because it was obvious that, without the extension, ERA would have died on March 22, 1979. But Phyllis Schlafly quickly turned that fleeting taste of victory to ashes.

She stepped up her appearances before television cameras and state legislative hearings to denounce the extension as "unfair and unconstitutional." Congress did not have the right to extend, she argued, because the right wasn't specifically or implicitly granted by the Constitution. What really irked Schlafly, though, was that Congress passed the extension by a simple majority. Original approval of ERA had required a two-thirds majority and so, Schlafly said, citing the Constitution, do all decisions on constitutional amendments. For the first time in her career, the New York *Times* and Washington *Post* and other major newspapers, all of which had been solidly behind ERA, agreed with her. In fact, the country's most prestigious papers opposed the extension editorially.

"If ERA were a cat," quipped one Missouri legislator after a Schlafly speech, "it would be dead by now." "These ERA folks," groused an Arizona legislator, "have forced us to spend as much time on ERA as we have on rewriting our state's entire criminal code. But the only effect on me and other ERA opponents is that it makes us dig in our heels."

Illinois League of Women Voters President Janet Otwell explained the extension's *raison d'être:* "They [legislators] are going to say, 'Oh my God, another three years. I'm going to vote for it and get it over with.'"

---

[6] Chief Justice Charles Evans Hughes explained why a limit was necessary: ". . . ratification must be sufficiently contemporaneous in the required number of states to reflect the will of the people in all sections at relatively the same period of time."

Schlafly pleaded with legislators to hold their ground. They did. In 1978—the year the extension passed—the proponents did not win a single state, while Phyllis and troops racked up a string of small but crucial victories—defeats on the floor or in committee—in Nevada, Virginia, Arkansas, Arizona, South Dakota, North Carolina, Illinois, and Oklahoma— despite a well-financed lobbying campaign in the last three states. In 1979, the extension in effect, ERA was defeated in nine states and passed in none. Utah's Senate took the un- precedented step of passing a resolution notifying Congress that Utah refuses to ratify ERA.

Another League of Women Voters official—Alice Kin- kead, the League's ERA director—concluded sadly, "Phyllis has taken the extension and hit us over the head with it. Per- sonally I don't think we'll pick up a single new state."

When Congress was debating the extension, it also took up the even more sensitive question of rescission—whether legis- latures that had ratified ERA could vote to withdraw their ratification. Congress refused to pass the so-called "fair-play amendment," which would have guaranteed the right of states to rescind during the extension period.[7]

In other words, a state like Illinois that had voted down ERA every year for seven years would have until June 1982 to change its mind and vote yes. But a state like Kansas that had voted yes—*sans* debate or hearings—could not change its mind from yes to no. "If this policy were applied to women individually, in other contexts, it would surely and properly be denounced as the height of male chauvinist sexism," stated the Chicago *Tribune* in an editorial titled, "Unequal Rights for ERA."

[7] By March 22, 1979, five states had already rescinded. Congress did not address itself to that issue, but rather to the issue of whether, dur- ing the three-year, three-month extension, states would be allowed to rescind as well as to ratify.

Yale Law School professor Charles Black vigorously lobbied against an extension that did not allow rescissions. "The extension of time for ratification but not for rescission would be so grotesque that I should think one would not have to reach the constitutional question, but . . . I am firmly of the opinion that lopsided extension would be unconstitutional."

And so, irony of ironies, ERA may end up being the first constitutional amendment whose fate, instead of hinging on the fifty states, will hinge on nine U. S. Supreme Court justices—all men.

As women's groups prepared for the final ratification push, the editors of thirty-six women's magazines agreed (as they had in July 1976) to devote space in their November 1979 issues to discussing how ERA would benefit women.

Ms. titled its article "ERA—What if It Fails?"

What if it does? Unless Congress passes an extension to the extension, ERA leaders would have to take their case to Congress all over again. "It will be much harder than it was six years ago," predicted Rep. Don Edwards (D., Calif.), who masterminded the extension, "because of Phyllis Schlafly and all the opposition she has generated."

Former Senator Sam J. Ervin, Jr., who seemed to out-Schlafly Schlafly in finding monstrous defects in ERA, wrote in a congratulatory letter to the STOP ERA leader that even if ERA got past Congress again, proponents "probably couldn't get half a dozen states to ratify."

How did Phyllis Schlafly do it? That was the question that a lot of people wanted answered.

17

How She Did It

That Phyllis Schlafly somehow did it and did it alone was a given. In the minds of friends and foes alike, Phyllis Schlafly was the reason for ERA's misfortunes. Depending on which side one was on, Schlafly was a supervillain or a superstar, but she was always larger than life. And that accounted for a good part of her power. She inspired women. They loved her. They idolized her. They would do anything for her. They waited in line for her autograph.

In 1973 Phyllis Schlafly led a contingent of STOP ERAers to Springfield, where ERA was scheduled for a vote in the Illinois House. There was barely one chair for every thirty women waiting—many for hours—outside the House chamber. Suddenly heads turned, murmurs swept the crowd. Phyllis had arrived, and judging by the stir she created, she might have been Phil Donahue dropping by the Capitol rotunda.

Immediately a chair became available. Phyllis sat, knees together, back never touching the back of the chair, an open briefcase in her lap, out of which she worked, oblivious to the commotion around her. When any of the women had a question, she came to the chair to ask. "There was no more need for Schlafly to move than for a colonel to leave his command post," observed one reporter.

Six years later, November 1979, her "girls" remained star-struck. The luster had still not dulled.

The rain had been falling since before dawn, and with temperatures dropping, it would soon be safer to negotiate the roads with ice skates than with the galoshes the women assembled in Sally Matthews' Downers Grove kitchen wore.

It was 6:30 A.M., the Tuesday before Thanksgiving, but it was obvious that the fifteen women were not assembled to make fresh cranberry sauce or to bake bread—although the suburban bilevel was filled with the glorious fragrance of freshly baked whole-wheat bread.

"OK, the windows are clear," said a stocky man wearing a slush-coated Chicago Bears beanie. "Now you girls remember," he advised the middle-aged women, "this is a van and it'll tumble if you take it too fast."

The women boarded a rented van parked in the driveway, each carrying several loaves of the foil-wrapped bread. Sally got behind the wheel, waved to her husband, and they skidded off to Springfield to fill the House gallery—at the request of Phyllis Schlafly, who had warned that ERA might come up for a vote.

"I've got twenty-four people coming for Thanksgiving," said Dorothy Meyers of Rolling Meadows, "plus all my kids coming home from school and relatives coming from Peoria. I'll just stay up all night Wednesday."

"My husband was just mad as the blazes," chirped in Nancy Callaghan of Downers Grove. "It's two days before Thanksgiving and you're gallivantin' off to Springfield. Are you nuts?" she mimicked him. "I'd better make his chestnut stuffing from scratch or I'll never hear the end of it," she said, giggling. "It really should set a day. I'll have to do it tonight when I get home."

"When Michelle called me," said Sally, "she mentioned Phyllis was counting on a thousand people. Leave it to the libs to threaten to bring up ERA before Thanksgiving. Oh well, I guess it's better than just before Christmas."

Closed roads and treacherous roads and collision-caused gaperblocks made the trip to the state Capitol take twice as long as it should have. The women climbed down from the van, bones cracking, to join a group of some fifteen hundred women under a sea of umbrellas.

"It was an empty threat," Phyllis Schlafly was telling the crowd. "But it will come up before Christmas, and so I'll have to ask you all to wait for a call and come out again." Then she unleashed a complicated set of instructions and divided her women into "combat teams" with legislators as their targets. "Be sure to attach the 'from the breadmakers to the bread-winners' stickers. Let's huddle back here in two hours 'cause the TV crews will be back and we can make their deadline for the evening news. And don't forget to smile."

The women finally boarded their van for home long after dinnertime. They shared one loaf of leftover bread and agreed to rerent the van whenever Phyllis' call came. "I'd no sooner skip this than I would my son's Little League debut. Some things just take priority," Nancy said.

"I have nothing to offer the people who work for me. I've never had a dime from the government or any company," Phyllis claimed at every opportunity. "I don't have any paid STOP ERA staff, a public-relations agent, a press secretary, or a professional fund-raiser. I have no paid lobbyists—no goodies to hand out. The only reason somebody would work against ERA is because she really believed in what she was doing. She's not going to get any free trips, or any nice, paid staff job in Washington like the ERAers have to offer."

Unquestionably Schlafly's supporters believe in what they're doing, but even more so, they believe in Phyllis Schlafly.

Sibyl Bellis, an East Alton resident and active ERA backer, touched on the key to her opponent's success. "You find ERA people just as committed but they can't get all that excited about it. They get mad, but it's not the same sort of thing because it isn't personal loyalty. I don't feel a personal loyalty to Ellie Smeal [president of NOW]. I support NOW and everything it does, but I can't see myself traveling around to do things for Ellie Smeal, just because it's Ellie Smeal."

Phyllis Schlafly because she's Phyllis Schlafly had a lot to do with ERA's unexpected woes. There was no question in the minds of the people who licked STOP ERA envelopes and manned the phone banks and carried the placards that but for the grace of Phyllis Schlafly went STOP ERA. If Schlafly were to disappear tomorrow there were not many STOP ERAers—from the lowliest doorbell ringers to Phyllis' top lieutenants—who doubted that the opposition would somehow eke out a victory.

Not even the most talented STOP ERAers, such as Shirley Spellerberg, a Florida leader, or Elaine Donnelly, a thirty-two-year-old Michigan leader—aggressive, attractive, and a whiz on television—were able to name anyone who could fill Phyllis' shoes. "There is no replacement for Phyllis Schlafly," said Spellerberg. "It takes a special talent to do what Phyllis has done, and I don't know anyone else who has it."

Her supporters become positively misty-eyed when talking about their Phyllis. Every year, Schlafly holds a leadership conference that climaxes in a Saturday-evening banquet at which the STOP ERA commander formally addresses her lieutenants. "That's the time she gets her troops really revved up and inspired for the next year," explained Virginia STOP ERA leader Kathleen Teague. She also presents her "Eagle Awards." "That's the big event," said the thirty-one-year-old career political activist (executive director of a national organization of conservative state legislators). "Eagles who have done outstanding work that year get an award—the personally signed framed Eagle award. That's a big event," she repeated, pointing to her own hanging in a prominent spot in her office. "That's really an honor to win that. This year Phyllis instituted her Super Eagle Award, for service to the cause above and beyond. That's the bronze eagle I have on my file cabinet there and it was really a thrill to have won it. I think it means more to me than anything I've ever gotten from anyone. Phyllis Schlafly is . . . well, she's just one of a kind, irreplaceable."

Is it possible that these women were afraid to mention a successor? That Phyllis Schlafly had some power over them that made them unwilling to entertain the possibility that Phyllis, as divine as she is to many of her followers, does not rule by divine right?

"Of course," said Schlafly's opponents. But were that the case, it would seem that some disenchanted STOP ERAer would, from time to time, have taken a shot—anonymous, perhaps, but still a shot—at "Madame Queen," as one ERA activist called Schlafly. Yet, in eight years of operation, a disgruntled member has yet to surface.

Reporters who could always dig up some one disillusioned member of any organization wondered, as Alton *Telegraph* reporter Doug Thompson put it, "why some lady in Ohio who's sick of doing all the work so Phyllis can have all the glory" hasn't gone public. It's been eight years now and I've never heard a public denunciation of Phyllis by any of her own. I just can't believe someone's not out there. I could go out this afternoon and find, without hardly trying, eighteen prominent feminists who hate Bella [Abzug], but I'm sure I couldn't find one anti-feminist who hates Phyllis Schlafly—in fact, who doesn't *love* Phyllis Schlafly."

In every organization, Schlafly said, there has to be one person on top pulling the strings, and in STOP ERA—she founded it and appointed herself chairman—there was never any doubt who had the control, or who was going to keep it. Schlafly created no mechanism for transfer of power, no board of directors, no annual meetings where new officers are elected. There are no resolutions, no tangents, and, apparently, no backbiting, infighting, plotting. There are not even any dues (just contributions). Schlafly described STOP ERA as more of a movement than an organization in the usual sense of the word.

The movement, paradoxically, is quite decentralized. Hundreds of little groups flourish in towns or cities or suburbs, some essentially block clubs, others covering a whole town, some having coed memberships, some church-related. The groups raise their own funds, elect their own officers, lobby their own state legislators in their own way. STOP ERAers in Miami don't have to do things the same way they do them in Little Rock. There is no central bureaucracy to issue policies or standards or paperwork or red tape. There is only Phyllis Schlafly who sets a national strategy, who makes STOP ERA visible by her constant appearances in the national media, and who serves as a consultant, a resource person, on call day or night.

At the Schlafly home, three phones ring incessantly, and the callers, when they aren't reporters, are bound to be STOP ERAers with questions—a woman in South Carolina who was testifying before the state legislature and needed to know what effect passage of ERA would have on her state's divorce law; a woman in Virginia who was holding a fund raiser for an anti-ERA state legislator and needed tips on publicizing it.

"She spends the night at my house all the time," said Kathleen Teague. "We'd get home at eleven at night and she'd say, 'Let's see, North Carolina was going to have a vote in committee today on such and such. I better call our gal up there and see how things went. The girls in Florida are going to have a big press conference in Tallahassee tomorrow and I better call up to see if everything's OK.' So she'd get on the phone to Tallahassee and she'd say, 'Pat, is everything set? Now, read me your press release. Fine . . . good, that's good . . . fine.' Then they'd ask a question and she'd say, 'Now, the answer to that is that the Supreme Court ruled in 1973 that da, da, da, da. That's how you answer that question. That's right,' and then she'd repeat it and it was obvious that it was being written down."

Just how important is Phyllis Schlafly?

"Indispensable," said Illinois Congressman Henry Hyde. "She's the Howard Jarvis of ERA. Individuals don't make that much difference anymore. I can think of only two in the last decade—Howard Jarvis (Proposition 13) and Phyllis Schlafly. Without her, I can say without a twinge of doubt, ERA would be part of the Constitution—unquestionably."

Columnist Ellen Goodman wrote recently, "I have a friend who once said that the quickest way to pass the ERA would be to send Ruth Carter Stapleton into Alton and have her convert Phyllis Schlafly."

Joseph Llyvejd, writing in the New York *Times Magazine,* agreed: "Fred Schlafly should be given his due as the man who made possible the movement that has battled ERA to a virtual standstill. ERA would have been ratified . . . if only he had kept his wife and mother of his six children at home in Alton in her place."

"Phyllis Schlafly *is* the STOP ERA movement," said Martha Shirk, a Washington correspondent for Schlafly's hometown St. Louis *Post-Dispatch.* "There don't seem to be any other leaders in the organization. She's the spokesman on everything. Any question you have on ERA, you call STOP ERA, which is Phyllis' home, and you get Phyllis, who defines their stands. I think it's a single-person organization with a mass following. I've never seen anything like it."

In November 1977 during the International Women's Year Conference, Phyllis Schlafly and Eleanor Smeal appeared on

PBS's "MacNeil/Lehrer Report." Robert MacNeil introduced the program: "To satisfy our own curiosity as to who really does speak for America's women we commissioned the Roper Organization to do a nationwide poll." 48 percent of the respondents, he reported, "did not identify with the women's-rights movement or Phyllis Schlafly. . . . Clear support for Phyllis Schlafly seems to hover around 20 percent for all groups." So here on the one side, at least according to a leading political commentator, was the women's-rights movement with hundreds of leaders and factions. Here on the other side was Phyllis Schlafly.

In public, ERA backers blamed a right-wing conspiracy for ERA's woes; a conspiracy controlled by a combination of anti-abortionists, John Birchers, Mormons, corporate honchos, the Catholic Church, etc. Phyllis Schlafly, they claimed, was a mere tool. "If it weren't Phyllis, it would be some other Barbie Doll of the right," said one ERA leader. In private, and off the record, most blamed Phyllis Schlafly, which may explain why she is so frequently called a "witch."

Even male conservatives, whom one might expect would now want to grab a piece of the credit, pointed to Phyllis Schlafly as the reason for ERA's transformation from "a sure thing" to "a very dubious proposition." "If Phyllis Schlafly hadn't gotten involved with ERA, I think it's unquestionably true that it would today be part of our Constitution," said Representative George Hansen (R., Ida.). "A single person can change the destiny of history sometimes. . . . When everybody else kind of gives up—they see they're losing and figure, 'I'll go fight somewhere else'—Phyllis is the kind of person who hangs in there. The fiercer the odds, the tougher she gets."

If her supporters considered Schlafly superhuman, Schlafly herself was more realistic. If her fans thought their leader's charisma could move mountains, Schlafly knew that charisma starts fading with the first defeat.

When Phyllis Schlafly took on ERA, she had been active in politics for twenty-five years. She understood the nitty-gritty of organizing. She understood that while a Schlafly-at-center-stage rally was bound to grab headlines, it would not, necessarily, change votes. She had spent enough time studying military strategy to know that a general, even the most invincible, is powerless without properly trained troops; troops that could do the only thing that counts in politics—turn out the vote.

"It's fun to come to Springfield and bring your sandwiches and mill around the Capitol," Schlafly told her troops on a very cold, damp day in February 1975. "But where the issue will be decided is in the ballot box in November."

Schlafly may sound like an ideologue, but she doesn't act like one. She may claim "God is on our side" but, as she told Illinois STOP ERAers in a 1980 "action" letter, "We should not expect God to stuff the ballot box for us; it is *our* job to get the votes."

Every October since 1968—four years before ERA—she has held "political-action leadership conferences" in a St. Louis hotel, attracting three hundred to four hundred of her top lieutenants from all over the country. The program offers not a single fashion show or museum tour—just three mornings, afternoons, and evenings packed with meetings and workshops and inspirational speeches—all designed to train women in the fine art of political organizing; in getting "pro-family" (that is, anti-ERA) candidates, regardless of party, elected on every level, no matter how local.

Schlafly's reason for calling the first conference was one any feminist would applaud. She told a reporter at the time that the women who would attend—mostly veterans of her unsuccessful race for the presidency of the National Federation of Republican Women the year before—"are tired of doing all the menial work and being told they have to accept the candidate presented to them."

A decade later, Carol Alexander, a reporter for the Lind-

Phyllis Schlafly obviously doesn't know what's about to hit her as she chats with Nancy Borman, editor of *Majority Report,* at a 1977 Waldorf-Astoria reception for the Women's National Republican Club. At right is Yippie Aron Kay, an agent of Pie Kill Unlimited, who explained that he chose to hit Schlafly with an apple pie instead of his usual cream concoction because "it was in the tradition of motherhood and apple pie." Although injured in the attack, Schlafly declined to press charges. (Credit: Wide World Photos)

The Perils of Pauline

One view of Schlafly's role in the ERA battle, by award-winning political cartoonist Bill Mauldin. (By permission of Bill Mauldin and Wil-Jo Associates, Inc.)

Phyllis Schlafly, who leaves most debating partners speechless, meets a worthy opponent in William F. Buckley. The subject was the Panama Canal treaties and conservative Buckley was for turning the Canal over to Panama. Schlafly opposed. (Credit: Jan Lukas)

Phyllis Schlafly on "Meet the Press" from Houston during the International Women's Year Conference in November 1977. Schlafly was the only guest who opposed the conference itself as well as ERA, which the conference later endorsed. Here she displays what reporters call her "schoolmarm posture." (Credit: NBC's "Meet the Press")

Phyllis Schlafly answers a question during a debate at the University of Illinois, Chicago Circle campus. Her debating opponent Betty Friedan (right) author of *The Feminine Mystique* and founder of NOW, looks thoroughly disgusted. Betty Wood is the moderator. (Credit: Wide World Photos)

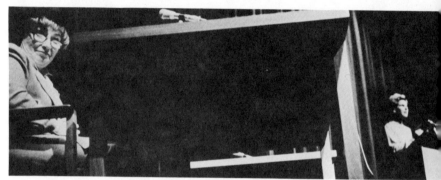

Bella Abzug and Phyllis Schlafly at Center College, Danville, Kentucky — the first time the two opponents appeared on a platform together. School officials pleaded with Abzug for an hour before she agreed to join Schlafly on stage. (Credit: Danville *Advocate and Messenger,* Danville, Kentucky)

The "Phil Donahue Show," summer 1979. Guests Phyllis Schlafly and NOW President Ellie Smeal disagreed on just about everything, making this show one of Donahue's most lively. (Credit: St. Louis *Globe-Democrat* photo)

Phyllis Schlafly escorts the late Cardinal Mindszenty of Hungary on his trip to St. Louis in 1974. The Cardinal, who spent much of his life in prison for resisting both the Nazis and the Communists, long had been a hero to Schlafly. She had written *Mindszenty the Man* two years earlier. (Credit: Arteaga Photo Ltd.)

Phyllis Schlafly and her daughter Anne with Mother Teresa, a year before the nun won the Nobel Prize for her work with lepers and other untouchables in the slums of Calcutta. Mother Teresa and Schlafly were both speakers at the Institute on Religious Life in St. Louis, summer 1978. (Credit: *St. Louis Review* photo by Richard Finke)

1980: The fight continues. At the rotunda of the Illinois State Capitol Phyllis poses with a young (female) friend as she gathers her forces for another crucial vote on the ERA. (Credit: Wide World Photos)

In the Schlafly living room on Christmas Eve 1979. From left to right: Bruce (seated) Fred, Phyllis, Andy, John, Anne, Roger, Liza. (Schlafly Collection)

say-Schaub News Service, observed: "This year could be the time females arrive in the American mainstream by a route long familiar to men: political muscle. That's the route anti-feminist Phyllis Schlafly is leading her grass-roots forces in Illinois and elsewhere this election year." Schlafly's Eagles would still be stuffing envelopes, but they would also be parceling out campaign dollars.

The first "training conference" in 1968 had, according to an Alton *Telegraph* reporter, "undertones of mapping guerrilla warfare against the liberals, especially Governor Nelson Rockefeller." The women, all wearing eagle pins to symbolize their self-reliance and also their loyalty to Schlafly, learned how to prevent liberal control of local party conventions. They heard Senator Strom Thurmond and Representative John Ashbrook urge them to "resist the Rockefeller blitz" and support either Ronald Reagan or Richard Nixon for President.

The conferences really started to hum when Schlafly found ERA, an issue around which to rally her troops. She called them "training conferences" and she meant it. The training ran the gamut from how to get your anti-ERA message on the "boob tube," mount an effective letter-writing campaign, testify at public hearings, hold a press conference, set up a phone bank, hold a fund raiser (Schlafly recommended brunches to avoid serving alcohol), infiltrate the feminist camp to learn ERA strategy.

A video room was open at all hours so participants could watch tapes of Phyllis debating Barbara Walters and Phil Donahue and Birch Bayh and Betty Friedan and a multitude of others. The purpose was not to provide entertainment or a much-needed break. The next day Phyllis would evaluate the women's performance in mock ERA debates.

She'd also lead workshops packed with advice on what colors and styles look best on television ("Always wear a scarf around your neck even if you have a short neck"), what kind of makeup looks best, and how to apply it. The sessions were never academic and seldom ended without an evaluation. Each woman would be videotaped making a two-minute speech and then watch "instant replays."

At another session a Schlafly aide handed women evaluation forms as they entered the room. Schlafly commanded a leader from every state to stand before the group and, in precisely two minutes, summarize a year's worth of STOP ERA and other "pro-family" activity. Speakers ultimately got their evaluation forms back, on which their peers anonymously evaluated their appearance, the content of their presentation, their knowledge, poise, hand movements, etc., and then summed it all up with a grade. The person with the highest grade got a prize.

"Television puts twenty pounds on you," Schlafly stressed at the television workshop as she demonstrated a daily exercise regimen. She also held another contest with a prize going to the Eagle who, since the last conference, had lost the most weight.

Schlafly understood the value of appearance, of public relations, much better than her opponents. And so there were always sessions on staging eye and TV-camera-catching rallies, on monopolizing the media. But Phyllis Schlafly had still another weapon, even more lethal than her home-baked apple pies, her frilly-gowned lobbyists, her brigades of doorbell ringers, her talent for upstaging the opposition.

In 1967, during her race for the presidency of the National Federation of Republican Women, columnist David Broder dubbed Phyllis Schlafly "the heroine of the right wing." When she lost that election and went into a self-imposed exile from establishment politics, she needed some way of communicating with her stalwarts—among them the three thousand women who hissed, booed, and wept when the election results were announced. And so, in 1967, she launched the monthly *Phyllis Schlafly Report*, which she has published every month since. Packed with her opinions, endorsements, ideas, and advice, it proved the perfect means for getting conservatives up in arms over some new concession to the Communists or curb on free enterprise.

By 1972, the *Report* was long established, successful beyond Schlafly's wildest expectations. And so it also proved the perfect means of rousing her women, of telling them why and how they must fight ERA and fight it now. Schlafly debated ERA for the first time in December 1971 and then recycled her research into the February 1972 *Phyllis Schlafly Report,* devoted exclusively to "What's Wrong with Equal Rights for Women?"—the first of a long line of *Reports* aimed at demolishing a sure thing.

Soon after that issue appeared, Ann Patterson, an Oklahoma subscriber, called Schlafly: "We beat ERA in Oklahoma today and all we had was your *Report.* I just went to the Capitol and passed it around and we beat it." That was the first state to turn down ERA. To the dismay of ERA backers, who thought Schlafly's arguments were preposterous, it wasn't the last.

Armed with cartons of her newsletter, Schlafly started testifying before state legislatures. She testified in Georgia, Virginia, and Missouri, and all three states rejected. Arkansas was scheduled to debate the issue, but the ERA was so popular there that cosponsors alone comprised clear majorities in both houses. A group of *Phyllis Schlafly Report* subscribers convinced the legislators, at least for form's sake, to hold hearings. They suggested that Phyllis Schlafly testify. She did, and there went what ERA backers assumed would be the thirty-first state in the "yes" column.

That first anti-ERA *Report* became a collector's item among feminists—like the first issue of *Playboy.* Women read it and ridiculed it and howled over it until it became obvious that state legislators were reading the *Phyllis Schlafly Report* and they weren't laughing at all; they were just voting "no." The *Report* subscription list grew from three thousand to thirty-five thousand, with a readership that was actually much larger because Schlafly urged subscribers to copy it and pass it out to members of their bowling team, their church, their state legislature, etc.

"It's the women in the states who should get the credit for beating ERA," Schlafly said. "What I've done is provide them with the ammunition to fight it via my newsletter." Paradoxically, the fact that ERA decreed a blanket equality meant that it was also inexact, and the amendment's vagueness turned into one of Schlafly's best allies. The twenty-four words of ERA's first section were so open-ended that ERA's potential effects were endless and so were Schlafly's arguments against it.

"She has faithfully provided the information needed to fight this battle," said Florida STOP ERA leader Shirley Spellerberg. "You can't just keep talking about the same thing over and over and over and Phyllis keeps coming up with new ammunition."

It is obvious that Schlafly's readers have enormous confidence in her monthly newsletters—as does Schlafly. "What power I have is the power of truth," Schlafly said in 1977 after being chosen one of the ten most powerful people in Illinois. "I have not sought power, period. . . . I have no way to reward people. . . . So where is the power? I think it's the power of the truth. I really do. I think it's the truth, plus the fact that I can put it out in a way that is understandable to anybody."

The *Phyllis Schlafly Report* is a somewhat scholarly but still feisty, printed, four-page, national-issues-oriented newsletter with a readership that is both male and female. In 1975, Schlafly founded the Eagle Forum and added the *Eagle Forum Newsletter* to her anti-ERA arsenal. It is more colloquial—a mimeographed, moralistic compendium of news, very heavy on the local, with instruction, inspiration, incitation, and advice. Its audience is mostly female.

If the *Phyllis Schlafly Report* is the movement's journal, the

Eagle Forum Newsletter is its primer. In a simple, spicy style, Schlafly provides step-by-step instructions on everything the neophyte needs to know about raising funds, influencing elected officials, demonstrating, letter writing, making a good impression, etc.

In her August 1976 newsletter, for example, Schlafly issued a directive to women who volunteered to sell STOP ERA buttons at the Republican National Convention: In the interests of looking dignified at all times, only those under twenty-five years old should wear STOP ERA T-shirts. In October 1977, the month before the "Pro-Family Rally" in Houston, Schlafly instructed her Eagles: "Our rally is not designed to promote any particular group, but merely to show grass-roots support of pro-family principles. Therefore, any signs you carry to this rally should identify *issues* and your *home state only—not* organizations." Some of her Eagles are probably also John Birchers and members of other right-wing groups, and Schlafly did not want network camera crews relaying that message across the country.

That same year, she instructed her readers in the fine art of pressuring the local librarian to balance the library's collection by acquiring "pro-family" (anti-ERA) books (such as *The Female Woman, Sex and Power in History,* and *The Retreat from Motherhood*). She directed readers to insist that their librarians acquire *The Power of the Positive Woman* by Phyllis Schlafly.

Most important, the *Eagle Forum Newsletter* has proven a surefire means of raising funds—essential because the organization's dues of five dollars a year barely bring in enough to pay the printer and postmaster. What brings in the dimes and dollars are Schlafly's personal appeals in the pages of her *Eagle Forum Newsletter*. Before ERA votes in Nevada, North Carolina, Florida, and Illinois, for instance, Schlafly pleaded for funds and netted thirty thousand dollars—enough for her unpaid workers to win in all four states.

If one local group or person stages a particularly ingenious fund raiser, Schlafly describes it in detail in her *Newsletter*. In April 1977, she reported that a Missouri Eagle named Vickie Harvey "personally made over four hundred Easter cakes in the shape of a lamb (hand-beaten, no mixes), sold them for $6.00 each, and donated the receipts to help defeat ERA in Florida."

Every year, Schlafly herself hatches some fund-raising scheme. One year she used the *Eagle Forum Newsletter* to hawk mother-baby pendants. "Everyone who has seen the pendant is thrilled with it. It carries our pro-family message in a handsome and powerful way."

In a *Newsletter* plug for subscribers to the *Phyllis Schlafly Report,* she asked her flock, "How will you and your friends know what action to take unless you receive the *Phyllis Schlafly Report?* How will you know what to pray for unless you receive the *Phyllis Schlafly Report?*"

Just why have Schlafly's newsletters been such potent weapons? "My writing is designed to make things happen, to make people act," she answered—and that it did, because Schlafly's writing has always been steeped in morality, whether she was deploring the state of the family, the public schools, or the Pentagon. "Is Our Welfare System Immoral?" read the headline of the lead article in a 1975 *Report*. "Our Moral Duty to Build Nuclear Weapons" read the headline of a 1973 *Report*.[1] (Since 1972, Schlafly has written double issues—one devoted to ERA and the other to her pre-ERA *Report* topics, such as defense, SALT, foreign policy, education, and economics.)

---

[1] Her world view has certainly not changed. "Disarmament in the face of any enemy whose purpose is to bury Western civilization is morally wrong," wrote Schlafly in 1963, opposing the Nuclear Testban Treaty between the United States and Soviet Union. "We must stamp out moral illiteracy if we are to retain the moral leadership of the world," she wrote back in 1952 during her congressional campaign.

The people who populate Phyllis Schlafly's newsletters are either good guys or bad guys, moral or immoral. And if the world is basically black and white, acting with single-minded energy and conviction against an issue like ERA becomes a lot easier. And solutions to complicated problems become a lot simpler.

Schlafly offered advice to the middle-aged woman "who has too much time on her hands because of a successful and indulgent husband" and who is thus "a ripe candidate for the disease called women's liberation. . . . The worst thing that such a woman can possibly do is take a 'women's studies' or some other sociology or psychology course in college. Some of these courses should be called 'How to Break Up a Marriage.' . . . The best cure for women who are limited in their own self-esteem is to stop reading women's magazines."

What to do about the increasingly publicized problem of battered wives? Feminists advocated establishing taxpayer-funded rest and recuperation centers in every community. No, wrote Schlafly, "After a wife returns from her R&R, the husband would probably beat her again with impunity knowing that the taxpayer, not he, would foot the bill for the damage." Her solution was to follow the example of the state of Delaware which, early in the century, sentenced a man who beat his wife to "thirteen lashes on his bare back while his hands were tied to a post in the courthouse square. The public whipping was a rare occurrence because the threat of it had made Delaware one of the most crime-free states in the country."

Saying that Schlafly's style is seldom subtle or understated is, well, an understatement in itself. In Schlafly's lexicon, "pervert" is an acceptable synonym for homosexual. "NOW is for pro-lesbian legislation," Schlafly wrote in her June 1976 *Report*, "so that perverts will be given the same legal rights as husbands and wives such as the right . . . to adopt children and the right to teach school. Surely the right of parents to control the education of their children is a right of a higher order than any alleged right of, say, the two college-educated lesbian members of the Symbionese Liberation Army to teach our young people."

In July 1978, when ninety thousand men and women marched in Washington in support of the ERA extension, Schlafly described the demonstrators as "a combination of federal employees and radicals and lesbians."

"Phyllis doesn't believe a word she writes," said state Senator Susan Catania, a leader of the pro-ERA forces in Illinois. "She scares those poor women. That's why she's so successful. She makes them believe that if they don't run out and fight ERA for all they're worth, their husbands are going to run off with the baby-sitter and they'll be stuck with no alimony or child support or maybe even no children."

The notion that Schlafly's followers are a bunch of drip-dry automatons who are too dumb or too dazed to reject Schlafly's preachings is as ridiculous as the notion that Schlafly is too smart to believe what she preaches. The ERA battle has been long and brutal. Only someone who believed in what she was doing—with a passion—could have carried it off.

"Nothing in the history of constitutional amendments quite matches this story. . . . Never have we had a proposal that shot off with greater enthusiasm than the ERA, only to grind to such a sudden, head-snapping halt," wrote columnist James J. Kilpatrick on March 22, 1979—the day that ERA would have died had Congress not agreed to a three-year, three-month extension of its lease on life.

That day, Phyllis Schlafly held her "Gala" in Washington to celebrate her self-styled "victory" over ERA.[2] Fifteen hun-

---

[2] Schlafly's claim of victory in the ERA battle is possibly premature because ERA's extension does not expire until June 30, 1982. On the other hand, Schlafly's claim has some substance. Even if ERAers win the three more states they say they need (because of rescissions, STOP ERAers claim their opponents need at least eight), the amendment

dred people, mostly women, jammed Washington's Shoreham-Americana Hotel ballroom. They came from all over the country, paying their own way from as far as Hawaii, for what was essentially a one-night bash. Many came on chartered yellow school buses; in their suitcases were the pastel chiffon gowns they would wear that night.

On the way into the ballroom, they filed past a wreath of yellow-and-white mums, a black ribbon draped dramatically across: "Rest in Peace—ERA." The "Triumphal March" from *Aïda* boomed in the background.

Virginia STOP ERA leader Alyse O'Neill clutched the evening's program, which featured a full-faced portrait of Phyllis. "We're literally watching a miracle happening and that's the miracle woman," she said, pointing to Phyllis, who was autographing programs for some star-struck fans.

"Three years ago," O'Neill recalled, "I thought, no way. The day Betty Ford came out for ERA, my husband told me to quit. 'Stop spending all my money, running up the phone bill. We're Republicans and our own Administration is backing ERA. It's going to pass.' When I told Phyllis what my husband said, she said, 'Oh no, we'll just fight harder.'"

Finally, dinner over, it was time for Phyllis to address her fans.

"They thought they won a great victory with the extension," Schlafly bellowed. "But in the state capitals it has turned peo-

---

may be tied up in court for years to come—on questions of the legality of rescissions and of the extension itself.

The attorney general of Idaho (a rescinding state), the attorney general of Arizona (an unratified state), and legislators from Washington and other states have already filed suit in federal court on the issues of rescission and extension. They claim that the ERA their states ratified expired on March 22, 1979. (All but five of the thirty-five legislatures that voted "yes" on ERA specified in their ratification resolutions that the measure would become part of the Constitution if ratified by the legislatures of three quarters of the states by March 22, 1979.)

ple off. Legislator after legislator who voted yes for seven years, as of tomorrow will start voting no, because they know the extension is wrong, crooked, and unfair."

"We are the most powerful, positive force in America today," she concluded, "because we have been able to give the bureaucrats and the politicians a stunning defeat."

"I live in a mobile home and coming to Washington to this celebration wasn't easy for me," said a heavy woman from Tennessee as she attacked her restuffed baked potato hoarded from dinner. "I came for Phyllis because I think she's such an outstanding lady. Look at her," she said, her mouth finally still as she gazed at willowy Phyllis in her salmon chiffon gown. "She looks blessed. I do believe she's been our Savior."

Coming from that woman, a staunch Southern Baptist, that was quite a tribute. For Phyllis Schlafly is as staunch a Catholic, and Catholics and Baptists are supposed to be deep-down suspicious of each other. Yet here was a purebred Baptist who seemed to think that Phyllis Schlafly was the next best thing to Jesus Christ.

And the Tennessean was not the only one in the room who thought so. Phyllis Schlafly surprised political observers by stopping ERA. But she shocked them by stopping ERA with what has to be recent history's most unlikely and powerful coalition.

18

The Sweetheart
of the Silent Majority

For the ERA battle, Phyllis Schlafly forged a coalition that most political strategists would have considered a contradiction in terms—a coalition of Catholics, Fundamentalists, and Orthodox Jews. In this improbable alliance, party affiliation was a moot point, as was the ancient suspicion between Catholics and Fundamentalists, not to mention Jews and Fundamentalists.

Schlafly, said former NOW President Karen DeCrow, was "the perfect one to do it because in many ways she thinks like a Fundamentalist."[1] DeCrow recalled being "shocked" the

---

[1] In setting goals for her Eagle Forum, Phyllis Schlafly wrote, "We support the Holy Scriptures as providing the best code of moral conduct yet devised. . . . We support the family as the basic unit of society, with certain rights and responsibilities, including the right of parents to insist that the schools permit voluntary prayer, teach the 'fourth "r"' (right and wrong) according to the precepts of the Holy Scriptures."

first time she sat at the same predebate dinner table with Schlafly and a group of local supporters—hard-core Fundamentalists.

"My view of Catholics," said DeCrow, "is that they're quite restrained. They don't talk about God at the dinner table. So it was very interesting at a dinner with some born-again people who were talking about God. I expected Phyllis to be really uncomfortable, but she wasn't at all. She was joining right in talking about what God wants. The Catholic God as far as I can see just doesn't sit around saying, 'Don't pass this piece of legislation.' God and Jesus and the Holy Ghost just aren't worried whether Arkansas is going to pass the ERA."

It was an unbeatable combination. In February 1979 ERA proponents from all over the country concentrated their energies and dollars on North Carolina, where Governor James Hunt was a strong booster, as was actor Alan Alda and columnist Erma Bombeck. Jimmy Carter worked the telephone.

What sealed ERA's doom, one legislator said, were over two thousand chanting, praying, hymn-singing anti-ERA demonstrators; the same mostly female crowd that two years earlier walloped ERA in the state Senate. "Our prayer chain did it," one woman explained. "We had women praying all night and all day. . . . We asked God that if this thing was not in his plan that he would see that it was defeated." "Our momentum of victory," Schlafly wrote to her Eagles in her July 1980 newsletter, is easily explainable. "We have the power of God's help. We have stormed Heaven with prayers."

Congressman George Hansen, a deep-voiced conservative from Idaho, looked and sounded like a fire-breathing preacher when he told a group of ERA opponents, "The rights of individuals come from God. We must fight against the abominable ERA."

In Oklahoma, the Church of Christ bused hundreds of devout lobbyists to the state Capitol. A Tallahassee demonstration drew over a thousand Church members, who arrived in car caravans organized by ministers. On a Florida radio talk show, the Reverend Bob Clark thundered, "Section II says the Congress shall have the power to enforce the article. There's Big Daddy Fed again. . . ." In Mississippi, soon after an ERA defeat, an AP reporter quoted one woman as saying, "We were told in our church that ERA meant the end of marriage, that school books would show pictures of people having sex with animals, and we've got to protect our children."

Evangelist Jim Brasher, pastor of the South Sulphur (Church of Christ) Congregation (Louisiana), reported in the church bulletin that sixty members went to Houston for the 1977 "Pro-Family Rally" (held the same weekend as the International Women's Year Conference). "While the family-rights people were emphasizing our need of God's guidance, the IWY Conference opened its session without any recognition of God, and proceeded to push through its socialistic Plan of Action and to wildly and enthusiastically place its stamp of approval upon the killing of unborn children, lesbianism, ERA, and a host of other highly questionable resolutions. . . . Moral rottenness filled the hall with the stench of death. . . ."

Schlafly's contention that ERA would force the Catholic Church to abandon its single-sex schools, and could bring litigation to force the Church to ordain women, also made powerful allies of hundreds of priests. Although the Catholic Church took no official position on ERA, all the large Catholic lay organizations took strong anti-ERA stands and were considered to have helped defeat ERA in Illinois, Missouri, and Florida.

The Mormon Church was credited with stopping ERA in Utah, Nevada, and Arizona, where Mormons represent a sizable portion of the population. The Mormons joined the anti-ERA battle late—in 1976—but when they joined it, they *re-*

ally joined it. Six days after the Senate passed the extension, Spencer W. Kimball, Church president, directed his 4.5 million members to lobby actively against ERA. A directive from Kimball, considered the Lord's mouthpiece on earth, was nothing less than a divine command.[2]

If an alliance between Catholics and Fundamentalists was surprising, an alliance between Fundamentalists and Jews was downright incredible. Yet Orthodox Jews worked ardently with Schlafly during the 1975 New York referendum on ERA, and have continued working. The Orthodox, strictly observant Jews, believe in a sharp division in the roles and responsibilities of the sexes. Men are the scholars and women the homemakers. Men and women are even assigned separate and far from equal seating during services.

Like Catholics and Fundamentalists, Jews feared that the First Amendment would not stop the federal government from insisting that women be ordained as rabbis and that Hebrew School classes and seminaries be sex-integrated, and—horror of horrors—that women sit anywhere they please during services. The Orthodox want equality in the marketplace, not in the synagogue.

Bernard Fryshman is a physicist and chairman of the Commission on Legislation and Civic Action of Agudath Israel of America, a national organization of Orthodox Jews. His young wife, who has five children "so far," believes it is "a woman's duty to stay home and make a warm home for her husband and children."

---

[2] In December 1979, the Mormon Church excommunicated a fifth-generation member who had campaigned for ERA. Sonia Johnson, a mother of four, was accused of knowingly preaching false Church doctrine. The excommunication sparked much bad publicity, and Church officials hastened to deny any connection between ERA and her excommunication. Many Mormons in good standing with the Church, they said, publicly support ERA.

"As a Jew," said Fryshman, "I never expected to be working with Phyllis Schlafly any more than she expected to be working with me. But what we've got works. It's a winning combination and when ERA's dead and gone it'll work for other issues. As long as we've got Phyllis at the head, I feel we can move mountains. We finally have someone who speaks for us; who understands that we've had just about as much interference from the government as we're going to stand."

In 1974 *Ms.* magazine titled a profile of Phyllis Schlafly "The Sweetheart of the Silent Majority"—certainly not intending any compliment to the subject. The coiner of the headline undoubtedly didn't know that back in pre-ERA 1970, Phyllis, running for Congress, proudly dubbed herself just that—"The Sweetheart of the Silent Majority."

Almost all the words spilled over ERA have been over Section I—"Equality of rights under the law shall not be denied or abridged by the United States or by any State on account of sex."—twenty-four simple words that, proponents contend, do nothing but guarantee women equal rights under the law.

Schlafly's power in the ERA battle stemmed from her focus not so much on Section I as on Section II—"The Congress shall have the power to enforce, by appropriate legislation, the provisions of this article."

"If you like ERA," Schlafly warned, "you'd better like congressmen and Washington bureaucrats and federal judges relieving you of what little power you have left over your own life." She sent that message loud and clear, and she sent it at a time when increasing numbers of Americans had begun to believe that Washington had grown too big and arrogant and gratuitously meddlesome.

"In case you haven't heard," Schlafly testily told a Washington bureau chief, "the people out there don't want to give any more power to Washington, and that's precisely what Section II does."[3]

Congressmen and bureaucrats were not the only demons Schlafly raised. Foes of ERA called those twenty-four words of Section I imprecise; friends of ERA called them uncompromising. Both sides agreed that this one, short sentence could call into question thousands of federal, state, and municipal statutes and that, in the end, it would be up to federal judges to interpret ERA.

Milling around the "pro-family" rally in Houston in November 1977, it was difficult to determine if the conservatives' public enemy No. 1 was Jimmy Carter or Ted Kennedy or Bella Abzug or federal judges—the latter lumped into one massive threat.

Kansas City attorney Matthew Nozinger said he came to Houston to show his opposition to ERA which, he explained, will require endless interpretation by "unelected, appointed-for-life, unresponsive" federal judges. "There's nobody more out of touch than a federal judge unless it's a federal bureaucrat." He carried a placard, "Phyllis go to it! The grass roots won't be stepped on anymore."

"If you liked Judge Garrity, you'll love ERA," read another placard, carried by a young woman carrying an infant in a backpack and leading a little girl by the hand.

"What's the connection?" asked a reporter.

"I'm from Southie and I ought to know," she said in a thick

---

[3] It's true that seven other amendments to the Constitution have identical second sections. But five of those deal with only one right, voting rights, and so there is no room for interpretation. The other two are the 13th and 14th, both of which, like the ERA, have open-ended and vague first sections and consequently have resulted in Supreme Court interpretations that the drafters of those amendments and the legislators who ratified them probably never intended. For example, in 1973, the Supreme Court found the right to an abortion under an amendment (the 14th) that had been ratified in 1868 for the purpose of giving full citizenship rights to blacks.

Boston accent. "Judge Arthur Garrity is the federal judge who took over the school system when Boston didn't bus enough children to please him. So now we've got a school system run by a federal judge whom nobody elected. Parents on every block who grew up in Southie, married someone from the same parish, and planned on their kids walking to the same schools they walked to, are putting their kids in private schools. That's why I support Phyllis Schlafly and that's why I oppose ERA. For a lot of these ERA people giving the feds control over the family doesn't matter because they're not having families. They're having abortions."

Minutes later, Dr. Mildred Jefferson, a black physician from Boston and a leader in the anti-abortion movement, addressed the fifteen thousand people packed into Houston's Astro Arena. "The silent majority isn't silent. It's grumbling and mumbling and will be heard to the corners of the country." Phyllis Schlafly sat on the dais savoring the wild applause as she awaited her turn to speak.

"The little people—people such as you and I—we can sew up the moral fabric of the country," Phyllis Schlafly said.

"Phyllis is one of the little people like Princess Grace of Monaco is one of the little people," said a leader of ERA-Illinois as she watched Schlafly's performance on television. "She suddenly became one of the little people when she read the polls on ERA and realized that the greatest support for ERA came from people with the most money and education. Before ERA she was one of the Republican country-club set and she still is."

Yes and no. Schlafly—Junior Leaguer, DARer, Radcliffe graduate, to be sure—has never been part of the Republican Ivy League establishment, perhaps first and foremost because she's a woman, but perhaps also because her anti-communist views have always been too unfashionably strident, her passion for free enterprise and big defense budgets too steadfast, and her isolationist tendencies too midwestern. Perhaps also because she believes America needs to be saved from the establishment—Henry Kissinger and Robert McNamara, the Rockefellers and the Kennedys—if it is to be saved from the Soviet Union. To Phyllis Schlafly politics is a mission, not merely a career, and she undoubtedly makes "the striped-pants boys," as she calls them, downright nervous.

A Choice Not an Echo was, after all, Schlafly's appeal to the "grass roots"—the "overwhelming majority of just plain hard-working Americans" to seize back control of their party from the eastern establishment, the "kingmakers," the very few and very rich elite who were, Schlafly charged, more concerned about their own financial interests than about a "strong America."

Three years later, in 1967, the race for the presidency of the National Federation of Republican Women also turned into a battle of the grass roots vs. the eastern establishment, decentralized vs. Washington control of the party, "the thousands of women out there who do all the tedious work for the party" vs. ten or so liberal, male Republicans who, Schlafly charged, were trying to hand-pick the women's president.

"The NFRW," Schlafly wrote during the campaign, "should always be an organization where the control comes from the bottom up—not from the top down. . . . I believe that the big decisions in the Republican Party should be made by the grass roots who labor in the precincts."

Those appeals to the "just plain people" were nothing new. Phyllis Schlafly has always found her support in the working-class and middle-class families whose sons fought in Korea and Vietnam; the people who felt fleeced at one end by inflation and at the other by taxes that paid for "foreign give-aways"; the people who stewed over welfare cheaters and federal bureaucrats and felt increasingly impotent under an increasingly complicated and centralized government. They're mad as hell and they yearned to say, "I'm not gonna take it anymore," but they didn't know who to tell. They found their voice in Phyllis Schlafly, who may not really have ever been one of them, but who certainly was not one of the ruling elite.

"Her column is quite successful," said John Moon, sales manager for Copley, the San Diego-based syndicate that distributes her semiweekly newspaper column. "She writes straight from the gut for the lunch-bucket carriers of America and they love her."

Back in 1952, when she was running for Congress, Schlafly raised an issue that would not come into vogue until the end of the Vietnam War. "During two years of the Korean War, white-collar trainees, college boys, have been deferred, but skilled-labor trainees have been drafted. Now we learn that fathers will be drafted after the November election but college students will continue to be deferred. Thus even laborers who are fathers will be called before well-to-do college students. Labor has had to pay the taxes made necessary by New Deal wars . . . waste and graft. Labor is unable to hedge against higher prices by buying real estate and corporate stocks as can middle-class and wealthy families. . . . The New Deal has given us government by rich men who never had to wait for a paycheck. . . . As long as the New Deal continues to be led by men like Averell Harriman, heir to forty million dollars, who believe that 'we can stand higher taxes,' labor will be taxed and taxed, drafted and drafted, expended and expended."

When ERA's original seven-year deadline expired, NOW president Ellie Smeal held a press conference to announce the game plan for the final push for ERA. "Those political leaders and business leaders who wager that a hard-core minority of right-wingers can keep down forever a surging majority of women and men who know they are equal do so at their peril."

Smeal and other pro-ERA leaders refused to believe a genuine grass-roots movement existed. They claimed that the anti-ERA movement was no movement at all, but a conspiracy by a few right-wing nuts, funded by giant corporations that wanted to keep women in their place. But that conspiracy theory had about as much substance as the "commie conspiracy" theory of the 1950s. A great social revolution was—and is—brewing. The fact that it was brewing on the right instead of the left made it no less a revolution.

Phyllis Schlafly's world view—Mom baking pies and changing diapers, and Dad dashing to the commuter train and later mowing the lawn—is about as realistic as a Norman Rockwell painting, or so goes a standard criticism.

Only 17 percent of American households include a father who is the sole wage earner, a mother who is a full-time mother, and one or more children—a statistic that ERA backers frequently mentioned (but that ERA opponents challenged because of the absolute words "sole" and "full-time"). A large percentage, ERA backers said, of all married women are eventually divorced or deserted, and most of those who escape divorce or desertion can expect to be widowed. The divorce rate doubled in the past decade and nearly half (45 percent) of all children born in 1979 will spend a portion of their childhoods with only one parent. During the past decade, households headed by women increased by 32 percent. More than half of all mothers with school-age children worked outside the home. In a Norman Rockwell world ERA is not necessary. In the real world, ERA backers argued, it is.

The statistics made a poignant point—but not necessarily to the millions who still lived in traditional nuclear families in neighborhoods full of traditional nuclear families. It was primarily from this group—women who were tired of feeling guilty for living a life very similar to their mothers'—that Phyllis Schlafly drew her support. And it was still a big group. Statisticians said nearly half of the women in the United

States work. Schlafly said nearly half of the women in the United States are full-time homemakers.[4]

Dr. Joyce Brothers and Phyllis Schlafly were in the midst of a heated debate on "The Merv Griffin Show." Dr. Brothers, obviously exasperated, snapped, "The idea that a woman can sit home and be supported by her husband, that has long ago died out."

"Forty million women are being supported by their husbands today," Schlafly countered. (Dr. Brothers appeared stunned by the number and didn't respond.)

In June 1978, Schlafly appeared on "The Phil Donahue Show." The almost entirely female audience gave her a very warm reception. Donahue seemed surprised. He asked, finally, "Who here supports the ERA?"—a feeble response. "Who here does not support the ERA?"—a lusty burst of applause.

If women really supported ERA, Schlafly argued, it would have long since passed. They don't and "I'm not about to let state legislators forget it." The audience cheered.

At about the same time, Rosalynn Carter was in Chicago to call on newly elected Mayor Jane Byrne and ask for her help in pushing ERA through the Illinois legislature. "We tried working through legislators," the First Lady explained, "but

---

[4] In a 1980 article in *The New Republic,* Diane Ravitch, associate professor of history and education at Teachers College, Columbia University, pointed out that while 40 percent of all marriages end in divorce (meaning that for every ten couples who married last year, four couples got divorced), 80 percent of all married couples have never been divorced. And, Ravitch added, about 90 percent of all Americans live as members of families related by blood, marriage, or adoption: forty-seven million families (out of a total of fifty-seven million families) are composed of the conventional husband-wife relationship. Schlafly collects statistics like these and always has several on the tip of her tongue.

invariably they told us they couldn't vote for ERA because their constituents didn't support it."

Gene Howard, president of the Oklahoma Senate, which has not passed ERA, was shocked, he said, when he started receiving piles of letters from women: "I want to remain a woman." "I want to remain on a pedestal." "I want to remain a homemaker."

A Washington press conference was packed with reporters, mostly women, and mostly, obviously, not fans of Phyllis Schlafly's.

"Mrs. Schlafly, how can you say that women don't want the ERA when every major poll has shown that they do want it?"

"The polls are wrong," Schlafly said flatly. "The best polls are at the ballot box."

In November 1978, both Florida and Nevada put ERA-related questions on the ballot. In Florida, where the federal ERA had been rejected repeatedly, voters resoundingly rejected a state version. In Nevada, voters were polled to "advise" the state legislature, which also had repeatedly rejected ERA. Voters advised their legislators, by a margin of more than two to one, to continue rejecting it.

"But Mrs. Schlafly, those are both conservative states," the reporter argued. "They don't represent any national grass-roots movement."

The perfect opening for Schlafly to mention her sweetest success.

In November 1975, liberal New York and New Jersey, both of whose legislatures had long since passed ERA, asked voters if they wanted a state ERA. The question quickly became a referendum on ERA in general. Schlafly saw her chance and grabbed it.

In a colossal political upset, voters in both states defeated the referendum. Suddenly ERA was headline news, and political commentators who had predicted an easy victory for the amendment now were predicting that the defeat signaled a change in the national mood.

Ever since, Schlafly has jumped at the chance to get ERA on the ballot anywhere, any time. And every time a legislature defeated a referendum proposal, Schlafly had another missile in her arsenal to explode the "myth that women want ERA."

In June 1978, a member of the Illinois House sponsored a resolution to put an ERA advisory referendum on the November ballot. Representative Michael S. Holewinski, an ERA backer from Chicago, explained why he voted against the resolution. "I estimate that a referendum on ERA would lose in forty-five of Chicago's fifty wards." In 1979 and 1980 identical proposals also failed. (A poll, taken by the Chicago *Tribune* a month before the referendum resolution failed, found the percentage of ERA supporters in Illinois down from 52 percent in February 1980 to 40 percent in May 1980.)

"She [Schlafly] is in the minority in her own state—she doesn't even speak for Alton," said Ellie Smeal. In the fall of 1978, Schlafly's next-door neighbor, ERA activist Gladys Levis, ran for the state Senate against a strong ERA opponent. Levis lost by a margin of about ten to one to the Schlafly-backed Democrat.

In one sense, Phyllis Schlafly's success in the ERA battle was quite understandable. She called feminists (in her mind and the public's mind synonymous with ERA activists) "a bunch of anti-family radicals and lesbians and elitists"—and feminists seemed to go out of their way to prove her right.

Some of their leaders' statements might have been written by Phyllis Schlafly—so sure were they to strike fear and suspicion in the hearts of housewives (and their husbands) anywhere west of Manhattan's Upper West Side.

"We're talking about a revolution, not just reform," said Gloria Steinem in a speech to college students. "It's the deepest possible change there is. We're working to overthrow the caste system." "The definition of women's work is shit-work," she said on another occasion.

"The care of children," said Kate Millett, "is infinitely better left to the best-trained practitioners . . . rather than to harried and all too frequently unhappy persons with little time or taste for the work of educating minds however young or beloved. . . . The family, as that term is presently understood, must go."

"Feminism is lesbianism. . . . [It is] only when women don't rely on men to fulfill sexual needs that they are finally free of masculine control," said Jill Johnston in *Time*.

On a Sunday afternoon in November 1977, thousands were watching live television coverage of the International Women's Year Conference in Houston when the delegates voted to endorse the "sexual preference" plank (that is, homosexual rights), and suddenly the balcony became a sea of gas-filled balloons with the message "We Are Everywhere." Hundreds of young women hugged and cheered and raised clenched fists. The television cameras zoomed in on one woman wearing a button with the message "Mother Nature Is a Lesbian," another "The Pope Has Clitoris Envy—He Wears Skirts, Doesn't He?" and another "A Woman Without a Man Is Like a Fish Without a Bicycle."

To the casual viewer of the IWY Conference, lesbians did indeed seem to be everywhere.

When Phyllis Schlafly wrote, "If man is targeted as the enemy, and the ultimate goal of women's liberation is independence from men and the avoidance of pregnancy and its consequences, then lesbianism is logically the highest form in the ritual of women's lib," women, not to mention men—which happens to be the sex of most state legislators—believed her.

Illinois Representative Edward E. Bluthardt said he switched from voting for ERA to voting against it in 1978 because of the IWY "and the resolutions adopted there that showed me what those people think the ERA stands for. . . . I can't tolerate those things." "I had hoped it would have passed last year," said Cook County Democratic Chairman George Dunne. "Unfortunately, some of the fellows who come from districts who oppose it were somewhat aroused after the women's convention in Houston about some of the resolutions that were passed about homosexuality and lesbians. Some of them would have wanted to vote for it, but now they say, 'What am I going to do?'" Illinois Representative Ronald E. Griesheimer argued against the amendment because he said it was supported by "a large group of bisexual or unusually sexual people."

Phyllis Schlafly probably didn't even have to bother linking ERA to homosexuality and abortion. ERA backers did it for her.

"There's a certain amount of liberal tsk-tsk-ing," stated a Washington *Star* editorial, "over the way the anti-ERA forces have organized their campaign around the idea that a vote for equal rights is a vote for lesbian quotas on school faculties, junior-high abortion clinics, compulsory round-the-clock day care, and the overthrow of capitalism. But the fact is that Phyllis Schlafly didn't have to make it up. Leaders of the National Commission on the Observance of International Women's Year, an official body set up by Congress and paid for with federal funds, have put the package together for her. . . . There's already an IWY priority list that links many of the emotionally charged issues quite the way an increasingly alarmed opposition fears. Yes, publicly financed abortion on demand, equality of everything for homosexuals . . . full-time day care, guaranteed incomes, and unilateral disarmament."

When the states held conferences to elect delegates to the IWY, many included controversial programs and exhibits. In Honolulu, for example, feminists presented leotard-clad women performing simulated sex acts in a pay toilet. "In many minds," observed Nicholas Von Hoffman, an ERA supporter, "the belief persists that the women's movement will celebrate the passage of the amendment by banqueting on roast fetuses."

Two popular buttons sported at the IWY Conference demanded "Wages for Housework" and "Women, Stop Giving It Away." Housewives, some feminists argued, should be paid an hourly wage just like bus drivers or lawyers. Evelyn Kaye, writing in *Parents' Magazine* in 1979, calculated that an American housewife with children is worth more than thirty-five thousand dollars a year or about seven hundred dollars a week. Husbands, she wrote, should pay their wives a weekly salary.

The author acknowledged that most husbands could not afford to pay their wives seven hundred dollars a week. She suggested that the government could pay the balance "because the United States is the wealthiest nation in the world. Women who are full-time homemakers are worth considerably more than men who are bus drivers."

That statement angered women whose husbands were time-clock punchers—Are full-time homemakers also worth "considerably more" than lawyers?—and it also angered women who realized that when the author suggested the government pay the balance, she was really suggesting that the taxpayers pay the balance.

Financial columnist Sylvia Porter raised one by-product of this new philosophy of marriage. If chauffeuring the kids to piano lessons and doing the laundry were assigned financial values, then the homemaker should contribute Social Security taxes just like any other self-employed person. Those taxes, of course, would have to come out of the earnings of the husband and, Porter conceded, "It might be charged that he would be paying taxes twice—once on his own earnings and once on the assumed earnings of his wife as a homemaker.

But this would be fair and equitable." If the husband had to hire a housekeeper, Porter explained, he would have to pay taxes on his employee's earnings. "If some change along these lines is not enacted sooner," she concluded, "the ERA, when finally passed, will require it."

Schlafly made hundreds of photocopies of the column and distributed it every chance she got. Many of the housewives who read it were outraged. In the face of double-digit inflation and high taxes, they already had enough trouble stretching their husbands' paychecks to cover essentials. Why in the world would they want to give still another chunk of it to the government?

At a press conference during the IWY, Bella Abzug introduced the forty-six IWY commissioners: "Thirty-four of us are married, four are widows, and one is engaged. . . . Among us, we have seventy-four children and seventeen grandchildren."

Why such a strange introduction?

An attempt—but too late—to offset a deep public fear that ERA supporters believed the true liberation of women required their liberation from traditionally paternal, sexist, male-dominated institutions, such as the corporation, the military, the university—and the family.

It wasn't male chauvinist pigs who were blocking ERA. It was women; women who had grown alienated from a movement whose goals and literature seemed elitist and totally disconnected from their lives and, worst of all, contemptuous of their values and aspirations. Too many feminists had appeared on too many talk shows implying that there was something wrong with being "just a housewife."

As columnist Russell Baker wrote, "The woman who preferred creating a family rather than going to the office and becoming a success was made to feel inferior and guilty. Making people feel guilty is a good way of getting political results in the short run. In the long run, it is a good way of making them despise you."

And it wasn't only the housewives whom the ERAers were losing in droves to Phyllis Schlafly, it was also the blue-collar women, who saw even less connection between ERA and their daily toils. In the late seventies, ERA advocates attempted to recoup their losses; to reach out to the woman who was working for the money, not the prestige. But it appeared to be too late. The following scene, with slight variations, was undoubtedly repeated many times all over the country.

The shift had just ended at a leather-tanning factory on West Armitage Street in Chicago; an area so grimy, ugly, industrial, so grim that it looked gray even on a bright summer day. That Tuesday was a windy November late afternoon, the sky a monochromatic slate.

"Ya wanna get somethin' to warm us up?" one woman asked her companion.

"I'd love to but I gotta go talk to my kid's teacher. He's in trouble for a change."

And so the shift of mostly women drifted to the bus stop and home, where there was still cleaning and cooking and children to tend to.

Standing at the gate, in the bus stop's path, were two middle-aged women in warm wools and tweeds, both wearing high leather boots and "ERA: It's for All of Us" buttons. They looked uncomfortable and the reason was more complicated than the merciless wind.

The first woman to pass by was black. She eyed the two white women suspiciously and didn't even shake her head "no" when one cordially, raising a black-leather-gloved hand, asked, "Can you spare a few moments?"

Eventually one woman stopped long enough to accept an

ERA brochure with a hand as lined and cracked and imperfect as the raw leather she spent eight hours every day treating. She had never heard of ERA, she admitted, as she stuffed the brochure in her shopping bag with yesterday's newspaper.

Finally, a live one. "Listen," said a very young but worn and fragile woman, "I heard Phyllis what's-her-name on TV and she said that ERA would mean we'd lose special benefits that we get and the guys don't—you know, like we've got a couch in the girls' room and we get an extra break in the afternoon, and it's easier for us to go to the john cause 'ya know the foreman never knows, it may be that time of the month, for all he knows. So I don't want no part of ERA," she said, her voice rising. "You come and work in a factory like this hole and I don't mean for a week. I mean for a year, at least, day in and day out, and I guarantee you won't want ERA either.

"Oh and the other thing this what's-her-name, Phyllis, said is that ERA will mean overtime forced on us like it's now forced on men. What's equal about that? I don't want to be equal if it means overtime. Who wants that? I've got two kids and a third on the way, and my husband works nights and sleeps days."

One of the ERA women handed her a brochure. "Keep it," the working woman said, walking away. "I don't work cause I enjoy it, you know," she snapped over her shoulder as she ran to catch her bus.

The NOW representatives looked frustrated. They wanted to point out that the protective labor laws were often used to keep women in their place and, besides, they wouldn't necessarily be taken away from women; they might be extended to men. "If women need special protection, so do men," was their standard line, but they didn't get a chance to use it. It probably would have made no difference. The factory woman wouldn't have agreed that the hefty, beer-bellied men she worked with needed any special protection.

In 1977, NOW organized an ERA convention boycott that did anything but endear ERA activists and their amendment to working women. The boycott was designed to put the squeeze on the fifteen states that still hadn't ratified ERA by convincing organizations not to hold conventions in those states' largest cities—Chicago, Miami, Atlanta, New Orleans, St. Louis, Kansas City, and Las Vegas.

As it turned out, although the boycott was literally successful—some two hundred of the nation's largest associations and organizations voted to honor it, depriving those cities of millions of dollars of convention business—it did not produce a single new ratification for ERA.[5] (Between 1978–1982, Illinois alone will have lost 25 million dollars.)

And, on top of that, it made new enemies among the waitresses and hotel maids who lost tips and sometimes even their jobs as hotels that were ordinarily booming with convention business were only half booked. Those working women who had never heard of ERA already felt hurt by it, and if they were hurt in such a concrete way now, who could predict the horrors that lay ahead if ERA were actually ever ratified?

Although the boycott drew support from nearly every mainstream organization in the country—the American Association of University Women, the American Home Economics Association, the B'nai B'rith Women, the National Coalition of Catholic Nuns—two of the biggest organizations, the

---

[5] The reason for this apparent paradox was that legislators from those big convention cities were already overwhelmingly pro-ERA. The rural areas—not the cities—were the sources of most of the anti-ERA sentiment. Because the rural legislators' constituents did not reap any direct reward from convention business, there was no pressure on those legislators to change their vote. If anything, the boycott provided them with a good reason to stick to their guns: "I will not yield to this blackmail," said one downstate Illinois legislator. (He might have if his constituents were losing money.) "It's a matter of principle."

National Council of Catholic Women, with eleven million members opposed ERA, and the Southern Baptist Convention, with twelve million members, opposed the ERA extension and the boycott.

Those are the people whom Phyllis Schlafly calls "the silent majority"—a new majority, the millions who she claims have traditionally been ignored or belittled by politicians, bureaucrats, liberals, and, especially, by the press.

When it comes to this "silent majority," maybe she's right. But, as for herself, she would have to admit that, in the ERA battle at least, reporters may have belittled Phyllis Schlafly, but they have seldom—very seldom—ignored her. Had they only ignored her, ERA backers often lament, STOP ERA just might have been stopped cold.

19

Phyllis Meets the Press

"Today [March 22, 1979, the day ERA's original deadline expired] is the greatest victory that American women have had since the ratification of the women's suffrage amendment in 1920." With that, Phyllis Schlafly opened a Washington press conference to an audible groan from a crowd of reporters—mostly women.[1]

"If there were a God in this world, Phyllis would have just been struck by lightning," said a young ABC newswoman to a reporter from the Washington *Post*. "Her saying that takes about as much *chutzpah* as if Barbara Walters held a press conference to complain she can't afford to buy her daughter school supplies."[2]

---

[1] Schlafly said that had she been a state legislator in 1920, she would have voted for the 19th Amendment. "The suffrage amendment gave women a right they did not have in some states (half the states allowed women to vote). ERA, on the other hand, gives women no new rights and takes away rights they currently have."

[2] Reporters simply don't believe that Phyllis Schlafly *really* opposes ERA. Toward the close of an interview on "Good Morning America," Sandy Hill asked, in exasperation, "I would really like to know,

Anti-ERA press conferences starring Phyllis Schlafly resembled nothing so much as Watergate press conferences starring Richard Nixon. Reporters were suspicious of Phyllis Schlafly, very suspicious.

The feeling was mutual.

Shortly before her marriage, Phyllis Stewart was explaining the origin of the title "Esquire" to attorney Fred Schlafly, who was preparing to debate a reporter. "I am sure that after giving this matter your impartial consideration," wrote Phyllis, "you will readily admit the poetic justice of referring to a lawyer as Esquire and to a newspaper man on the same platform as just plain mister. Certainly the two cannot be considered in the same class."

By 1964, Phyllis Schlafly came to view much of the media as just another link in the chain that strangled Barry Goldwater's presidential hopes. The press, in her writings, became a "tool of the kingmakers"—part of a conspiracy to use any and all tactics to defeat the Arizona senator. The "kingmaker-controlled" print media, Schlafly claimed, ranged from the New York *Times* to *The Saturday Evening Post;* from *Newsweek* to *Scientific American;* from *Time* to *The New Yorker.*

As deeply as Phyllis Schlafly distrusted the press, she was not above exploiting it. She intended to get her message out and she realized that only via the mainstream media—"kingmaker-controlled" or not—could she do so. Typically, when Phyllis decided to meet the press, there was nothing haphazard about it.

"Mrs. Schlafly is a creature of the media," wrote Alton *Telegraph* reporter Walt Sharp after she led him and a photographer into the kitchen to show off the apples she was baking for lunch. ". . . she is careful to sit in just the right chair

personally, Mrs. Schlafly, what you get out of this campaign." ("I don't get anything out of it except a lot of abuse," Schlafly answered, "And it has meant a tremendous amount of personal sacrifice to me.")

when she is going to be photographed. . . . Like an eager actress she's concerned that the light be adequate for a photograph and that she's always wearing an affable smile."

"The last time we did an article on her and Fred," recalled *Telegraph* editor Doug Thompson, "the photographer came back and said it was impossible to get a candid shot of her because she was always aware of the camera. She's always on, she's very serious about that image. She's deadly serious about it, and that's what makes her so dangerous."

Television proved to be the medium that suited Schlafly best. Perfectly poised, perfectly groomed, perfectly at ease, and in perfect command of her subject, Schlafly had a way of making her opponents—no matter how well-informed—appear half-baked. She was never at a loss for words and seldom at a loss for a clever comeback; a comeback so perfectly suited to the occasion that it rendered her opponents speechless—literally.

In 1973, Schlafly appeared on William Buckley's "Firing Line" with Dr. Ann Scott, then NOW's chairperson for legislation.

BUCKLEY: Suppose one took the position that the full field pack tends to be too heavy for a woman to carry. Would that be grounds under the amendment to exempt women from service in the infantry?

DR. SCOTT: It would probably not be grounds now. I think Phyllis, as a mother of six, can attest to how many pounds women have to carry, particularly young mothers.

SCHLAFLY: Yes, but I don't carry them for twenty miles.

Four years later, she appeared on "The Merv Griffin Show" opposite Dr. Joyce Brothers.

SCHLAFLY:	We cannot stop wars altogether.
BROTHERS:	Why not?
SCHLAFLY:	Well, maybe we can, you can keep on trying, but meanwhile . . .
BROTHERS:	If wars are right, then women have as much right and obligation to fight them as the men do.
SCHLAFLY:	Oh, which war did you serve in?
BROTHERS:	I don't know. . . . Have you ever known of a war that is right?
SCHLAFLY:	But if you think it is your obligation to be treated just like men, I really think you should have served.

Frequently her frustrated opponent would begin attacking Schlafly instead of her position on ERA. Schlafly would just sit, smiling, of course, posture perfect, hands folded in lap, savoring every second of the outburst. At the proper time she'd say calmly, still smiling, "If my opponent had any substantive case for ERA, she wouldn't have to spend so much of her time attacking me."

Frequently, Schlafly turned an outburst into an occasion for a long lecture, delivered so smoothly, so articulately that her attacker usually sat as transfixed as the audience—for example, during a debate in Bloomington, Illinois:

BETTY FRIEDAN:	I'd like to burn you at the stake, as far as that's concerned.
SCHLAFLY:	I'm glad you said that, because that just shows that the intemperate, agitating proponents of ERA are so intolerant of the views of other people that they want to burn us at the stake.
FRIEDAN:	I consider you a traitor to your sex. I consider you an Aunt Tom.

SCHLAFLY: You know, there is an old saying about the advice that the old lawyer gave to the young lawyer. If you are weak on the law, argue the facts; if you are weak on the facts, argue the law; and if you are weak on both the law and the facts, abuse your opponents. So you notice that the ERA proponents have almost given up arguing for affirmative or constructive consequences that the amendment would have. They have resorted to abusing the opponents, and to hurling epithets at them, or making false and phony charges about their being part of a conspiracy, or having finances from mysterious sources.

"She's as cool as an icicle," said a member of the production team for "The Phil Donahue Show." "We see people coming apart here all the time especially under the sort of hostile, personally insulting questions she gets. Now I personally think she deserves every dig she gets, but I have to say I admire her composure. During her last appearance—a joint appearance with [NOW president] Ellie Smeal—at one point Smeal started sort of weeping. Phyllis would have been as likely to do that as she would have been to take off her dress."

Which is not to deny that Schlafly is a virtuoso at rousing her audience with talk of abortions and homosexuality and divorce and the "Brave New World" that lies in wait under ERA.

In November 1979, thirty-six women's magazines, from *Cosmopolitan* to *Ms.*, from *Vogue* to *Ladies' Home Journal*, ran pro-ERA articles. The magazines' combined circulation was sixty million, but still, as reported in *Time*, "One editor at least had few illusions about their collective clout, especially head to head with Opposition Leader Phyllis Schlafly. Says *Cosmo*'s Helen Gurley Brown: 'All the women's magazines together may not be as effective as Phyllis Schlafly with her rabble-rousing TV appearances.'"

Schlafly complained incessantly about reporters' "deliberate distortions," yet she manipulated the media with the skill and flair of William Safire promoting Richard Nixon; with the expertise of the most savvy PR man. And like a good public-relations agent, she would never fail to return a reporter's call or to make herself available to the press at all hours of the day and night. "A large part of what I do," Schlafly said, "is answering the telephone. The calls come in all the time, sometimes as early as 6:00 A.M. or as late as midnight. I talk to reporters by the hour."

"If we've been working all day," said STOP ERA leader Kathleen Teague, "and it's 10:00 P.M. and we're finally sitting down to our first real meal of the day, Phyllis will always say, 'I've got some press calls to make before I eat. I've got to call back that reporter from the Los Angeles *Times* because it's seven o'clock in L.A. and I know he has a deadline for the morning edition.'"

As loudly as reporters grumbled about what they called Schlafly's media megalomania, they kept calling her; out of laziness or inertia, they kept calling her for the pithy opinion on subjects ranging from ERA to the Ayatollah Ruhollah Khomeini's treatment of women. They knew they could call Schlafly's home and that, more often than not, she'd answer the phone and cheerfully offer a concise, fact-filled answer to any question. (Connecting with Ellie Smeal, in contrast, was as difficult as connecting with Rosalynn Carter. The reporter would get shifted from switchboard operator to secretary to administrative aide to scheduler and, only occasionally, to the president of NOW herself.)

"We're sending Missouri STOP ERA newsletters and press releases to the papers and TV stations all the time," complained STOP ERAer Ann McGraw, "and they have my name and phone number right there. But even St. Louis reporters always call Phyllis because they know their readers are more interested in Phyllis Schlafly's opinion of an ERA vote in the Missouri legislature than in Ann McGraw's.

"When they say there are no leaders on the STOP ERA side, it makes my blood boil," she added. "When reporters want to get the pro-ERA side, they'll spend a whole morning calling everyone from Bella Abzug to the leader of the local ERA block club. When they want to find out what's happening on our side, they'll spend ten minutes calling Phyllis Schlafly. I think they just figure that anyone who is sincerely opposed to ERA—and they're convinced Phyllis' opposition is a power play—isn't smart enough to give a coherent answer."

Considering the enthusiasm with which the press embraced ERA, it was odd that reporters tended to be so ill-informed about the amendment. The reason, perhaps, was that most newspapers and networks didn't have one reporter assigned to covering ERA from a national perspective (that is, assigned to becoming the in-house ERA expert). Consequently, papers with reporters who had grasped the fine points of SALT II and the Mideast conflict and inflation had no one person who was thoroughly informed about ERA—about its legislative history, its wording (that is, the fact that it has three sections, not just one), about congressional testimony by constitutional authorities on possible ramifications, about the difference between 14th Amendment language ("equal protection of the laws") and ERA language ("equality of rights under the law"),[3] and about the fact that ERA referred only to action by the federal government and the states, not by private employers, and so did not mean equal pay for equal work.

Most reporters were just no match for Phyllis Schlafly—simply because they had not spent the months, years dissecting ERA and everything surrounding it. Schlafly had, of course, and she skillfully exploited the press's ignorance. Their errors in discussing the amendment gave her the ideal and dramatic opportunity to voice her objections to ERA—again. Uninformed—and thus frequently unfair—reporting gave her the opportunity for a letter to the editor or an on-air protest, dripping with self-righteousness and undoubtedly generating sympathy for Phyllis Schlafly and her cause.

In May 1979 Timothy Schellhardt of *The Wall Street Journal* wrote an article about ERA, stating unequivocally, at the start, that ERA did not mean equal pay for equal work. Fine, but Schlafly was still dissatisfied and she shot off an angry letter to the editor.

She denounced the article as "just a federal propaganda handout" because the reporter "omitted all reference to Section II" (which gives Congress the power to enforce and thus, in Schlafly's mind, gives massive power to the federal government). "Every person quoted . . . is living at the taxpayers' expense except one. Not a single expert who opposes ERA was quoted. . . . That's not objective reporting. That's just

[3] According to former Senator Sam J. Ervin, Jr., the equal-protection clause of the 14th Amendment differs from the language of ERA because the former does not require "identity of treatment. It permits a state to make distinctions between persons . . . if the distinctions are based on some fair or reasonable classification and all persons embraced within the classification are treated alike." The 14th Amendment language is also used in Illinois' state ERA, which Schlafly endorses, and in several other state ERAs. Only six states have ERAs that use the same language as the federal ERA and, in those states, Schlafly claims, "women are already starting to lose rights."

swallowing government handouts and passing them off to your readers as though you had done your usual objective research when you did not."

Phil Donahue opened a June 1978 program by announcing he would read ERA, and then read only Section I. "That's all it says," he concluded confidently, gazing intently at Schlafly. "There's no more or less to that."

"Oh yes, there *is* more to it," replied Schlafly, eyes flashing. "There's another section," which she proceeded to recite. The same summer, a month later, Schlafly appeared on both "Today" and "Issues and Answers." Both times, only Section I was read, and both times, Schlafly grabbed the chance to recite the second section.

When thirty-five women's magazines agreed to run ERA articles in their August 1976 issues, Schlafly complained, "Not a single one of the thirty-five magazines discussed the effect of Section II of ERA. They all acted as though Section II did not exist. It is a sham and a fraud to pretend to discuss ERA, but refer only to Section I"—and she seemed to have a good point.

"Isn't it true that some of the states that have ratified ERA are now providing benefits to women that did not exist before?" asked Richard Whitcomb, "Florida Forum" moderator, displaying a fundamental lack of understanding not only of ERA, but also of the amending process itself. (An amendment, as Article V of the Constitution specifies, does not take effect until three quarters of the states have ratified.)

"ERA is not in effect in any state. . . . It doesn't go into effect anywhere unless they get thirty-eight states," Schlafly responded, leaving Whitcomb nonplused, not knowing enough about the subject to respond to her response. So he changed the subject.

Later in the same program, Schlafly listed the five states that rescinded their ratification.

WHITCOMB: That would mean that the other side would
            need eight states to win it [apparently not
            realizing that, although Schlafly would love
            to think that eight more states need to ratify,
            the legality of rescissions is an open question;
            ERA backers say they need only three more
            states]. "That's not too many states." [A naïve
            statement, considering that proponents ex-
            pressed strong doubt that they could get even
            three states, much less eight.]

SCHLAFLY: ERA came out of Congress on March 22,
            1972. They got thirty states within twelve
            months. In the next six years they got five
            states and they lost five others [through re-
            scission].

WHITCOMB: You don't think they can get eight states in
            three years?" he persisted.

SCHLAFLY: No, because they haven't got any in the last
            six.

On the show "Chicago Feedback," the subject was the
draft. Co-moderator Marty Robinson asked: "How about the
young ladies who are presently enrolled in the U.S. military
academies?

SCHLAFLY: Well, what are they complaining about?

ROBINSON: You said before you didn't think there were
            any women who wanted to go into service in
            an active combat role.

SCHLAFLY: They don't want combat. Nobody wants com-
            bat. I don't know any man who wants combat.

ROBINSON: These women who are in the service acade-
            mies will be sent into combat.

SCHLAFLY: No, they won't. There are federal laws against
            it.

ROBINSON: That's not my understanding, but I'll take your word for it.

SCHLAFLY: [exasperated] There's a federal law against putting women in combat. The military has to obey the law. And if ERA goes into the Constitution, the military will have to obey the Constitution.

ROBINSON: [sourly] Obviously.

Barbara Walters didn't seem to know much about Phyllis Schlafly—or the ERA—when she interviewed the STOP ERA leader on the "Today" show in 1973. Expecting a slightly more serious version of Marabel Morgan, she instead got a more combative Bill Buckley. Schlafly's unstoppable stream of facts and figures left Walters sputtering. "But, but, this is perhaps. I, I mean, uh. I'm arguing both sides" [indecipherable mumbling].

Near the end of the encounter, Schlafly said that under ERA, women would no longer enjoy the legal right to be supported by their husbands.

WALTERS: They still have that right. The ERA . . .

SCHLAFLY: But not under ERA.

WALTERS: . . . does not take that away.

SCHLAFLY: But not according to law. According to the best constitutional authorities and the debate in the Senate, this would remove and wipe out the laws of the fifty states which make the husband primarily responsible for the financial support of his wife and children. It is shown in the legislative history and in the leading constitutional lawyers.

WALTERS: [frantically] Our time is *up!* And it's about time someone like you had the last word.

Phyllis Schlafly, obviously not one to let television commentators intimidate her, would continue to get the last word.

During the International Women's Year Conference, Schlafly and Ellie Smeal were waiting to go on the nationally broadcast "MacNeil-Lehrer Report." Two minutes before air time, the show's producer handed both guests a copy of a Roper Poll of six hundred women, to which MacNeil would refer during the program. It was the first time either Schlafly or Smeal had seen or even heard of the poll. Smeal, looking unconcerned, just glanced at it. Schlafly, looking furious, started reading it quickly, trying to digest as much as possible before the cameras clicked on.

Watching the proceedings was writer Gail Sheehy, who had accompanied Smeal to the studio. "Was it the imagination or was Schlafly's alabaster composure beginning to crack at the edges?" she later wrote in a strongly anti-Schlafly article in *Redbook*. She was angry, all right, but Sheehy needn't have worried about Schlafly's composure.

During the program, Robert MacNeil reported the poll's findings, that "clear support for Phyllis Schlafly seems to hover around 20 percent. . . ." A wide smile crossed Ellie Smeal's face, as the result seemed to contradict Schlafly's major criticism of the IWY—that delegates were not representative of the average American woman.

SMEAL: I think a really remarkable thing about the statistics you just released is that 20 percent of the people identify with the anti-movement and that is exactly the proportion of delegates who are here who are anti.

MACNEIL: Mrs. Schlafly, that's a remarkable observation. . . . Doesn't that demonstrate that the women's conference is in fact representative of your views?

SCHLAFLY: [glaring] No, it doesn't demonstrate that at all, and if you didn't get NOW to pay for the poll you really got gypped. I have seen a lot of loaded questions but I seldom have seen one so loaded as the one you didn't read but is on there—Roper asked women if they were "for women's rights or for Phyllis Schlafly"—and really in effect accuses Phyllis Schlafly of being against women's rights. Now to phrase the question that way is really completely dishonest. I am for the rights of women. The right of women to be exempt from the draft and from military combat duty. . . . The right of a woman to be supported by her husband. . . . If you ask me if I am for wommen's rights I will say, "Yes, I am for women's rights" and therefore your poll is absolutely invalid.

MACNEIL AND
LEHRER: [both stuttering, finally one managed meekly] I don't understand your complaint.

SCHLAFLY: I don't understand why you're giving so much time to a poll of six hundred people. If you want to talk about a real poll on ERA, look at the vote in New York, where the ERA proponents had everything going for them and it was overwhelmingly defeated.

MACNEIL: We're quite satisfied to stand by the poll. We have every faith in the Roper organization. . . .

SCHLAFLY: It is all a matter of how you ask the question.

MACNEIL:	Well, that is their business, not ours, Ms. Schlafly, and they're professionals in the business.
SCHLAFLY:	You should get NOW to pay for it.
MACNEIL:	[Indecipherable stuttering.]
SCHLAFLY:	If you ask people, "Are you for women's rights or are you for Phyllis Schlafly?" that is the silliest, dumbest question I've ever heard.
MACNEIL:	[regaining his composure] How about the actual issues, Mrs. Schlafly? How about support for ERA, for example?
SCHLAFLY:	Oh good. I'm glad you brought that up. ERA has been defeated in every state that's considered it in the last two years except one. Those representatives who have been voting no over the last six years have been facing the voters every two years and they keep getting re-elected because their constituents like the way they're voting.

In the *Redbook* article, Gail Sheehy complained, "She [Schlafly] used up more than five minutes of precious air time attacking the Roper people and then the methods and motives of MacNeil and Lehrer themselves. Her composure was coming apart," Sheehy repeated. Wishful thinking.

When Schlafly returned to her headquarters at the Houston Ramada Inn, her composure seemed intact and her expression triumphant. "What a performance," she congratulated herself. "You know these TV people have set themselves up as gods, as beyond reproach. They're not used to having a mere mortal question them, especially on the air."

Unquestionably, Gail Sheehy and other women reporters were enraged by Phyllis Schlafly and they often didn't bother to hide it.

"There's nothing I like about Phyllis Schlafly," said Martha Shirk of the St. Louis *Post-Dispatch*'s Washington bureau, "but I'm always appalled at press conferences and breakfasts with her how the rest of the press corps treats her. It is so unprofessional. You just never see this with anyone else. They cannot contain their outrage. It's certainly more true of women reporters. For a profession that in Washington is still predominantly male, Schlafly's Washington press conferences attract all the women reporters. They are just so hostile.

"At Houston [during the IWY conference], for example, the men reporters were mostly senior political correspondents. The women were younger and for the most part feminists. The men knew that the ground rules were that you're just not hostile to the subject at the press conference. You don't let your own opinions show on your sleeve. I get outraged when I listen to Phyllis. She really makes my blood boil, but you can't do your job when you're yelling at the subject."

During Schlafly's press conference after the Senate passed the extension of time for ERA—which Schlafly lobbied against fiercely—one young woman reporter walked passed the dais and hissed, "Eat your heart out, Phyllis."

Another woman reporter, on the New York *Daily News*, capped a lengthy interview by looking Schlafly in the eye and asking, "Just one last question, please: What would you like to have inscribed on your tombstone?"[4]

---

[4] As any politician or social crusader knows, unpopularity with the press can be a major—even a fatal—liability. But Phyllis Schlafly and her cause seemed to thrive on the hostility. As Los Angeles *Times* syndicated columnist Joseph Sobran observed in a July 1980 column, "The Equal Rights Amendment is dead. She [Schlafly] did it. Nobody else has so monopolized an issue since Ralph Nader took up auto safety. But there's a difference: The media liked and admired Nader. None of the giant editorial voices in the land supported Mrs. Schlafly. Enlightened young things like Ellen Goodman scorn her. They're all a little annoyed with her for not being extinct."

March 1, 1979, was the day after the Democratic primary in Chicago; the biggest news day in the city since Mrs. O'Leary's cow kicked over the lantern. Jane Byrne—an outsider, an enemy of the city's power elite, and a woman to boot —had toppled the supposedly invincible Chicago machine.

Phyllis Schlafly was in Chicago that day completing the Illinois Bar exam. As she was leaving the room, she found her path blocked by Karen Engstrom, a Chicago *Tribune* photographer. On most days being trailed by the press would have been just fine, with Phyllis, but on this day, she was drained and, worst of all, wearing a garish black wig. She looked— well, un-Phyllis-like. She wasn't even wearing her usual smile when Engstrom snapped her picture.

The next morning, the *Tribune* ran the photo next to one of a flawlessly coiffed Phyllis. It was an amusing juxtaposition. "I've raised six kids and I can do whatever I want," Schlafly was quoted as saying in response to a question about whether practicing law wasn't contrary to her preachings on a woman's proper place.

Apparently, someone taking the bar exam recognized Phyllis Schlafly under the wig and tipped off the *Tribune*. "We just couldn't resist it," said the editor who assigned the story. "Whenever Phyllis is in town there's never a shortage of women who want to cover her. Masochism, I guess."

Having courted Schlafly diligently, now, apparently, many reporters are beginning to regret it; to believe that Schlafly would still be home in Alton babbling about the Communist conspiracy if the press hadn't built her a platform and handed her an audience.

"In some ways she [Schlafly] might be called an artificial creation of the fairness doctrine," wrote Lisa Wohl in *Ms*. magazine. "Wherever pro-ERA views of the vast majority of Americans are presented, Schlafly—the only nationally known spokeswoman against it—is brought out in the name of objectivity."

"After the Supreme Court announced that alimony was not for women only," wrote columnist Ellen Goodman, "the media rounded up their usual suspects to make their usual statements about this unusual case. Front and center, of course, was Phyllis Schlafly, a person created by the media, in its relentless pursuit of what is called balance."

"Press Should Not Be So Darn 'Fair' " was the rather shocking headline of a column in the Chicago *Sun-Times*. The column's author was Grace Kaminkowitz, chairwoman of public information for ERA-Illinois.

"I am fed up with the efforts of the press to bend over backward to be fair and balanced in its coverage of the struggle to ratify the ERA," Kaminkowitz wrote. "As a result of sincere good intentions, the media have provided a forum for the lies and distortions of ERA opponents, frequently without providing an opportunity for rebuttal. . . . Sometimes I think members of the press are actually so pro-ERA that they forage for these unfavorable comments just so no one can accuse their news columns of being biased in behalf of the amendment."

Phyllis Schlafly just smiled when she read Kaminkowitz's column—and there wasn't a photographer in sight—thought "great," photocopied it, and sent it to her troops. It was a great way to stir them up. "We have to work twice as hard," she exhorted, "because the libbers' latest tactic is to try to censor us. They've got the press in their pocket, and reporters just might decide that objectivity—telling both sides of the story—is essential on every issue but ERA."

20

After ERA, What?

"For a long time," said Virginia STOP ERA leader Alyse O'Neill, "Phyllis Schlafly was a voice in the wilderness. People thought she was crazy; a right-wing nut. Everyone sneered at her. Who's laughing now? Now everyone's agreeing with her."

Well, not everyone. But undoubtedly, after thirty years of political activism, Phyllis Schlafly, who sometimes seemed to have a self-defeating knack for being out of sync with the times, appeared, finally, to be at the right place at the right time. Vietnam was the issue of the sixties; the environment was the issue of the seventies; the family appeared to be the issue of the eighties—the preservation, the security of the family, which, in Schlafly's terms, is synonymous with the security of the nation.

Until 1980, Schlafly had never quite succeeded in tying together those two concerns that had dominated her public life. Then, in his February 1980 State of the Union message, Jimmy Carter tied the knot for her by calling on Congress to revive military registration (defunct since 1973 when the voluntary Army replaced the draft) and, for the first time in U.S.

history, to require both men and women to register. In so doing, he handed Phyllis Schlafly a tailor-made controversy—tailor-made because it linked security of the family (mothers conceivably could be drafted and sent to combat) and security of the nation (Schlafly believes that female troops would be less fit for battle than male because women on the average have only 60 percent of the upper-body strength of men and because of the high rate of pregnancy among women in the volunteer army).

It also gave Schlafly's long-running STOP ERA campaign a shot of adrenalin for the final stretch. The President's speech sparked unexpectedly emotional debate. If ERA were in effect, Schlafly observed correctly, Congress and the public would not even be debating whether to send women into combat, much less merely to register or to draft them. The federal laws that exempt women from compulsory military service and combat would become unconstitutional.

Meanwhile, ERA activists claimed that Carter's call showed precisely why ERA should be ratified posthaste. Congress always has had the right to change the laws exempting women and, they predicted, Congress was about to do just that, without ERA to compel them.

Once again, they underestimated the power of Phyllis Schlafly. Congress was not about to do anything of the sort—thanks, at least in part, to Schlafly, who had seen the President's announcement coming and vowed, "Any congressman who wants to get re-elected will not vote for registering women." The previous Father's Day she launched a movement called Dads Against Drafting Our Daughters—a nationwide petition drive to "let our congressmen know that the grass roots opposes changing laws that exempt women from registration, the draft, and combat."

By the time Carter made his address to the nation, Schlafly's Eagles (and their husbands) had bombarded congressmen with letters, petitions, telegrams, and phone calls. Within days, House Speaker Thomas O'Neill warned that the House would definitely defeat any proposal to register women. The chairman of the House Armed Services Subcommittee on Military Personnel agreed, as did most members of the House and Senate Armed Services committees and, apparently, many other members of Congress. One Illinois congressman was in Washington when he told a reporter conducting an informal poll of the state's delegation that he favored registering women. He called the reporter as soon as he returned to his district, pleading to change his mind before the story broke. "Everyone who has walked in the door and everybody who has telephoned is opposed to registering women. I'll be killed if I support it. It's coming from women and men. There are a lot of men who don't want to see their daughters go to war."

In March 1980, the House Military Personnel Subcommittee voted 8 to 1 against registering women. The lone yes vote was cast by the representative from Guam. "We don't have any Eagle Forum Members in Guam," Schlafly explained. The next month, the full House, by an overwhelming voice vote, defeated a motion to register women. In June both the House and Senate approved registration—of men only.[1]

"The phones have been ringing off the hook ever since

[1] The ACLU immediately filed suit, claiming that men-only registration was unconstitutional because it discriminated against men on account of sex. The ACLU would not have had to bother filing suit, Schlafly said, were ERA already in effect. "Single-sex registration would be clearly unconstitutional. There is nothing now in the Constitution that requires that men and women be treated exactly alike." Three days before registration was to begin, a panel of federal court judges disagreed. They ruled in the ACLU's favor that draft registration of men only is unconstitutional because it excludes women. The next day, Supreme Court Justice William J. Brennan, Jr., ruled that registration could proceed as scheduled. The full Supreme Court was expected to rule on the case in the fall of 1980.

Jimmy Carter stabbed the women of this country in the back," Schlafly proclaimed. "Women who hesitated to join us because they thought we were using scare tactics—like warning that Carter had it up his sleeve to draft women—are joining us now. The draft issue has lowered the average age of our movement by about 20 years."

Even if she does not stop ERA, Phyllis Schlafly has a very hot issue for the eighties. In an increasingly security-conscious America, in an America to which the Russians again seem a real threat, drafting women is an issue that is not going to fade away. It will be a very hot issue indeed, an issue that has ramifications in national and international affairs. The perception that most people had of Phyllis Schlafly as a one-issue activist was about to change. And it was the draft that was proving such a sturdy bridge, over which Schlafly could cross from the ghetto of women's issues into questions of national security, into anything and everything.

"Phyllis Schlafly is training leaders who could work for her if she ran for something," said Alyse O'Neill. "I think she could run for President. She has an organization nationwide all the time working for her. Her organization is growing by leaps and bounds. On just the Virginia level, we started out six years ago with a hundred people. We now have over two thousand in Virginia alone and we're still growing."

Just before Christmas 1979 a new bumper sticker hit the road: "SAVE AMERICA—SCHLAFLY FOR PRESIDENT."

Phyllis Schlafly insisted she isn't interested in breaking into that boy's club called the U. S. Senate or even in becoming the first woman ever to man the Oval Office. "I really think I have more power right here, with this organization," she said in 1979, scanning her flock of Eagles who had traveled to St. Louis from as far as Hawaii to attend her annual Eagle Forum Leadership Conference.

At that conference, three hundred STOP ERA activists

plotted plans for the eighties—rebuilding U.S. military strength, passing a constitutional ban on abortions, ensuring parental control over school textbooks, and, of course, preventing women from being included in any future draft.

They also plotted strategy for burying ERA, but they obviously had moved on to other issues.

"The ERA was a blessing in disguise because we'll be mobilized for further causes," explained Alyse O'Neill as she cheered the first of many pep talks Schlafly would give during the weekend conference. "We know the contacts and where the troops are. There's a bottomless pit of issues we're waiting to sink our teeth into."

Moments later, Senator Paul Laxalt (R., Nev.) assured them, "Ladies like you can move political mountains." He was soliciting their help in passing his "Family Protection Act." The act would, among other things, deny federal funds for purchase of textbooks that "belittle women's traditional role in society." It would also cut off funds to schools in states that prohibit voluntary prayer in public buildings. The ladies liked what they heard and promised, as a first step, to write letters.

"There's no question that Phyllis and her ladies are getting increasingly successful on Capitol Hill on all kinds of issues," lamented Vicki Otten of the liberal Americans for Democratic Action. "Congressmen are finding their mail running ten to one against busing, abortion, homosexual rights, drafting of women."

It could even be said that, as the seventies moved into the eighties, Phyllis and her Eagles appeared to be moving into the mainstream—without a bit of moderating or mellowing. It was the nation that seemed to be changing direction and priorities, to be taking, if not a sharp, then at least a slight, right turn.

Consider:

• In October 1979 President Carter declared that "the

American family is in trouble" and announced a new "Office for Families."

• In 1978, *Good Housekeeping* conducted a poll and found, to its profound surprise and embarrassment, that the woman its readers admired most in the world was anti-homosexual crusader Anita Bryant. To add insult to injury, Anita was first again in 1979 and 1980, years when Phyllis Schlafly also made *Good Housekeeping*'s top ten.

• "We are the wave of the future," proclaimed Phyllis Schlafly with unmitigated confidence. If the future is today's high-school students, she may be right. *Seventeen* magazine polled a national cross section of two thousand teens and found that the person they admired most was Bob Hope. Columnist Garry Wills called the results the "Teen Girls' Idiot List" and observed, "It seems clear that Marlo Thomas got on the list for 'That Girl' repeats [on television] after school, not for ERA agitation."

• A 1978 survey of teen achievers (those included in Who's Who Among American High-school Students) found only 57 percent favoring ERA, down from 1974, when 74 percent were in favor. In 1979, only 52 percent favored ERA, and 63 percent said that homemaking could be a totally rewarding career for women. Two thirds said they favored censorship, and only 8 percent favored living together before marriage, down from 47 percent in 1971.

On the foreign front, too, Phyllis Schlafly began to feel that the tenor of the times was on her side.

• "I really think the Soviet Union is dedicated to the destruction of the civilization of which we are the major power," said Norman Podhoretz, editor of the influential magazine *Commentary*.

• In the fall of 1979, politicians of all stripes—especially those up for re-election in 1980—were making campaign noises about the Soviet Union's just-discovered three-thousand-man combat brigade in Cuba. Frank Church (D.,

Ida.), chairman of the Senate Foreign Relations Committee and until very recently one of the most enthusiastic champions of détente, was the most militant of all.

• By late 1979, in the face of the Soviet invasion of Afghanistan, SALT II, which Schlafly denounced as "one more craven attempt to appease the unappeasable Soviet barbarian who is determined to rule the world" had become about as popular as the price of gasoline. *The Wall Street Journal* called for the United States to get serious about "meeting the Soviet threat." Henry Kissinger, the architect of détente, warned that the United States is in "grave peril." Paul Nitze, a onetime disarmament advocate and a member of the SALT I negotiating team (he was one of the "gravediggers" in Schlafly's book by the same name), was traveling around the country denouncing SALT II and predicting a Soviet "march toward world domination" and the possible obliteration of U.S. cities by Soviet nuclear warheads.

• Every presidential candidate—including Ted Kennedy—called for an increase in the defense budget.

• The proprietor of a trendy San Francisco boutique couldn't keep up with the demand for his latest T-shirt. The Ayatollah Khomeini is clutched in the claws of an angry American eagle above the caption, "We're Mad as Hell and We're Not Gonna Take It Anymore!" In Southern California, it was becoming chic to be patriotic. American-flag merchants enjoyed their best year since 1942.

In 1979, Phyllis Schlafly won another poll, this one taken by a magazine for senior citizens called *50 Plus*. She was chosen one of the twenty-five most influential Americans—over fifty.

When does Phyllis Schlafly begin to slow down? No time soon. "I'll just keep on working. None of my children is married. [In early 1980, Bruce Schlafly announced his engagement.] I don't know when I'll have any grandchildren. I'll just keep working," she repeated. And anyway, one can't imagine that grandchildren or anything or anyone would change the pattern of a lifetime.

"I know some of my fellow feminists are just praying for Phyllis to retire," said Karen DeCrow, a lawyer, former president of NOW, and frequent debating opponent of Schlafly's. "But I see Phyllis Schlafly as a power for the next twenty years. Knowing Phyllis, maybe I'd be safer in saying the next twenty-five."

Reflecting on what she just said, DeCrow signed and admitted she is "in a bind about Phyllis Schlafly."

"I think that what Phyllis is doing is absolutely dreadful. Yet I admire her. Friends are always asking me, 'God, how can you be on the same stage with her?' But I just can't think of anyone who's so together and tough. I mean, everything you should raise your daughter to be. . . . She's an extremely liberated woman. She sets out to do something and she does it. To me, that's liberation."

Setting out to do something and doing it, working, planning, leaping obstacles. That, coupled with Phyllis Schlafly's belief that she has goodness and God on her side, have made her invincible.[2]

Even if ERA ultimately becomes the 27th Amendment to the Constitution, Phyllis Schlafly will not fade away. She believes that she can accomplish just about anything, including a constitutional amendment banning abortion, another allow-

---

[2] In comparing the media's treatment of John Anderson (1980 independent presidential candidate) and Phyllis Schlafly, Joseph Sobran, a Los Angeles *Times* syndicated columnist, wrote, "Nobody even laughs when Anderson hauls out the dustiest liberal clichés and offers them as 'new ideas.' Phyllis Schlafly will outlast him and a hundred more TV-promoted avatars of new ideas. In fact, liberals should brace themselves for some news they will regard not merely as bad but as incredible: The wave of the future is rolling in, and its name is Schlafly."

ing voluntary prayer in the public schools and, if it came to that, a constitutional amendment, perhaps the 28th, repealing the 27th.

Love her or hate her, Phyllis Schlafly is a power to be reckoned with, a woman whose inevitable impact on the eighties dismays her foes almost as much as it delights her fans.

Index